Educational Enactments in a Globalised World

Intercultural Conversations

Kathleen Quinlivan
University of Canterbury, Christchurch, New Zealand

Ruth Boyask
University of Plymouth, UK

Baljit Kaur
University of Canterbury, Christchurch, New Zealand

SENSE PUBLISHERS
ROTTERDAM/BOSTON/TAIPEI

A C.I.P. record for this book is available from the Library of Congress.

ISBN 978-94-6091-008-1 (paperback)
ISBN 978-94-6091-009-8 (hardback)
ISBN 978-94-6091-010-4 (e-book)

Published by: Sense Publishers,
P.O. Box 21858, 3001 AW
Rotterdam, The Netherlands
http://www.sensepublishers.com

Printed on acid-free paper

ACKNOWLEDGEMENTS

The idea of this book builds on the joint work that the three of us at various points in our careers has done with Jean McPhail as a friend/colleague or teacher. We would like to acknowledge our intellectual debt to her.

To our contributors, thanks for engaging seriously with our intent and purpose despite some of our false starts and somewhat tardy timelines. We are also grateful to the audience participants at various national and international symposia, particularly at AERA 2009 where significant and extended intercultural conversations did occur, some of which form a part of this text. We would like to specifically mention Lia de Vocht van Alphen, Shane Darmody, Vanessa Andreotti, and Libby Cohen.

Our thanks are due to the New Zealand Association for Research in Education for selecting our symposium for presentation at AERA 2006, giving us the platform from which we contemplated this book. We would further like to acknowledge the financial support from our respective universities to facilitate our attendance at AERA. To Professor Greg Lee, the Head of School of Educational Studies and Human Development, Baljit Kaur and Kathleen Quinlivan thank you for your genuine support of our work.

We are thankful to Paula Wagemaker for suggesting the name of Tanya Tremewan. We could not have completed this book in a timely fashion but for Tanya's energetic support in meticulously copy editing the manuscript.

Finally, our sincere thanks to Michael Peters and John Freeman-Moir, and to Peter de Liefde for seeing the relevance of this book for their Series and the Publishing House respectively, without which this book will not have been a reality.

Kathleen Quinlivan, Ruth Boyask and Baljit Kaur
July 2009

TABLE OF CONTENTS

Acknowledgements v

Introduction: Educational Enactments in a Globalised World: Intercultural
Conversations ix
    Baljit Kaur, Kathleen Quinlivan and Ruth Boyask

1.   Provocations: Putting Philosophy to Work on Inclusion 1
    Julie Allan

2.   Children Navigating Home–School Relationships: Strategic Compliance,
    Resistance and Other Survival Strategies 13
    Baljit Kaur

3.   Contradictory Representations of Identity Formation: Race and Class
    at Western High 27
    Andrew Gitlin and Frances McConaughy

Conversational Interlude One. Hopes, Dreams and Slippages 41

Interstice One: Māori Aspirations in Contemporary Times: Old Narratives,
New Articulations, Uncertain Outcomes 45
    Hazel Phillips

4.   Place, Power and Pedagogy: The Potential that a Critical Pedagogy
    of Place May Hold for Enhancing Cross-cultural Conversations
    in New Zealand 51
    Richard Manning

5.   Perspectives in Equity: What Progress Have We Made? 65
    Didi Khayatt

6.   When 'Everything Collides in a Big Boom!' Attending to Emotionality
    and Discomfort as Sites of Learning in the High School Health
    Classroom 77
    Kathleen Quinlivan

Conversational Interlude Two: Emotionality and Learning? 91

Interstice Two. Globalisation and Language Diversity: Implications
for the Enactment of Identities and Intercultural Relations 95
    Gill Valentine

7. Journeying on the Frinj of Outdoor Education 103
    Mary Lou Rasmussen and Lou Preston

8. Changing Concepts of Diversity: Relationships between Policy
    and Identity in English Schools 115
    Ruth Boyask, Rebecca Carter, Hazel Lawson and Sue Waite

Interstice Three. Educational Enactments and the 'New Aid Era': Implications
for the Pacific 129
    Eve Coxon

9. Discovery Meets Inquiry: A Cross-cultural Essay 137
    Jean Claire McPhail and Annemarie S. Palincsar

Conversational Interlude Three. Engaging With Dilemmas and Possibilities 151

Notes on Contributors 157

Index 163

BALJIT KAUR, KATHLEEN QUINLIVAN AND RUTH BOYASK

INTRODUCTION: EDUCATIONAL ENACTMENTS IN A GLOBALISED WORLD

Intercultural Conversations

What does it mean to learn and educate in these social and historical times? This text represents the result of a series of ongoing conversations about this fundamental question that began with the development of a symposium proposal for the American Educational Research Association Conference (AERA) (Boyask, Kaur, McPhail & Quinlivan, 2006). Since that time, the project has taken the form of ongoing and evolving conversations, a work in progress that spans geographic boundaries and a range of educational contexts. These intercultural conversations put an international group of education thinkers to work on the challenges of education, difference and diversity in today's globalised world. We contend that in this era of globalisation with its concomitant complexities and uncertainties, education that acknowledges and grapples with difference and diversity is of singular importance as growing populations claim recognition of their differentiated identities and aspirations (Kaur, Boyask, Quinlivan & McPhail, 2008; McPhail & Kaur, 2008). Whilst governments around the world attempt to redistribute the public good of education amongst larger and more diverse groups of individuals, rising fundamentalist ideologies, instantiations of essentialist identities, and pervasive instrumental approaches appear to challenge such responses to issues of difference and diversity. These paradoxical global and local conditions require new approaches to education. This introduction charts our shifting and evolving thinking in relation to the issues raised by this book, before commenting on the organisation of the book and contribution each chapter makes to further intercultural conversations, despite the challenges that can characterise such undertakings.

BEGINNING THE CONVERSATION

In 2005 we, the editors and our then colleague Jean McPhail, felt that despite shifts towards a 'global village' culture that makes claims of accommodating diversity and providing for individual freedoms and consumer choice, issues of social justice and equity in schooling remained largely unaddressed. Our interests centred on unpacking the possibilities and dilemmas that emerge when working at the micro level of schools within the wider context of policy initiatives that, while appearing to address inequalities, can operate paradoxically to undermine social justice issues.

Cognisant of the extent to which 21st century rational-economic globalisation is currently informing a range of educational initiatives, we sought to broaden and deepen our understandings of the democratic possibilities of schooling through conversations with educational thinkers from the USA, the United Kingdom and Canada around specific themes that emerged from our analyses of data based on three research projects carried out in New Zealand schools. Our intention was to further our joint understandings for (re)imagining schooling based on the specifics of our situated experiences rather than to draw abstract generalisations across contexts and countries. In that vein, we conceptualised the symposium as an open '... text that resonates between author and audience, not to produce conclusions but to open up possibilities for imagination and creativity' (Gitlin, 2005, p. 21). Didi Khayatt from Canada and Andrew Gitlin from the USA engaged with the papers as discussants.

EXTENDING THE CONVERSATION

Like the symposium that inspired it, the book retains our focus on the contributors identifying examples of localised solutions to the problems of diversity for the practice of education in their own empirical and theoretical research work. These examples or cases, which we term 'educational enactments', are intended to illustrate the interactions of local and global discourses within particular contexts of educational policy and practice. Our emphasis on educational enactments challenges contributors to consider how abstract notions of education (for example, within theoretical or policy representations) are applied through education as a practice and/or subjective experience.

A second AERA symposium (Boyask, Kaur & Quinlivan, 2009) provided another opportunity for several of the book contributors to engage in an embodied conversation in San Diego, USA. The themes emerging from that exchange of ideas have been woven into the text in the form of three conversational interludes, which speak to, and at times question the themes emerging from various chapters and the main conceptual underpinnings of the book itself. Mindful of the structural limitations imposed by the regime of globalisation, our intention is to explore the challenges and the agentive possibilities of working across cultural and material boundaries, and to provide multiple venues in which to transcend the limitations of addressing educational issues through a single lens. So how are we to understand the notions of educational enactments, globalisation and intercultural conversations and the relationships among them?

We use the notion of educational enactments, as it is conceptualised in this volume, in a number of ways. First, it can speak to the possibility of framing a broad range of formal as well as non-formal educational sites as 'educational contexts', in contrast with a narrower 'what works' focus on school practices, which can admittedly be seen as dangerous in these instrumental and (neo) pragmatic times (Lather, 2007).

Second, we are interested in employing it for an exploration of the slippage between the intended discourses operating at the macro level and what actually gets enacted on the ground within a micro context; for instance, the slippage between intentions of a policy and its enactment in a particular context. An emphasis on an enactment 'on the ground' can provide a more complex analysis in terms of under-standing the ways in which global discourses take on particular shapes in specific contexts.

Third, attending to the discursive formation of globalisation as a rule-governed set of material practices (Foucault, 1972) and its understanding 'from above and from below' (Singh, Kenway & Apple, 2005) can enable insights into how macro discourses of globalisation are enacted in the lived realities of individuals in ways that are problematic, and yet can also provide some possibilities (Willis, 2003). Framing globalisation as a discursive formation engages with the ways in which individual subjectivities can be constituted by discourses of globalisation yet, at the same time, exercise some agency in relation to the discourses that constitute them.

In the current global economic recession, the limits and discontents of a globali-sation discourse, particularly the neo-liberal variety prominent in the world in recent decades, have been brought into focus. While the destructive influences of neo-liberal globalisation are being justly enumerated, our concern is to simul-taneously mobilise the networks created by the technologies of globalisation to counteract these effects and explore the possibilities of facilitating social justice for diverse peoples (Chan-Tiberghien, 2004).

On the one hand, educational globalisation has meant that education the world over is geared towards preparing young people for participation in a global market, and the success of such economic participation is taken as a measure of the quality of education. On the other hand, it is also true that educational globalisation is not a monolithic entity or an absolute phenomenon despite the widespread discourse that gives an impression to the contrary. Such a totalising conception in its extreme form makes local resistances or creative challenges invisible, seemingly rendering the actors in any enactment into mere puppets. We believe that both the 'dead ends and the opening spaces' of globalisation need to be kept in view while considering educational enactments in a globalised world. An interconnected two-way approach seems a reasonable way to proceed. Therefore, we invited fellow researchers to engage in investigating 'the deep politic of everyday life' (Gitlin, 2005) in the local contexts of their own research with reference to the relevant macro discourses operating therein. At the same time, recognising the 'in-process' 'never finished' nature of this endeavour, we engaged with one another around mutually significant issues across disciplinary and national/geographical boundaries to seek possibilities for change through multilayered intercultural conversations.

The extent to which such a double move is productive remains to be seen, particularly in view of some globalisation discourses that assume intercultural conversations to be easy and desirable for all concerned. Such discourses present intercultural encounters as unproblematic and neutral, masking the power dynamics involved. Steiner-Khamsi (2004), for instance, suggests that learning from another culture is generally construed normatively – as unproblematic borrowing or lending 'what works' from one culture and transferring it to another. She favours more complex analyses that probe '… the politics of educational borrowing and lending ("why"), the processes ("how"), and the agents of transfer ("who")' (p. 2). This approach enables the study of '… transnational transfer, globalization, and international convergence' (Ibid.). In this book, we attempt to go beyond this, or perhaps inside these macro-level dynamics, to examine their production through micro-level relationships – that is, intercultural conversations between micro-cultures of schools, between subject-disciplinary cultures or between individual, culturally embedded subjectivities.

The intercultural dimension of these conversations challenges us as educationalists to draw upon the insights of our cultural others to reveal the limitations and possibilities inherent within our own sites of investigation that we may not otherwise notice. As the authors in this collection reveal, finding productive possibilities in a global world for an equitable and just education is not easy. At both the levels of subjectivity and culture, globalisation unsettles hitherto determined identities (Rattansi & Phoenix, 2005) and constructs new and uneasy associations or hybrid identities (Lucey, Melody & Walkerdine, 2003). These challenging conditions provoke yearnings for stability and constancy, intended to act as a social good. Paradoxically, in the current world context, they are also associated with rising fundamentalisms that can work against the recognition of diversity to make meetings between cultures more challenging.

Some of the questions that arise for us in considering the possibilities of productive or successful intercultural conversations include: Whose initiatives do such conversations reflect? Are all parties to the conversation interested in such an engagement, with similar objectives? How is having the possibility or freedom to disengage, an exit strategy if you will, enacted within intercultural conversations? Are all parties expected to change to the same extent and to understand and value each other's world-views? To what extent does the assumed mutuality of interest and reciprocity of desire to engage mask the hierarchical inequalities of knowledge and beliefs across cultures and contexts, and with what consequences? How can such inequalities be mediated, and by whom? And of course, what constitutes a productive or successful conversation?

Finally, what relevance do such questions have for a continuing dialogue along the lines this book pursues? We see this book as one attempt to grapple with these complex issues, not with a quest for definitive solutions, but with a hope for possibilities. As Greene (2000) argues:

> If spaces can be opened that disclose alternative realities or ways of being, individuals are far more likely to break with the ordinary and the taken-for-granted. Visions may appear before their mind's eye – visions of what might be, what ought to be. Experiences of this kind are what direct attention to deficiencies, the inequities in lived situations; they may, in fact, provoke persons to take action together – to transcend the deficiencies, to transform. (p. 8)

ORGANISATION OF THE BOOK

We have aimed to organise this book so that it embodies multilayered intercultural conversations that deliberate upon localised educational enactments and global discourses that take the shape of all-encompassing theories and/or policies. As such we employ a dialogic structure within the text for *intercultural conversations* that shift between global/local interests and micro/macro contexts. There are nine chapters, three interstices, and three conversational interludes – all responding to and framed by one another to a certain extent. The authors of the chapters drew on their own research to engage with any or all three of the main concepts underpinning the book as outlined below.

For the interstices, three educational thinkers were invited to respond to the issues arising from the overall themes of the project. Drawing upon their own theoretical and/or empirical positionings, they move across macro and micro contexts to pose questions and raise challenges for educational practice and theory, each with focus on a specific question:

Hazel Phillips: How might attention to the interaction of global discourses within localised teaching and learning relationships produce better educational experiences and/or outcomes for diverse learners?

Gill Valentine: How are diverse subjectivities constructed and enacted through local and global discourses and associated practices, both historically and within post-modernity?

Eve Coxon: How are policies and practices that aim to address difference and diversity within a globalised culture enacted through global and local contexts?

As already noted, two conversations that we engaged in at AERA 2009 were audio-recorded. Edited excerpts from these conversations, along with reflections from one author who could not be present are included in the book as three conversational interludes. These reflect our thinking after the chapters had been written and serve to highlight the ongoing and open nature of these conversations.

The opening chapter, by Julie Allan, speaks to one of the most crucial challenges we see as confronting education today: what does it mean to grapple with issues of diversity and difference? Shifting between theory and practice contexts, she puts a number of philosophers of difference to work in order to reframe inclusion as a social, ethical and political activity. Her application of a complex theoretical frame to problems that emerge through the enactment of universal ideals, leads us to consider how the global and the local impact upon the subjectivities of learners in schools. Such an approach, Allan suggests, could enable teacher educators, teachers, student teachers and children and young people to see themselves as capable of enactments of inclusion.

In Chapter Two, Baljit Kaur also discusses the implications of the ways in which children positioned differently within school systems are currently constituted. She uses data from a longitudinal study to identify roles that children enact to illustrate how home–school relationships can interact problematically with the subjectivities of diverse children. Calling into question the universal advocacy of home–school partnerships for effective schooling, and the theorisation of children that underpins it, Kaur draws on the children's cultural perspectives to show how they actively negotiate an issue that has been unproblematically framed and driven by adult concerns.

In the next chapter, Gitlin and McConaughy continue the focus on young people – in their case, adolescents – to provide a complex view of student representation and identity formation that challenges the macro-level discourse of taken-for-granted categories of race and class. Utilising an extended case methodology, they trace more than a decade of significant staff and structural changes within the micro context of a high school in the USA. Gitlin and McConaughy discern contradictions between the school's responsibility to support the achievement of all students, and the effects of the shifting school culture on their diverse subjectivities.

The first conversational interlude, Hopes, Dreams and Slippages contemplates the difficulties associated with enacting aspirations at both personal and social levels. Not only are the outcomes of dreams of self-determination and autonomy affected by context, but the nature of dreams is also dependent upon location. To understand such dissonances, it is suggested that it may be useful to cultivate an (admittedly transgressive) interest in a comparative analysis of educational research as failure.

In the first of our interstices, Hazel Phillips echoes the conversational themes as she considers the extent to which it is possible for the cultural aspirations of the indigenous Māori population of Āotearoa New Zealand to be achieved within a global context dominated by economic imperatives. She suggests that there needs to be a fundamental questioning of the hegemonic neo-liberal discourses and structures that underpin economic globalisation in order for the aspirations of Māori to be met.

In Chapter Four, Richard Manning also speaks to Māori issues as he notes disjunctures between the ways in which Māori elders and high school history teachers viewed the teaching of local, Māori, environmental and New Zealand history, particularly in relation to their own life experiences of learning about past and place. He suggests that the notion of a 'critical pedagogy of place' may hold some potential in enabling further intercultural conversations about the teaching of history and social studies in New Zealand secondary schools within the Port Nicholson Block area, in the southwestern corner of New Zealand's North Island.

Staying with an exploration of the ways in which diverse subjectivities are engaged with in learning contexts, in the next chapter we move to Canada with Didi Khayatt. She delineates her personal praxis as a teacher educator over several decades, showing how she has responded when intersecting or contrary perspectives in relation to sexuality, gender and diversity have been enacted in her classroom over time. Khayatt suggests that although there is a great deal more discursive noise about the topic of equity and social justice in our schools, and a deeper theoretical engagement with understanding and accounting for diverse sexual and gendered subjectivities, the issues in schools largely remain extant.

Kathleen Quinlivan speaks to the challenges raised by Khayatt in the following chapter as she explores what it means to engage with normative understandings of gender and sexual diversity enacted within the micro world of a high school classroom. She suggests that working intentionally with student emotionality and discomfort as a site of learning in the classroom might have enabled the teacher, the students, and herself as a researcher to engage more closely with the destabilisation of subjectivities that can characterise 'thinking otherwise' in relation to genders and sexualities.

The second conversational interlude, Emotionality and Learning? explores the extent to which engaging in 'learning otherwise' for students, teachers and researchers is a strongly emotional as well as intellectual endeavour. Acknowledging ways in which these constructs might be usefully brought into relation with one another, rather than treated as oppositional, may enable us to engage more deeply with the roles that emotionality and desire play in learning and unlearning, and the challenges involved.

While the preceding interlude highlights the need for emotional engagement in education for diversity, Gill Valentine's concern in the second interstice is with the ways in which language constructs identities. Considering the ways in which diverse subjectivities are constructed and enacted through local and global discourses within post-modernity, she draws on Somali children's everyday practices in the United Kingdom to demonstrate the need for language to take centre stage in debates about cultural connectivity in schools. Valentine suggests that fostering a more diverse range of language practices as part of wider social and economic processes of cultural hybridity might also lead to the development of 'intercultural citizens' who have positive attitudes to diversity.

In Chapter Seven Mary Lou Rasmussen and Lou Preston explore notions of indigenous location as a non-formal site of education through reconceptualising the pedagogy of the outdoors in ways that might prompt students to think differently about relations between people and places of learning. Through the metaphor of a journey, they advocate for making explicit connections between education and location, offering possibilities for outdoor education that can transcend its construction as a discrete 'activity'.

In the next chapter Ruth Boyask, Rebecca Carter, Hazel Lawson and Sue Waite move between the contexts of policy analysis and the lived experience of student difference within a UK schooling context. They explore the conceptual underpinnings of equity-related policy reform since the mid-20th century to reveal a recent global policy discourse that homogenises difference. The authors suggest that in a climate of proliferating identities, closer attention to the subjectivities of learners and how they are constructed, and how they construct themselves as different from one another, may provide policy-makers with a new venue to explore in the search for more equitable social provision.

The third and final interstice, from Eve Coxon, extends the discussion from the individual interests and psychologies missing from the globalisation rhetoric, to its evisceration of local knowledge and culture within a non-formal educational context. Coxon explores the effects of globalisms imported through the rhetoric of development and aid upon small Pacific Islands countries and cultures, and their subsequent strategies of resistance.

The last chapter is an intercultural essay from two academics from the USA, Jean McPhail and Annemarie Palincsar, both of whom, to different extents, experienced local resistance to their globalised identities when they took their culturally embedded beliefs about educational theory and practice to their work within a primary school in New Zealand. McPhail and Palincsar suggest that although economic ideas may readily cross national boundaries, educational ideas are much more difficult to transport because they are integrally bound with cultural and moral values.

The book closes with a conversational interlude, Engaging with Dilemmas and Possibilities, that speaks to the challenges and the complexities of intercultural conversations in relation to issues of diversity and difference. We acknowledge the limitations of the ways in which dominant discourses of globalisation can homogenise and further silence diverse populations. However we also recognise that our role as educators compels us to engage with the productive possibilities, as well as the dilemmas of what it means to learn and to educate within such 'interesting times'.

REFERENCES

Boyask, R., Kaur, B., McPhail, J., & Quinlivan, K. (2006, April). *Engaging in intercultural conversations on participation, diversity and social justice in schooling.* [Chair: Andrew Gitlin] NZARE-sponsored symposium at the American Educational Research Association Conference, San Francisco, USA.

Boyask, R., Kaur, B., & Quinlivan, K. (2009, April). *Educational enactments in a globalized world: Intercultural conversations.* [Chair: Annemarie S. Palincsar] Symposium at the American Education Research Association Conference, San Diego, USA.

Chan-Tiberghien, J. (2004). Towards a 'global educational justice' research paradigm: Cognitive justice, decolonizing methodologies and critical pedagogy. *Globalisation, Societies and Education, 2*(2), 191–213.

Foucault, M. (1972). *The archaeology of knowledge* (A. M. Sheridan Smith, Trans.). New York: Pantheon Books.

Gitlin, A. (2005). Inquiry, imagination, and the search for a deep politic. *Educational Researcher, 34*(3), 15–24.

Greene, M. (2000). The ambiguities of freedom. *English Education, 33*(1), 8–13.

Kaur, B., Boyask, R., Quinlivan, K., & McPhail, J. (2008). Searching for equity and social justice: diverse learners in Aotearoa New Zealand. In G. Wan (Ed.), *The education of diverse populations: A global perspective.* The Netherlands: Springer Science and Business Media.

Lather, P. (2007). *Getting lost: Feminist efforts towards a double(d) science.* New York: SUNY Press.

Lucey, H., Melody, J., & Walkerdine, V. (2003). Uneasy hybrids: psychosocial aspects of becoming educationally successful for working-class young women. *Gender and Education, 15*(3), 285–299.

McPhail, J. C., & Kaur, B. (2008). In search of a participatory democratic vision in teacher education. In A. Scott & J. Freeman-Moir (Eds.), *Shaping the future: Critical essays in teacher education.* Rotterdam, The Netherlands and Taipei, Taiwan: Sense Publishers.

Rattansi, A., & Phoenix, A. (2005). Rethinking youth identities: modernist and postmodernist frame-works. *Identity: An International Journal of Theory and Research, 5*(2), 97–123.

Singh, M., Kenway, J., & Apple, M. (2005). Globalising education: perspectives from above and below. In M. Singh, J. Kenway, & M. Apple (Eds.), *Globalising education: Policies, pedagogies and practices.* New York: Peter Lang.

Steiner-Khamsi, G. (2004). Introduction: Globalization in education: real or imagined? In G. Steiner-Khamsi (Ed.), *The global politics of educational borrowing and lending.* New York: Teachers College Press.

Willis, P. (2003). Foot soldiers of modernity: The dialectics of cultural consumption and the 21st-century school. *Harvard Educational Review, 73*(3), 390–341.

Baljit Kaur
School of Educational Studies and Human Development
College of Education
University of Canterbury

Kathleen Quinlivan
School of Educational Studies and Human Development
College of Education
University of Canterbury

Ruth Boyask
School of Secondary and Further Education Studies
University of Plymouth

JULIE ALLAN

1. PROVOCATIONS

Putting Philosophy to Work on Inclus

INTRODUCTION

Inclusion is currently characterised by confusion about what it is supposed to be and do; frustration at the way the current climate of standards and accountability constrains teachers' work; guilt at the exclusion created for individual pupils; and exhaustion, associated with a sense of failure and futility. This chapter considers the 'impossibility' of inclusion in the current context and how it has become a highly emotive and somewhat irrational space of confrontation, with questions about how we should include being displaced by questions about why we should include and under what conditions. An attempt is made to rescue inclusion from its valedictory state and to reframe it as an ongoing struggle and a more productive form of political engagement. This reframing takes some of the key ideas of the philosophers of difference – Deleuze and Guattari, Derrida and Foucault – and puts them to work on the inclusion *problem* (Allan, 2008).

THE IMPOSSIBILITY OF INCLUSION

Questions raised by teachers' unions about whether inclusive education can realistically be achieved have emanated from concerns about teachers being unprepared for inclusion (Macmillan, Meyer, Edmunds, Edmunds & Feltmate, 2002) and about the 'collision course' between high-stakes testing programmes and inclusion (National Association of Education, 2005). Researchers report that teachers are increasingly talking about inclusive education as an impossibility in the current climate (Thomas & Vaughan, 2004) and about their lack of confidence in their capacity to teach inclusively (Hanko, 2005). A dramatic U-turn by the so-called architect of inclusion from the United Kingdom, Mary Warnock (2005), who describes inclusion as a 'disastrous legacy' (p. 22), appears to have validated the resistance to inclusion. Although commentators have reacted speedily to the 'ignorant and offensive' nature of Warnock's comments (Barton, 2005, p. 4), this 'stunning recantation ... by a respected figure' (Hansard, 22 June 2005, col. 825) has clearly had an influence.

Smyth (2001) acknowledges the extent of the exclusion experienced by teachers as well as children and contends that if we are prepared 'to think radically outside the frame' (p. 239) then we need to find ways of bringing people *into* the frame. Philosophy offers lucrative possibilities for enabling teachers to step out of the

K. Quinlivan, R. Boyask and B. Kaur (eds.), Educational Enactments in a Globalised World:
Intercultural Conversations, 1–12.
© *2009 Sense Publishers. All rights reserved.*

that has developed with inclusion and into a new and productive frame. philosophers of difference offer a reimagining of inclusion as a social, ethical and above all political activity, which identifies everyone – including children and young people – as powerful and capable of enacting inclusion. It seeks to change the environments, the spaces and the people within them, to incite them to use this power in productive directions. This is likely to produce change not through revolution or 'grand plans' (Roy, 2003, p. 147), but through 'combat' (p. 147), 'looking out for microfissures through which life leaks' and opening up new possibilities for inclusion.

THE PHILOSOPHERS OF DIFFERENCE

Deleuze and Guattari, Derrida and Foucault, along with Irigaray, Kristeva, Lyotard and others, have been recognised as philosophers of difference because of their concern with achieving the recognition of minority social groups and their attempt to formulate a politics of difference that is based on an acceptance of multiplicity (Patton, 2000). All of these writers have in common an orientation to philosophy as a political act and a will to make use of philosophical concepts as a form of, not global revolutionary change, but 'active experimentation, since we do not know in advance which way a line is going to turn' (Deleuze & Parnet, 1987, p. 137). Their work is a philosophy of affirmation which is a 'belief of the future, in the future' (Deleuze, quoted in Rajchman, 2001, p. 76). It does not offer solutions, but rather produces new concepts, 'provocation' (Bains, 2002) and new imaginings, 'knocking down partitions, co-extensive with the world' (Deleuze, 1994, p. 22). The key elements of the thought of Deleuze and Guattari, Foucault and Derrida that are considered relevant to inclusion are set out in Allan (2008). This chapter shows the provocations at work and unpacks some of the key concepts as they are put to work on inclusion: Deleuze and Guattari's deterritorialisation, the rhizome and difference (Deleuze, 2004; Deleuze & Guattari, 1987); Foucault's practices of the self and transgression (Foucault, 1986; Foucault 1994); and Derrida's deconstruction (Derrida, 1997).

The concepts of the philosophers of difference are made to work in two ways. First, the concepts themselves can be taken and *used* to help with a different way of seeing, thinking about and practising inclusion. It is not, however, a simple task to see, think and do differently. Therefore it is necessary also to use some of the practices of the philosophers of difference to help us achieve a new orientation to knowledge about inclusion – and about ourselves. Put to work in these ways, the concepts of the philosophers of difference open up possibilities for the enactment of inclusion and involve two sets of propositions. The first set of propositions involves *subverting* the balance of power in schools in favour of the students to enable them to participate more fully and effectively, *subtracting*, in order to do less more effectively and *inventing* new ways of learning and engaging together. The second set of propositions is concerned with changes in the processes of learning to teach and in the opportunities available to practising teachers to enable a more politicised form of engagement. These propositions involve *recognition* of the double-edged and contradictory nature of inclusive teacher education, *rupture* of conventional approaches to learning to teach and attempts to *repair* the profession by encouraging teachers to work on their own selves.

TEACHERS AND STUDENTS: SUBVERTING, SUBTRACTING, INVENTING

The tasks of subverting, subtracting and inventing speak back to power but are also about redirecting the huge amount of energy that already exists in schools in more useful and productive ways.

The rigidly hierarchical and bounded relationships between teachers and children and young people, with the latter subjugated by the former's authority, knowledge and power, could be interrupted by the teacher him or herself. The shift in teacher–student relationships could be characterised as a move, in Deleuzian (Deleuze, 2004) terms, from communication to expression or from the sender–receiver mode, in which information flows along 'established power grids' (Roy, 2004, p. 298) that exist between teachers and their students, to more messy forms of exchange. The challenge for teachers is to try to think from within confusion (Britzman, 2002) without seeking closure through a demand for a clear distinction between the teacher and taught, and to be open to 'the ethically rich drama that runs through education' (Edgoose, 1997, p. 1). Although this may be unsettling to teachers because of its departure from the intended content and may produce anxieties about achieving learning outcomes, such 'failure of fluency' (Edgoose, 1997, p. 6) is more likely to produce inclusive practice.

Transgression, the concept of practical and playful resistance to limits as developed by Foucault (1994), is an important way for disabled people to challenge the disabling barriers they encounter. Transgression is not antagonistic or aggressive, nor does it involve a contest in which there is a victor; rather, it allows disabled individuals to shape their own identities by subverting the norms that compel them to repeatedly perform as marginal. Although it is necessary to continue to work to remove the barriers to inclusion that exist within schools and elsewhere, there is possibly a place for helping disabled and young people to recognise barriers, for example in the form of negative or patronising attitudes, and to find ways to challenge them. Teachers or other adults could work with children and young adults, individually or in groups, to plan transgressive tactics, either proactively or reactively. This could even be a project for disabled children and adults to work on with their non-disabled peers. More generally, students might be helped to become *readers of power*, learning to recognise how it is used to construct their identities and relationships with adults, and control their movements, learning and behaviour. Developing literacy in relation to power would perhaps enable students to understand how adults are also implicated in this way and perhaps make them feel less antagonistic towards them. The students could then direct their resistance towards more productive and positive ends, although this outcome will not, of course, be easily achieved.

The highly rigid and striated – territorialised – space of the school could be worked upon and smoothed out – deterritorialised (Deleuze & Guattari, 1987) – by

3

students. This involves inventing new ways for students to experiment with and experience inclusion and participation.

An example of effective work upon the school space was found in a school in which the headteacher had introduced children's rights (Allan, I'Anson, Priestley & Fisher, 2006). The headteacher's ambition was to explore the limits of children's rights under the terms of the United Nations Convention of the Rights of the Child. Having had limited success with various formal, bureaucratic activities such as assemblies and school councils, the headteacher decided to hand over some responsibilities to a group of children and a parent leader. The group called itself the Special Needs Observation Group, gleefully displayed its acronym (SNOG – a colloquial term for kiss) on T-shirts, and set about investigating inclusion and the right of all children to participate in school. One boy, Alistair, became a strong leader of the group, particularly in relation to shaping the others' understanding about inclusion. The group excelled in identifying the barriers to participation and encouraging the whole school community to think and act more inclusively. Interestingly the members of the group very quickly and comprehensively identified the need to examine inclusion by looking simultaneously at exclusion, a point that inclusion scholars have grasped only relatively recently in spite of enjoinders from Booth and Ainscow (1998), Ballard (2003) and others, and that continues to elude some. They operationalised intuitively the social model of disability, developed by disabled people, and recognised it as an important framework for understanding inclusion because of its shift away from student deficits and onto the environmental, structural and attitudinal barriers to participation (Barnes, Barton & Oliver, 2002; Barton, 2005). The students concluded that the biggest barrier to participation was the attitudes of teachers and students and made numerous suggestions for alterations that would remove the barriers.

The quest for certainty, closure and *outcomes* in learning could be replaced by a search for the undecidable, in which learning cannot be predicted. This alternative quest does, however, involve a considerable subversion of the expectations contained within policy documents that particular behaviours will lead to particular outcomes. It also requires some inventive thinking about the alternative kind of learning that is to take place. The metaphor for the shift in learning used by Deleuze and Guattari (1987), the rhizome, is particularly useful. The rhizome is posited as a contrast to the arborescent tree structure of learning in which knowledge is passed down in a linear fashion. The rhizome, in contrast, proliferates in unanticipated directions, requiring learners to undergo the 'disorienting jolt of something new, different, truly other' (Bogue, 2004, p. 341). The process of learning, thus, is the explication of these new encounters, an 'undoing of orthodox conventions' (ibid).

The invitation to students to narrate their own learner identities and experiences and map their own learning could assist them in becoming better learners, but they are likely to need help in managing the uncertainty associated with rhizomic learning. Experiencing uncertainty as positive, rather than as evidence of a lack of knowledge or understanding of the rules and expectations, could free students up to pursue their own 'new lines of flight' (Deleuze & Guattari, 1987, p. 161) and avenues of thought and could be enormously liberating. However, although this approach to learning need not pose a threat to the social order of the school, it may be perceived in some quarters as an unacceptable challenge to authority.

The experience of SNOG was a form of rhizomic learning in which the children experimented with and experienced inclusion. They took rights – literally – on a walk through the school in order to discover the points at which exclusion arose. Simulation exercises of this kind, in which non-disabled individuals pretend to be disabled, can be superficial and essentialist, but these young people – because they had in their minds the rights of students to be included – forced their gaze on the barriers that restricted participation and found themselves constantly surprised and capable of imagining more of the exclusion experienced by their disabled peers. This way of learning seemed to be particularly effective because it took them off in new and unanticipated directions. Having 'dealt with' disability, the group decided to move on to ethnicity, and identified some concerns about the level of participation of some individuals. They then decided to tackle 'fat' issues when they became aware of some of their peers' discomfort when changing for gym. Their experience and experimentation with rights had alerted them to new forms of exclusion that they wished to do something about.

For Alistair, mentioned above for his emergence as a leader of the group, the experience of being part of SNOG and of rhizomic learning was particularly significant in rescuing him from a downward spiral of misbehaviour and exclusion. He described himself as having formerly been out of control, often getting into trouble in the playground for fighting and being regularly excluded. Prior to joining SNOG, he had become a buddy to a disabled child and the experience of being responsible for others who had come with SNOG membership had made him alter his own behaviour. His membership of SNOG had, by his own account, transformed him into someone else, someone who had to have regard for others, and had allowed him to escape his deviant identity. It was a dramatic line of flight:

> Well, when I started to know [disabled students] I was, like, I need to show them I want to be good, 'cos I used to get into fights and stupid things like that but when I started to get to know them and got into the SNOG group I started my behaviour; I wanted to start again and be good … I didn't want everybody to know me as Alistair the bad boy. I want to be good now. So that's what I was trying to do when I went into the SNOG group … sometimes I'm amazing. (Allan & I'Anson, 2005, p. 133)

Alistair had transformed himself, but recognised that he had to police his own newly formed identity and occasionally he lapsed:

> I get into a fight or I get angry because it didn't happen. If I didn't get to sit beside my friends I start to get angry. I just want to be a good boy now. As everybody says 'good boy.' That's what I want to be – I want to prove them all wrong. They all think I [can't] behave but I want to prove them all wrong that I can behave … some people just know me as 'there's Alistair – stay away from him.' But I'm to prove them all wrong – that I'm good. I'm going to be good. I just want to be good now. (Ibid., p. 134)

Clearly such opportunities for escape would not be available to, or responded to by, every student with a label of behavioural difficulties. It is, nevertheless, a heartening transformation that delighted all with whom Alistair was connected – the headteacher, the teachers, the janitor, Alistair's mother and us, the researchers. Most impressed of all was Alistair himself who came to know himself as 'amazing'.

NOMADIC LEARNING TO TEACH: RECOGNITION, RUPTURE AND REPAIR

Although the philosophers of difference can help us to challenge standards and accountability, making headway with our challenges may be a long-term task and it may also be possible to find ways of practising teacher education differently and more effectively – as education – and producing teachers who are keen to participate in the struggle for inclusion. The philosophers of difference assist with the *recognition* of the double-edged and contradictory nature of inclusive teacher education and with the *rupture* of conventional approaches to learning to teach; and they offer opportunities to *repair* the profession of teaching and teachers' own selves.

The most significant challenge for teacher educators is accepting that the aspiration to be inclusive creates a number of responsibilities that pull them, and their students, in different directions. These divergent responsibilities produce tensions because they are assumed to be resolvable or reducible to one choice but might be framed as a series of double duties or 'aporias' (Derrida, 1992, p. 22), both of which must be fulfilled in each case:
– How can student teachers be helped to acquire and demonstrate the necessary competences to qualify as a teacher *and* to understand themselves as in an inconclusive process of learning about others?
– How can student teachers develop as autonomous professionals *and* learn to depend on others for support and collaboration?
– How can student teachers be supported in maximising student achievement *and* ensuring inclusivity?
– How can student teachers be helped to understand the features of particular impairments *and* avoid disabling individual students with that knowledge?
– What assistance can be given to student teachers to enable them to deal with the exclusionary pressures they encounter *and* avoid becoming embittered or closed to possibilities for inclusivity in the future? (Allan, 2003, p. 143)

If these aporias were accepted as an inevitable element of teacher education for inclusion and if the pressure to choose between the double contradictory imperatives was resisted, there would perhaps be less confusion, frustration, guilt and exhaustion. Student teachers could be taught to understand the nature of these contradictions and how to engage with the uncertainty they produce. Uncertainty, the greatest torment for the student teacher, could become acknowledged as an important element that beginning teachers have to enact, with the moments of undecidability being where they learn to do their most inclusive teaching.

Deconstruction, a process of reading texts with an eye out for their blind spots, contradictions and obfuscations (Derrida, 1997), could enable student teachers to see how they work to 'write the teacher' (Cormack and Comber, 1996, p. 119) in ways that are contradictory and oppositional (Honan, 2004) and constrain how they can act. Recognition of how they are regulated, and thereby controlled, and of the process of producing effective teachers who are 'elastic or infinitely flexible and ultimately dutiful figures who can unproblematically respond to new demands' (Cormack and Comber, 1996, p. 121) may make the passage towards full teacher status less of an ordeal.

The rigid content-driven programmes of teacher education, with their special education orientation, could be replaced through the process of deterritorialisation. The four strands of this activity, developed by Deleuze and Guattari (1987), could be undertaken as a collective task within higher education institutions or by individuals. The first of these, becoming foreigners in our own tongue, would involve scrutiny of the language used in lectures and materials, watching for where the language of special needs is prevalent and creating stutterings over words and expressions that have hitherto been familiar. Colleagues in my own institution developed a game of 'bullshit bingo' in an effort to pick up and subvert jargon in their written work. A similar exercise could be usefully undertaken with the teaching materials used with students.

The refusal of essences or signifieds is an important second strand of deterritorialisation which could be undertaken within teacher education programmes. Instead of attempting, in lectures and materials, to define inclusion, we could point to who is included and who is not. We might also ask not what inclusion is but what inclusion does. This question might take us closer to elaborating some of the consequences of inclusion for children and young people and their parents. We would then perhaps begin to understand how inclusion is experienced rather than how it is represented.

Creative subtraction would involve identifying what not to do within the curriculum. Instead of responding to the latest government imperatives to insert more content by looking to see where it can be squeezed in, there could be a search for what might be removed or reduced. An invitation to lose aspects of what we currently do in the name of inclusion and in education, in order to put some other things in, could be attractive. Such creative subtraction, of course, will not be easy as there will be opposition from those who insist that the items proposed for shedding will remain purely because they have always been there and are precious to the individuals who put them there in the first place.

The acceptance that there is no one behind expression, the final strand of deterritorialisation, is a refusal to attribute blame or responsibility for content to any individuals and to encourage the contribution of new and untried ideas. Greater use of brainstorming sessions could enable staff to roam through the kind of teacher education that they really want to do, rather than what they feel constrained to do, then to ask themselves, 'Why not?' The ruptures provided by deterritorialisation may create opportunities for more productive learning.

Adopting the rhizome as the means for learning to be a teacher ruptures the interpretation of theory (Deleuze, 1995) and privileges experimentation and experience, taking the student teachers on, in Derrida's (1992) terms, an 'empirical wandering' (p. 7). The rhizome allows student teachers to invent themselves as the

7

kind of teachers they want to become and, instead of absorbing and later replicating content, student teachers would be involved in 'experimenting with pedagogy and *recreating* its own curricular place' (Gregoriou, 2002, p. 231; original emphasis). Rhizomic wanderings, whilst extremely challenging because of the uncertainty they bring, could help to disrupt conventional knowledge about teaching and learning. They could also interrupt the dominant knowledge of *special needs* and enable student teachers instead to experiment with responding to difference in ways that are meaningful to the young people. This would force the student teachers to question what they know themselves, to 'ask what determinations and intensities [they] are prepared to countenance' (Roy, 2003, p. 91) and to abandon ways of working that seem unreasonable.

Student teachers' knowledge and understanding might be fashioned as a series of maps, 'entirely oriented toward an experimentation in contact with the real' (Deleuze & Guattari, 1987, p. 12). These maps do not replicate knowledge, but perform and create new knowledge. Reflexivity, which students are often demanded to practise but are rarely given guidance on how, could be directed towards producing maps of their journeys as becoming teachers. Maps of their school contexts could also be created by student teachers during their teaching practice. These could detail the exclusionary points, and openings for inclusivity, in the school as a whole, in lessons they observe and in their own classrooms.

Learning to be a teacher through the rhizome is not a journey towards a fixed end, as denoted by the standards; rather it involves wanderings along a 'moving horizon' (Deleuze, 2004, p. xix) that are documented visually. As well as creating new knowledge, these wanderings provide opportunities for student teachers to establish, in Rose's (1996) terms, new assemblages and new selves, as teachers. Students' wanderings need to be supported and responded to in a way that does not entrench further their novice and incompetent identity. Student teachers' 'creative stammerings' (Deleuze & Guattari, 1987, p. 98), questions and searches for links would be engaged with, rather than closed down as indicative of their failure to grasp content. It is in these spaces or schisms where complex thinking would take place and where 'a new experiment in thought could be inserted ... that might help teachers get an insight into the generative possibilities of the situation' (Roy, 2003, p. 2).

Teacher education has traditionally packaged difference for the student teacher in the form of lists of deficits, their causes and their cures. Even if this packaging is done with the caveat 'no two children are alike' and a discouragement of categorisation, it still facilitates a recognition of 'types' of failings in children and what they might expect from them. A rupture in this typing could be achieved by asking student teachers to turn the gaze back on themselves and on the schools in which they do their teaching placements. The refusal to explain children's pathologies to student teachers might provoke wails of protest from them, but the reasons for this refusal could be set out along with an exposition of the consequences of pathologies for those at whom they are directed. Having outlawed pathologies of children, student teachers' energies could be directed instead to trying an alternative – social model – reading of students' difficulties; a reading that identifies the environmental, structural and attitudinal barriers to their participation. Student teachers could be encouraged to engage with difference *in itself*, as opposed to in relation to identity, and in comparison with the normal. They could undertake the task of finding out about individual children's 'conditions', but could investigate how this description has been arrived at and by whom. Student teachers might also scrutinise their own fears about responding to individuals effectively and share these with more experienced teachers or with fellow students. They might be encouraged to think of their anxieties about responding to the other as precisely the point at which inclusion and justice becomes a possibility:

> As soon as you address the other, as soon as you are open to the future, as soon as you have a temporal experience of waiting for the future, of waiting for someone to come: that is the opening of the experience. Someone is to come, is *now* to come. Justice and peace will have to do with this coming of the other with the promise. (Derrida, 1997, p. 22)

This desire for, and openness to, the other privileges relationships over the delivery of content and makes knowledge of children's *needs* less important than knowing the children themselves. I have suggested previously that a concern for difference in terms of *needs* could be replaced with an attention to the *desires* of the child and young person (Allan, 1999). This is neither excessive nor radical, but simply involves asking the child or young person for guidance on the kind of support he or she is most comfortable with. There is clearly an enormous risk associated with bringing desire into educational conversations and doing so may be perceived as more or less dangerous within different cultural contexts. The Scottish school context is hardly the bedrock of permissiveness and indeed there was some disquiet among parents over the SNOG T-shirts, which also featured a picture of lips. The headteacher's determination to allow the students' enactments to be upheld prevailed but it is easy to envisage a less sanguine reaction to the introduction of desire in other schools.

The student teachers' own desires could be foregrounded in their identity as becoming teachers. Instead of their status representing a lack of competence, they could be encouraged to articulate their trajectory – emotional as well as in terms of their acquisition of skills – towards the kind of teacher they want to become. The narratives of experienced teachers could be a valuable resource in helping student teachers to understand the fractured, partial and embodied process of becoming a teacher and the centrality of desire, or at least emotion. Student teachers could be encouraged to offer and compare reflections on the intensities of their experiences and their 'percepts' and 'affects' (Deleuze, 1995, p. 164), the way they come to think and live as teachers.

Foucault's framework of ethics could be used by student teachers by, first, identifying the part of themselves as teachers that they wish to work on (determining the ethical substance). The second ethical dimension, the mode of subjection, could come from examining the rules that operate within schools or higher education institutions and that create barriers to inclusion. Self practice or ethical work, the third dimension, could be directed towards their professional conduct and attempts

9

to be inclusive. Taking on this task might necessitate identifying the way in which their own teaching practices and actions, carried out *in the best interests* of children, create barriers to inclusion, and modifying these. Finally, students could be invited to work out the overall goal, the telos, perhaps with guidance on this from children and young people and their families. The ethical project of inclusion is one which we undertake and practise upon ourselves, but on which we can seek advice from those who hold the greatest expertise and who are likely to know what their own best interests are.

Foucault's framework of ethics could also provide a structure for staff development and for supporting the work of practising teachers in becoming more inclusive. Staff development, instead of being a content-driven attempt to skill teachers up in response to the latest government imperative, could provide a smooth space for them to pause, think and repair some of the damage they have experienced. Teachers might be given an opportunity to examine the exclusionary pressures within the education system. By doing some of this collectively they may come to recognise the struggle for inclusion as something that is constant, shared and necessarily inconclusive. Determining the ethical substance, the part of teachers' selves and their schools to be worked on, could be done collectively, perhaps starting with 'confessions' of aspects of their practice that have been exclusionary. The mode of subjection could be identified by examining teachers' own school context and their experiences of exclusion and regulation. Self practice or ethical work could be focused on both making their classroom practice more inclusive and trying to tackle some of the barriers they themselves encounter. Finally they could be encouraged to think about the overall goal, the telos, for both inclusion and for themselves as teachers.

UNCANNY ENACTMENTS?

The philosophers of difference offer possibilities for rescuing inclusion from the impasse that it appears to be in and encouraging all of those involved – teacher educators, teachers, student teachers and children and young people – to see themselves as capable of enactments of inclusion. They allow a response to the demand for practical solutions to educational problems such as inclusion in the form of new routes through the problems. Teacher educators, in facilitating enactments are curious rather than knowing, acting to 'complicate rather than explicate' (Taylor & Saarinen, 1994, p. 7) and pursuing 'interstanding' rather than understanding (ibid., p. 3). The act of interstanding occurs when depth gives way to surface, in a search for what stands between and involves risking the personal (Ware, 2002). In other words, teachers and other professionals may find ways forward in those moments of undecidability when a new thought or a new kind of experiment emerges. These are unlikely to be new in the sense of never having been seen before, but 'uncanny ... a thing known returning in a different form ... a revenant' (Banville, 2005, p. 10). The provocations from the philosophers of difference allow us to make inclusion a more realistic possibility by 'acting counter to our time and thereby acting on our time and, let us hope, for the benefit of a time to come' (Nietzsche, 1983, p. 60).

REFERENCES

Allan, J. (1999). *Actively seeking inclusion: Pupils with special needs in mainstream schools*. London: Falmer.

Allan, J. (2003). Inclusion and exclusion in the university. In T. Booth, K. Nes, & M. Strømstad (Eds.), *Developing inclusive education*. London: RoutledgeFalmer.

Allan, J. (2008). *Rethinking inclusion: The philosophers of difference in practice*. Dordrecht, The Netherlands: Springer.

Allan, J., & I'Anson, J. (2005). Children's rights in school: power, assemblies and assemblages. *International Journal of Children's Rights, 12*, 123–138.

Allan, J., I'Anson, J., Priestley, A., & Fisher, S. (2006). *Promising rights: Children's rights in school*. Edinburgh, UK: Save the Children.

Bains, P. (2002). Subjectless subjectivities. In B. Massumi (Ed.), *A shock to thought: Expression after Deleuze and Guattari*. London and New York: Routledge.

Ballard, K. (2003). The analysis of context: some thoughts on teacher education, culture, colonisation and inequality. In T. Booth, K. Nes, & M. Strømstad (Eds.), *Developing inclusive education*. London: RoutledgeFalmer.

Banville, J. (2005). *The sea*. Basingstoke, Hampshire: Picador.

Barnes, C., Barton, L., & Oliver, M. (Eds.). (2002) *Disability studies today*. Cambridge, UK: Polity Press.

Barton, L. (2005). *Special educational needs: An alternative look*. Unpublished discussion paper.

Bogue, R. (2004). Search, swim and see: Deleuze's apprenticeship in signs and pedagogy of images. *Educational Philosophy and Theory, 36*(3), 327–342.

Booth, T., & Ainscow, M. (1998). From them to us: setting up the study. In T. Booth & M. Ainscow (Eds.), *From them to us: An international study of inclusion in education*. London: Routledge.

Britzman, D. (2002). The death of curriculum? In W. Doll & N. Gough (Eds.), *Curriculum visions*. New York: Peter Lang.

Cormack, P., & Comber, B. (1996). Writing the teacher: the South Australian junior primary English teacher, 1962–1995. In B. Green & C. Beavis (Eds.), *Teaching the English subjects: essays on English curriculum history and Australian schooling*. Geelong, Victoria: Deakin University Press.

Deleuze, G. (1994). *What is philosophy?* (H. Tomlison & G. Burchell, Trans.). London: Athlone Press.

Deleuze, G. (1995). *Negotiations*. (M. Joughin, Trans.). New York: Columbia University Press.

Deleuze, G. (2004). *Difference and repetition*. London: Continuum.

Deleuze, G., & Guattari, F. (1987). *A thousand plateaus: Capitalism and schizophrenia*. London: The Athlone Press.

Deleuze, G., & Parnet, C. (1987). *Dialogues*. (H. Tomlinson & B. Habberjam, Trans.). New York: Columbia University Press.

Derrida, J. (1992). Force of law: the mystical foundation of authority. (M. Quaintance, Trans.). In D. Cornell, M. Rosenfield, & D. Carlson (Eds.), *Deconstruction and the possibility of justice*. New York and London: Routledge.

Derrida, J. (1997). The Villanova roundtable: A conversation with Jacques Derrida. In J. Caputo (Ed.), *Deconstruction in a nutshell: a conversation with Jacques Derrida*. New York: Fordham University Press.

Edgoose, J. (1997). An ethics of hesitant learning: the caring justice of Levinas and Derrida in *PES Yearbook*. Retrieved April 27, 2005, from http://www.ed.uiuc.edu/EPS/PES-Yearbook/97_docs/edgoose.html

Foucault, M. (1986). *The care of the self: the history of sexuality, 3*. (R. Hurley, Trans.). New York: Routledge.

Foucault, M. (1994). A preface to transgression. In *Aesthetics: Essential works of Foucault 1954–1984*, Vol. 2. London: Penguin.

Gregoriou, Z. (2002). Performing pedagogy with Deleuze: the rhizomatics of 'theory of education'. *Philosophy of Education Society of Great Britain Conference Proceedings*.

Hanko, G. (2005). Towards an inclusive school culture: the 'affective curriculum'. In M. Nind, J. Rix, K. Sheehy, & K. Simmons (Eds.), *Curriculum and pedagogy in inclusive education: Values into practice*. London and New York: RoutledgeFalmer/The Open University.

Hansard (2005). *Debate on special schools and special educational needs*. 22 June.

Honan, E. (2004). (Im)plausibilities: A rhizo-textual analysis of policy texts and teachers' work. *Educational Philosophy and Theory, 36*(3), 267–281.

Macmillan, R., Meyer, M., Edmunds, A., Edmunds, G., & Feltmate, C. (2002). *A survey of the impact of funding cuts on inclusion: a report to the NSTU*. Halifax, UK: Nova Scotia Teachers Union.

National Association of Education. (2005). *Testing, inclusion on a collision course?* Retrieved August 1, 2006, from http://www.nea.org/specialed/research-specialed.html

Nietzsche, F. (1983). *Untimely meditations*. (R. J. Hollingdale, Trans.). Cambridge, UK: Cambridge University Press.

Patton, P. (2000). *Deleuze and the political*. London: Routledge.

Rajchman, J. (2001). *The Deleuze connections*. Cambridge, MA: MIT Press.

Rose, N. (1996). *Inventing our selves: psychology, power and personhood*. Cambridge, UK: Cambridge University Press.

Roy, K. (2003). *Teachers in nomadic spaces: Deleuze and curriculum*. New York: Peter Lang.

Roy, K. (2004). Overcoming nihilism: From communication to Deleuzian expression. *Educational Philosophy and Theory, 36*(3), 297–312.

Smyth, J. (2001). Managing the myth of the self-managing school as an international educational reform. In M. Fielding (Ed.), *Taking education really seriously: Four years hard labour*. London: RoutledgeFalmer.

Taylor, M., & Saarinen, E. (1994). *Imagologies: media philosophy*. London: Routledge.

Thomas, G., & Vaughan, M. (2004). *Inclusive education: Readings and reflections*. Maidenhead, Berkshire: Open University Press.

Ware, L. (2002). A moral conversation on disability: Risking the personal in educational contexts. *Hypatia, 17*(3), 143–172.

Warnock, M. (2005). *Special educational needs: A new look*. Impact No 11. London: The Philosophy Society of Great Britain.

Julie Allan
Stirling Institute of Education
University of Stirling

BALJIT KAUR

2. CHILDREN NAVIGATING HOME–SCHOOL RELATIONSHIPS

Strategic Compliance, Resistance and Other Survival Strategies

> The *concept* of childhood requires that children be distinguishable from adults in respect of some unspecified set of attributes. A *conception* of childhood is a specification of those attributes. (Archard, 1993, p. 22)

> Ultimately, the individual child is largely a tool to illuminate the nature of the autonomous adult citizen by providing the perfect mirror within which to reflect the negative image of the positive adult form. (Arneil, 2002, p. 74)

CONSTRUCTIONS OF CHILDREN AND CHILDHOOD

Children these days are widely construed as active participants in their own development. Yet paradoxically modern childhood is the most regulated and managed period of life (Prout, 2005). Young children in particular continue to be seen as incapable, ignorant, innocent and incompetent, and lacking the capabilities that they must be helped to develop over time. They are subject to hierarchical inequalities based largely on arbitrary distinctions between childhood and adulthood. A child, by definition, is not yet an adult (Archard, 1993), which means that the child has little agency or autonomy and no space in public debate about what is in the child's own best interests.

The predominant *conception* of childhood, to use Archard's term, is largely derived from developmentalism[1] (Wyness, 2006). Children are assumed to develop new capabilities as they move through a more or less linear set of age-related stages that are cumulative and universal. Adults are assigned the duty and privilege to assist in furthering this unfolding of capabilities by supporting the developing child, although the developmental process itself is conceptualised as largely internal to the child. Thus the younger the child, the lower the stage of development and concomitantly the poorer his/her abilities to think reasonably about issues confronting him/her (Cannella, 1997). At least two problematic consequences follow from this perspective. One, children might be conceded to actively create meanings of their life worlds but these meanings are not expected to be based on sound reasoning, and thus not considered worthy of serious attention in research, policy or practice. Second, the assumed nature of development conjures up an ideal global

K. Quinlivan, R. Boyask and B. Kaur (eds.), Educational Enactments in a Globalised World: Intercultural Conversations, 13–25.

hood, which denies and undermines the multiplicity of childhoods
n diverse backgrounds experience in their daily lives.
and global measures to rescue children from poverty and depri-
ng them under adult monitoring in specifically designated spaces
although enabling and well-intentioned, are not unproblematic given
g social and economic disparities in children's lives that remain
unmitigated. Within school systems children get positioned differently, by others as
well as by themselves, based on a range of criteria that reference back to the universal
ideal childhood, further marginalising those who already might be disadvantaged
on entry to school (James & James, 2004). To what extent do research, policy and
practice on home–school relationships take childhood diversity into account when
construing the roles of thus 'differentiated' children?

CHILDREN CAUGHT IN THE MIDDLE: HOME–SCHOOL PARTNERSHIPS

Existing approaches to home–school relations in policy and practice arenas
seem to have hardly begun to engage with the diversity of meanings 'home–
school relations' might have, the functions they might serve for children
and young people, and the underlying broader structural issues involved.
(Alldred, David & Edwards, 2002, p. 135)

The meta-narrative of the crucial significance of effective partnerships between
home and school for children's optimal development and learning is so widely
accepted today as to need no further comment or scrutiny of the claim or its assumptions (Delhi, 2003). As in many other countries, the current educational policy in
New Zealand advocates close working partnerships between home/ whānau[2] and
school. Several government policy and strategy documents emphasise the need for
schools to work in close collaboration with parents and community to enable better
educational achievements for all children in the wake of persistent gaps in the
measured achievement outcomes for children from diverse backgrounds (e.g.
Ministry of Education, 2005). On its website, the Ministry of Education offers a
whole section for parents to learn about becoming effective partners with their
children's teachers and schools, and close home–school relationships are listed
among the Ministry's eight priorities for schooling and early childhood education
(Ministry of Education, 2007).

Research on the importance of home–school relationships for children's effect-
tive schooling has a long, contested history. The arguments about whether teachers
or parents should have more power over shaping the lives and minds of children
have occupied researchers since the inception of mass schooling (Bastiani, 1993;
Cairney, 2000; Cutler, 2000 Hoffman, 1991). Researchers have elaborated the relative
roles of parents and teachers for effective home and school relationships, often
advocating interventions for parents, and making suggestions for teachers. Parents'
involvement in their children's education has been repeatedly shown to have
positive results. Children for whom there is a mismatch between home and school
might not do as well in school as those whose home and school hold similar goals,
values and beliefs (Biddulph, Biddulph & Biddulph, 2003; Bull, Brooking &

Campbell, 2008; Epstein & Sheldon, 2006; OECD, 1997). The overwhelming congruence between research and policy is reflected in teacher education programmes and teacher practices too. The goal of working closely with families is evident in school charters across New Zealand.

Despite the salience of home–school partnerships for effective schooling in policy, practice and research, children's own perspectives and experiences have been virtually absent till recently (Edwards, 2002). The vast majority of research in this area has been, and continues to be, driven by developmentalist assumptions, which posit that children might have little to add to our understandings about home–school relationships. In this view, children are more or less passive recipients of the concern and benevolence of adults, who act in concert to promote children's best interests. However, for the last decade or so, a new line of inquiry in child-hood studies has emerged that takes a critical view of the existing research (James & James, 2004; James, Jenks & Prout, 1998; Lareau, 2000; Qvortrup, Bardy, Sgritta & Wintersberger, 1994). Consequently more researchers have begun to investigate children's own perspectives on issues and contexts of their lives, including the issue of home–school relationships. Some studies have investigated the possibility that the meanings children create have a bearing on how they manage the adult regu-lation, monitoring or support of their school lives (Alldred et al., 2002; Ericsson & Larsen, 2002; Mayall, 1994).

In this chapter, I argue that the premise of children's rights of participation in their own lives needs to be examined seriously for all children. The unquestioned acceptance of the predominant constructions of universal ideal childhood, founded on the assumptions of linearity of development and deficit thinking about child-hood in general and about 'at risk' children in particular, makes us, educational researchers and practitioners alike, complicit in creating and authorising the silencing of children's voices. The normative discourse of childhood and schooling operates to produce children's silence for its own survival. My concern here is to '... search for the breach that permits the silent specter to enter our midst' (Mazzei, 2007, p. 15), by presenting data in young children's voices and actions that challenges the basic assumptions about their lack of competence to understand complex situations and respond in sophisticated ways.

However, let me clarify that while my argument is that children's meaning-making of their lives is worth serious consideration (James, 2007), we need to be cautious to avoid assigning unfettered meaning-making freedom to children, as indeed to any other person, because the meanings largely inhere within a broad cultural frame. Children do not speak in a single voice, nor are they better placed than other social actors to comment on schools. Just because it is the voice of a child it does not have more, nor should it have less, legitimacy than others parti-cipating in the home–school systems. Nevertheless, I take the position that children do have unique and so far largely undocumented perspectives on home–school relationships that can widen the current understandings in this area of research.

My overarching research question is: How do young children, positioned variously in the school system, according to perceived ability or cultural or class background, perceive and manage home–school relationships? Some corollaries of this question are: Do all children benefit equally from closer home–school relationships? Under what conditions might a close relationship work against rather than for a child's best interests? What do children, positioned differently in the school system, think about their parents and teachers collaborating, and what roles do they play in facilitating or impeding this relationship?

In the larger study on which this chapter draws, I was interested in investigating the relative positioning of three 'groups' of participants in home–school relationships: professionals, parents/caregivers and the children themselves. However, here my focus is on children's perspectives. I begin with a brief outline of the context of the larger study, followed by children's views, experiences and strategies of managing home–school relationships. I then consider what can be learnt from children's lived experiences and negotiation of home–school relations, and implications such insights might have for constructions of contemporary childhood.

CONTEXTUALISING THE RESEARCH STUDY: TEACHER–PARENT–CHILD TRIANGLE

Elm Tree Primary[3] was a Decile 3[4] school in a relatively poor neighbourhood with a highly mobile refugee and migrant population when I began my study. In 2000, the Education Review Office put the school roll of 5- to 11-year-olds at 225, with ethnic composition of Pākehā[5] 65%; Māori 25%; Others (including Somali, Ethiopian, Samoan, Chinese and Fijian) 10%. Over a two-year period, extensive data were gathered through school observations (in classrooms as well as in other spaces outside the classrooms) and multiple interviews undertaken with parents, teachers, board members[6] and support staff. In addition to the observational data on children and informal conversation with them over the course of the field work, most children in all classrooms in the 'senior' section (N = 60; aged 7 to 11 years) participated in a 'draw/write and tell' activity using nine prompts, each followed by focus groups. In addition, 23 children from these classrooms whose parents had given permission for further participation in the study were interviewed individually or in pairs at their discretion. This data from children was collected towards the end of the field work when children were familiar and comfortable with the researchers.[7]

The school had recently won a nationally contested award for its effectiveness despite its low decile rating. The principal held the school's close relationship with the community to be one of its main strengths. As the interviews subsequently revealed, the school professed a strong commitment to close home–school relationships depicted through a widely used metaphor, a triangle, which placed CHILD at the apex of an equilateral triangle with TEACHER and PARENT at the other two angles. Most of the school policy documents and communications to families used the triangle symbol prominently. The teachers often referred to it while talking with children and parents. The deputy principal and the principal considered the triangle a distinct characteristic of the school's philosophy and practice. Many children, too, mentioned it during my conversations with them. So how did home–school relationships get enacted in the lives of children at Elm Tree Primary, and what roles, if any, did they take up in such enactments?

LIVED REALITIES OF HOME–SCHOOL RELATIONS
THROUGH CHILDREN'S EYES

Trust was a strong theme in children's responses to the issue of contact between parents and teachers; trust they had in their relationship with their teachers or, in a few cases, whether they could trust any adult at all.

Children were clear about whether a teacher liked them and why teachers liked certain children. This perception often had an effect on their decisions on whether to sort things out for themselves or to seek adult help. They said that it took them less than a month to know whether this will be a good year for them or not, based on the teacher's verbal as well as non-verbal behaviour towards them and their classmates.

I:[8] Why do you think they [teachers] will do that [act mean towards you]? ...

C:[9] I don't know, because they know I am a real dick!

I: Who says that? ...

C: Me? Nobody, but I think they think I am, probably ... you know Sam in my class? He is real smart. He is the smartest kid in our class. [They'll write] probably good things about him because he is like real smart. He is brainy.

I: And you don't think that you are brainy.

C: Na. ...

I: So teachers would be nice to that kind of kid who is brainy and very good?

C: Well, they'll probably be nice to other kids like me too. Well, NOT REALLY!

Children as young as seven had well thought out and discerning answers that made sensitive distinctions between 'private' and 'public'. They used their perceptions, observations and experiences to justify their decisions about whom they would share their concerns or secrets with. Often their answers to questions about contact between their home and school, home visits by teachers, teachers and parents meeting, and children themselves sharing an issue that was troubling for them inside or outside the school, began with, 'it depends on who the teacher is' or 'I will tell this teacher because she cares', or 'No. I think that is just a waste of your time, ... because they won't listen', or 'Teachers will say you are bad, but you are not ... It depends on who the teacher is ... It is a matter of trust'.

Some children responded to their perceptions and experiences by saying that they did not care whether their teachers talked to their parents. 'I don't care, I think they talk rubbish.' Others decided to keep out of harm's way or to take a watchful stance, towards not only that teacher but the school in general, thus actively seeking to keep their parents away from school as evident in the roles described below. I discerned five distinct role clusters in these educational enactments and named these: Vigilant Sentinel, Goody Two Shoes, Little Atlas, Assiduous Protector, and Smart Tactician (Clayton, 1993; Lakoff & Johnson, 1980).

Vigilant Sentinel: 'I Always Keep an Eye on Them'

Many children accepted the reality of contact between their parents and teachers but they did not like them talking to each other without children's knowledge or participation: 'I would want to know what they are saying about me.' At least some of these children asserted their right to know given that the conversations were about them.

> I will not like my teacher to come to my house, because Mum will ask me to go to my room, and I won't know what he said and I'll wonder what he had to say to them.

> They should tell me [what they are saying] because it is an interview about me and no one else.

> It is a good thing that you [child herself] get to come along to parent interviews and I think that you should get to have your opinion.

When children feared that they were seen as achieving or behaving poorly, they thought about contact between parents and teachers in terms of consequences for their daily life. From their perspective, such contact was not necessarily benign. They were aware of the adults' sanctioning authority and, as is evident below, many wished for a low level of contact between teachers and parents or acted to minimise the chances of facing the consequences. Children often made strong connections between bad or naughty behaviour and the need, then, for parents and teachers to communicate. The punitive possibilities of such adult arrangements for monitoring were uppermost in their responses, and they acted judiciously to avoid such contact between their home and school, by staying vigilant or obeying rules.

> If my mum comes in to talk to my teacher, then she gets to know I am not doing my work well, so I don't get to watch TV. I don't like it.

> I do not want [teacher] to come home, because he gives too much homework and I don't like doing homework. So if he came home, he will tell my mum that I don't do my homework.

> If my mum found out I was naughty, I get grounded.

> I don't want my teacher to know that I am bad, that I can be naughty.

> I go to a friend and find out if his parents can take me to school. That is what I do [to avoid his parents coming to school].

> If you live close by, you can ask if you can walk to school with other children. That works.

These children strategically managed the demands of home and school in their lives, and did not want that balance disturbed by frequent contacts between home and school. The reality of the sorting function of school was not lost on those who lived its consequences. For children who were not seen as 'star pupils', the contact between home and school served to magnify the adult surveillance and regulation of their lives. While not always able to control it, they were quick to express displeasure.

A few children said that they neither trusted the teachers individually nor the school as a whole. For instance, a nine-year-old boy from a Pacific Island country had huge distrust of teachers. His father had passed away. He was close to his mother and other members of his extended family, and enjoyed independence and agency at home. He spent a good deal of time outside school with teenage boys who were his cousins or their friends. At school, he was teased by other boys and got into fights over that quite often, but he did not seek intervention. He wanted no contact between his home and school, and had none.

I: If you get into trouble, say, when you are out and about in town with your older friends, who will you talk to? … Would you talk to your mum?

C: Probably. If I want to …

I: Would you talk to a teacher?

C: NO. When I come to school I will be in deep trouble you see. You see that. I am pretty smart with teachers, eh. Because like, if they come to my house, and I talk to them about it, they come to school and report it on a piece of paper. When I go to high school, that'll get me in big trouble. You see? That is the problem.

I: Is that why you don't want them to come home? And you won't talk to them? [He had already stated these views]

C: Yes, that's right. That is right, because then I can't be my ordinary self …

I: So what do you do? … How are you smart with teachers?

C: I know, I know what they are up to.

I: What are they up to?

C: Ah, when you do your work, you give it to the teacher, eh. Then they write like how smart you are and everything … And then they write it down on a piece of paper. Then they will probably give it to like intermediate, whatever school I am going to. And then they'll kick me out of the school.

This child had very different self identities at school and outside it. He used his ample clout with his mother and extended family to keep the home and the school apart. He insisted, successfully, on no family visits to school. During the two years of field work, I never met any member of his family. He brought back consent forms signed for his own participation, but I never got permission to interview his mother.

Goody Two Shoes: 'We Don't Hide Our Trouble, Because We Don't Mostly Get Into Trouble'

Some children thought that it was fine if their teachers and parents talked to each other, in situations outside the formal parent–teacher interviews. Largely these were the children who thought that they were doing well at school, some academically, most behaviourally. Most, though not all, of these children were from relatively stable, typical middle class, two-parent families of Pākehā background.

> I get along with my teacher as well as my mum, so that's all right … I don't want to know what they are talking about because it is their time to speak. I don't have to worry about it. It is none of my business anyway.

> I do not get into trouble. I never lost privilege in my life. If any of them talk to each other, that is fine with me. I am not bothered by that.

> I love my parents coming to school because there is no problem.

> I: What do you think about teachers visiting students' homes?

> C: I think it's pretty cool. If she came into the lounge, I will just probably be sitting on the couch real lazy. At school, I'd probably be working real hard.

> I: So you think it will be interesting for her to see you in another way.

> C: Yeah.

Many children, particularly girls, managed minimal contact between their home and school by behaving well and staying within the rules, or being selective about what they shared with their parents about school and with any adult at school about their home life.

> Well, I just don't do it. I just stay out of trouble. If I think it'll get me in trouble, I won't do it.

> I like my teacher. I feel very close to her because she never tells me off. That's because I don't do bad things. I never get into trouble. I am Miss Goody Good.

> If my teacher calls her then I want my mum to come to school … I am never in big trouble, so she will not come for that reason.

> I tell my mum about what I did in school, but not if I get into trouble.

Little Atlas: 'I don't know what to draw. I don't have a normal life. I don't have much of a family. I want a better family but I don't have it'

In every class there were a couple of children who, given a choice, did not want to participate in the draw/write activity. The whole subject of pondering over home–school relationships was painful for these children in view of their tough family circumstances. One child felt so angry that he tore his pencil through the sheet of paper on which he was to write. After testing the limits of my commitment to listen to him should he choose to speak to me, he ended up telling me a woeful narrative of a succession of foster homes in his young life, and the anger he felt at his abandonment by his parents. 'They just don't know what can happen to a young child in foster homes', he finished in a small voice.

Some children carried burdens of poor relationships between the adults in their lives, within their families or between their parents and teachers, acting stoically to protect others or to avoid further dire consequences for themselves.

> I can't really tell you what he [my father] says. It will be wrong for me to say what my father says about the teachers in school. He has said many things about this teacher and other teachers that I can't tell you.

> If in trouble, he said, he did not tell his mum, 'because she gets REALLY sad. Yeah, she gets really sad, so I don't tell her anything about school or what happened at school.'

> I can tell [a teacher] but I am too scared to, and I don't like what is sort of going on in my life.

> No [I can't tell my mother]. I won't want her to come down [to school] ... People are mean ... it is just that I don't want to get in trouble the next day. Because like whenever you tell your mum, then the next day, 'Oh you have got problem [own name]!' They snap. You get shouted at and get bossed around a lot.

When asked who will she talk to, she said, 'Nobody. I'll talk to nobody.' Without being asked again, she returned to make this statement several times.

> I will talk to my sister [who was five years old] if there was a problem because we can together figure it out somehow.

> I will tell my friends. And that's about it.

These children sounded really sad when they spoke of not talking to any adults at home or school, as if they had nobody to turn to, or that they wished they could talk to someone but knew better.

Assiduous Protector: 'It is a Bit of a Personal Thing, Home Life'

A vast majority of children were adamant that their life outside the school was a personal matter, and the school had no reason to know about it. They expressed opposition both to the idea of home visits by teachers and to sharing information of any life events with teachers or others at school by the children themselves.

Some of children's reasons for disliking the idea of home visits by teachers are mentioned above. In addition, many children opposed the idea because they made a clear distinction between 'public' and 'private' in their lives. They were protective of what they perceived to be the private sphere, home. Teachers were not welcome at home because '... they could be invading your private space', 'they have no right to see your private life', 'It just doesn't feel right', 'It is none of their business', 'I think they should not know what goes on in my private life'.

A few students opposed the idea in the name of efficiency. More frequent contact would put more pressure on parents, teachers or children themselves. 'No, because it is too much time on a regular basis [for parents to spend on meetings at school]', 'No, because they usually give more homework [Wastage of time for the child]', 'No, they [teachers] aren't there to make house calls'!

The majority of children did not want to be 'embarrassed' by their parents' affections towards them in front of their peers or teachers or by their actions in general. Display of such affection, mostly maternal, definitely belonged in the private sphere. They actively sought to ensure that their parents did not come to the school by not telling them about some events, asking them to drop them off at the gate, choosing to walk to the school instead and other such strategies. Similarly some children thought they would be embarrassed by a teacher's visit if their room were not clean. Children from refugee families thought others might tease them about their way of life, so they did not want teachers or children to visit their home.

Both boys and girls often said that they would not involve adults, particularly teachers to help them sort any issues that they may face, deeming this a private matter. Several children felt that nobody really listens to them or cares about them, or that others will not understand. For some children it was a matter of trust as mentioned earlier. For others it was a matter of independence: 'I will not talk to anybody at all.' When asked why, this child said, 'Well, that's how I am. I won't talk to anybody.'

Smart Tactician: 'I do not Want to do Extra Work but I do Need to Know More'

A few of the older children (9–11 years old), who were doing well academically and thinking ahead to attending intermediate school the following year, used their voice and authority to create focused interactions between their parents and teachers. All of them were from middle class families with 'professional' parents. Two of them in a pair interview had this to say:

C1: I find the work too easy, so I talked to my mum.

C2: I do not want to do extra work but I do need to know more.

C1: I have been asking my parents to ask my teacher to teach us harder work in spelling. They have been teaching me harder stuff than we do at school.

C2: Me too.

It is good if they talk because it might be something good about me … because it is good to know what you have to do more of.

It is important if my teacher and parents talk, because my mum could tell the teacher to give harder work in subjects I do well in.

INTERPRETING CHILDREN'S RESPONSES

Contrary to the developmentalist assumptions about young children's inability to think logically, the foregoing account of children's responses leaves little doubt that they were capable of creating sophisticated and complex understandings of home–school relationships. Further, children acted intentionally and purposefully to negotiate the adult monitoring and interventions into their lives. They made sensitive and well-considered judgements about adult roles, guarding the distinctions of the private and the public in their lives. They actively subverted or facilitated interactions between parents and teachers depending on how they perceived their own positioning in the school and/or home, and flexibly took up a number of complicated roles in relation to those judgements and self/other-positionings.

Children who were from different minority cultures, who were not achieving well academically, who disliked school, or who were seen as problem children or as belonging to problem families, did not want close contact between home and school and acted overtly or covertly to achieve that goal. Logically that seems to be a rather smart move. Given that schooling with its sorting routines and rituals is compulsory and children are seen to be unfit for autonomy within school, it stands to reason to keep such a context as separate as possible from the rest of one's life.

Children who were happy with close relationships between their homes and school and those who sought yet closer relations did so based on their valorised positions within the system. They were doing well at school and were seen as good students. They had inherited the cultural and socioeconomic advantages reflecting their similarity to the universal ideal of childhood. The close home–school relationships enshrined in research and policy and promoted as best practice in teacher education worked to support effectively the schooling experiences of these children. They had nothing to fear from closeness between their parents and teachers.

The actions and reflections of children in the study cast serious doubts over the developmentalist assumptions of incompetence that underpin the widely accepted constructions of young children. The current models of home–school partnerships do not take sufficient cognisance of the diversity of schooling experiences for different children. Overwhelmingly researchers in this area continue to speak of 'the child', even as they fail to consider this mythical normal child's voice, and to recommend interventions driven by a deficit-oriented conception of childhood for those who do not fit the norm. Thus research, practice and policy based on the homogeneous conception of childhood fails to raise the question of whether close home–school relationships that are useful for some children might be necessary for all children. Young children in my study were clear eyed and strong voiced in expressing how they saw and managed the issues related to home–school relationships in their lives. The challenge for us – researchers, policy-makers, teachers, teacher educators and parents alike – is to question our own roles in sustaining the grounds on which children are subjected to hierarchical inequalities and rendered into silent and passive 'not yet' spectres, even as we struggle to find alternative conceptualisations of childhoods. I conclude with Baker (1999) who, citing Morrs (1996), argues that, '... perhaps it is time to operate in a space that is ambiguous and less clearly defined than what we may be used to and that this is a constructive, not destructive, outcome of antidevelopmental arguments' (p. 826).

NOTES

[1] For discussions of developmentalism see B. Baker (1999). The dangerous and the good? Developmentalism, progress and public schooling. *American Education Research Journal, 36*(4), 797–834; J. Morrs (1996). *Growing critical: Alternatives to developmental psychology.* New York: Routledge; V. Walkerdine (1993). Beyond developmentalism? *Theory and Psychology,* 3, 451–469.

[2] Whānau is a Māori word that roughly translates to extended family.

[3] Pseudonym. All participant and place names have been altered. The study was partially supported by the University of Canterbury (Internal Grant #U6363), and by several grants from the Research Committee of the School of Education.

[4] All New Zealand schools are assigned a decile rating on a scale from 1 to 10 by the Ministry of Education; 1 reflects the lowest socio-economic neighbourhood.

[5] Pākehā are Caucasian New Zealanders of predominantly British/European ancestry.

[6] New Zealand has one of the most devolved educational systems in the world with elected Boards of Trustees (mostly parents) holding the overall responsibility for administration and management of the each school locally. For more information see McPhail and Palincsar, this volume, or visit http://www.minedu.govt.nz/educationSectors/Schools/SchoolOperations/BOTOperationsAndSupport/ BOTElectionsCoOptionsSelectionToCasualVacancy.aspx

[7] Some interviews were conducted by Lynn Gardiner.

[8] Interviewer.

[9] Child.

REFERENCES

Alldred, P., David, M., & Edwards, R. (2002). Minding the gap: Children and young people negotiating relations between home and school. In R. Edwards (Ed.), *Children, home and school: Regulation, autonomy or connection?* London: Routledge Falmer.

Archard, D. (1993). *Children: Rights and childhood.* London: Routledge.

Arneil, B. (2002). Becoming versus being: A critical theory of the child in liberal theory. In D. Archard & C. M. Macleod (Eds.), *The moral and political status of children.* Oxford, UK: Oxford University Press.

Baker, B. (1999). The dangerous and the good? Developmentalism, progress and public schooling. *American Education Research Journal, 36*(4), 797–834.

Bastiani, J. (1993). Parents as partners: Genuine progress or empty rhetoric? In P. Munn (Ed.), *Parents and schools: Customers, managers or partners?* London: Routledge.

Biddulph, F., Biddulph, J., & Biddulph, C. (2003). *The complexity of community and family influences on children's achievement in New Zealand: Best evidence synthesis.* Wellington, NZ: Ministry of Education.

Bull, A., Brooking, K., & Campbell, R. (2008). *Successful home-school partnerships.* Wellington, NZ: Ministry of Education. Retrieved June 12, 2009, from http://www.educationcounts.govt.nz/ publications/schooling/28415/28416/1

Cairney, T. H. (2000). Beyond the classroom walls: The rediscovery of the family and community as partners in education. *Educational Review, 52*(2), 163–174.

Cannella, G. S. (1997). *Deconstructing early childhood education: Social justice and revolution.* New York: Peter Lang.

Clayton, M. (1993). *Living pictures of the self: Applications of role theory in professional practice and daily living.* Caulfield, Australia: ICA Centre.

Cutler, W. W., III. (2000). *Parents and schools: The 150-year struggle for control in American education*. Chicago: The Chicago University Press.

Delhi, K. (2003). 'Making' the parent and the researcher: genealogy meets ethnography in research on contemporary school reforms. In M. Tamboukou & S. J. Ball (Eds.), *Dangerous encounters: Genealogy and ethnography*. New York: Peter Lang.

Edwards, R. (2002). Introduction: Conceptualising relationships between home and school in children's lives. In R. Edwards (Ed.), *Children, home and school: Regulation, autonomy or connection?* London: Routledge Falmer.

Epstein, J. L., & Sheldon, S. B. (2006). Moving forward: Ideas for research on school family and community partnerships. In C. F. Conrad & R. Serlin (Eds.), *Handbook for research in education: Engaging ideas and enriching inquiry*. Thousand Oaks, CA: Sage Publications. Retrieved December 6, 2007, from http://www.csos.jhu.edu/P2000/research/index/htm

Ericsson, K., & Larsen, G. (2002). Adults as resources and adults as burdens: The strategies of children in the age of home–school collaboration. In R. Edwards (Ed.), *Children, home and school: Regulation, autonomy or connection?* London: Routledge Falmer.

Hoffman, S. (Ed.). (1991). Educational partnerships: home–school–community. *The Elementary School Journal, 91*(3), [Special Issue], 193–287.

James, A. (2007). Giving voice to children's voices: Practices and problems, pitfalls and potentials. *American Anthropologist, 109*(2), 261, 12 pp. Retrieved June 11, 2009, from http://proquest.umi.com.ezproxy.canterbury.ac.nz/pqdweb?PMID=27652&TS=1245337296&SrchMode=3&SrtM=1&PCID=36206871&VType=PQD&VInst=PROD&aid=1&clientId=13346&RQT=572&VName=PQD&firstIndex=0

James, A., & James, A. (2004). *Constructing childhood: Theory, policy and social practice*. New York: Palgrave Macmillan.

James, A., Jenks, C., & Prout, A. (1998). *Theorizing childhood*. Cambridge, UK: Polity Press.

Lakoff, G., & Johnson, M. (1980). *Metaphors we live by*. Chicago: University of Chicago Press.

Lareau, A. (2000). *Home advantage: Social class and parental intervention in elementary education*. London: Rowman & Littlefield.

Mayall, B. (1994). Children in action at home and school. In B. Mayall (Ed.), *Children's childhoods: Observed and experienced*. London: Falmer Press.

Mazzei, L. A. (2007). *Inhabited silence in qualitative research: Putting poststructural theory to work*. New York: Peter Lang.

Ministry of Education. (2005). *Making a bigger difference for all students: Schooling strategy 2005–2010*. Wellington, NZ: Ministry of Education.

Ministry of Education. (2007). *Education counts: Eight education priorities*. Wellington, NZ: Government of New Zealand. Retrieved January 27, 2009, from http://www.educationcounts.govt.nz/themes/eight_education_priorities

OECD. (1997). *Parents as partners in schooling*. Paris: Organisation for Economic Co-operation and Development.

Prout, A. (2005). *The future of childhood: Towards the interdisciplinary study of children*. New York: Routledge Falmer.

Qvortrup, J., Bardy, M., Sgritta, G., & Wintersberger, E. (Eds.). (1994). *Childhood matters: Social theory, practice and politics*. Aldershot, Hampshire: Avebury.

Wyness, M. (2006). *Childhood and society: An introduction to the sociology of childhood*. New York: Palgrave Macmillan.

Baljit Kaur
School of Educational Studies and Human Development
College of Education
University of Canterbury

ANDREW GITLIN AND FRANCES McCONAUGHY

3. CONTRADICTORY REPRESENTATIONS OF IDENTITY FORMATION

Race and Class at Western High

During the early 1970s Western High (fictitious name) was a predominantly white working class school (Paris, 1980). By 1988 Western had become the most racially diverse high school in the area while maintaining its working class character. In the same year it closed its doors. Even though Western has now been closed for two decades, it provides a powerful exemplar of a school that in a short period (15 years) went from being totally white and working class to a racially diverse school that was still working class. From a research viewpoint, this particular change in student population allows class to be held constant as race changes thereby potentially providing insights on the relationships among culture, schooling and issues of equity. Before trying to unearth these insights, we will begin by accounting for a few contextual issues surrounding Western High.

The months preceding the closing of Western were tumultuous. Many members of the community surrounding Western, including its students, parents, teachers and alumni passionately opposed the closing of the school (Oxaal, 1990) and these emotions still run hot two decades later. The passion for Western is somewhat puzzling given its inconsistent record of academic achievement and the constant decline (since 1970) in graduating seniors (Anderson, 1988; Sorensen, 1988; Wilson, 1987). Initially our research focused on why there would be such passion for a school that seemed to do little in terms of furthering educational opportunities. As we continued to probe this question, however, other queries arose; centrally how did race and class influence the type of education and student identities formed at Western?

Our initial take on race and class at Western supported much of the literature that speaks to the disjuncture of the dominant middle class white orientation to schooling, and students who come from cultural backgrounds that have been marginalised (e.g. Fordham, 1996; Grant & Sleeter, 1986; Ogbu, 1974; Valenzuela, 1999; Weis, 1990). However, on further reflection Western did not respond to students in a unified way (e.g. by marginalising the students). Instead, the school both marginalised students (an extreme form of uncaring) and yet also cared for them in profound ways. Put simply, Western's influence on identity formation (Davidson, 1996; Valenzuela, 1999; Weis, 1990; Wortham, Murillo & Hamann, 2002) represented a contradictory logic such that race and class,[1] markers of

K. Quinlivan, R. Boyask and B. Kaur (eds.), Educational Enactments in a Globalised World:
Intercultural Conversations, 27–40.

cultural identity, did not act in a singular direction, as reinforcing the marginalisation of particular groups. In many ways, our findings are consistent with the important work of O'Connor, Lewis and Mueller (2007), who argue that two of the dominant traditions in analysing race 'mask the heterogeneity of the Black experience and its relationship to the differentiated Black youth but also underutilize institutionalized productions of race and racial discrimination' (p. 541). Although our focus, which is on race and class, differs from that of these authors, whose sole concern is race, we build on their insights about heterogeneity and institutionalised production of discriminatory relationships imposed on students by school structures (e.g. race-based tracking) and school policies of surveillance, as well as teacher perspectives and practices.

To provide a sense of how these contradictory representations and identity formations developed, we begin with an abbreviated methodology section, and then provide evidence in the form of quotes from our interviews with teachers and a few administrators at Western to illuminate the contradictory representations and identity formations found there.

METHODOLOGY

Because we feel it is impossible to approach a study without bringing into the field some preconceived ideas (Agar, 1980), we will explain where we started, how we changed and the standpoint we ended up with after the collection of data.

Our approach to studying Western is informed by Burawoy et al.'s (1991) notion of an extended case methodology. Burawoy et al. follow many in the qualitative tradition when they argue that an extended case methodology begins with the specific, and then uses the variations and changes over time in the case study as a vehicle for understanding the working of social life. However, the extended case approach also makes an unconventional move by 'extending' the analyses beyond the data. Put differently, the data become a point of departure to consider conceptual questions.

The extended case approach also differs from some qualitative methodologies by arguing that the researcher should be changed by their involvement in the case study. Specifically, the data from the study should alter the researcher's conceptual lens and theoretical development. As part of our employment of an extended case methodology, we illustrate our conceptual theoretical development throughout the research process.

CONTRADICTORY REPRESENTATIONS AND IDENTITIES

Uncaring/Refuge[2] at Western

Many influential scholars have illuminated the way schools have often segregated cultural groups of students and fostered an uncaring environment (Davidson, 1996; Kozol, 1991; Noddings, 1992; Oakes, 1985; Ogbu, 1974; Valenzuela, 1999). What is interesting about Western High is that the school fostered a sense of class-identified caring, a refuge, when caring is viewed in terms of the relationship between students at Western and the middle class and dominant religious culture of the region. Simultaneously Western cultivated a race-based form of uncaring marginalisation, where particular students became objects of surveillance, and were provided limited opportunities due to racial forms of tracking and teacher perspectives that cast doubt on their abilities and character. The race-based uncaring, a form of marginalisation, was clearly the dominant influence of the school (i.e. the way the policies, practices and perspective of teachers influenced the identities of immigrants and students of colour). Moreover, White students benefited from White privilege in relation to class identified caring in ways the students of colour did not. Nevertheless, it is important to see that refuge (caring) and uncaring (marginalisation) were linked. The narrative that follows points to the ways schooling could be caring and uncaring at the same time for not only alternative groups of students at Western but more surprisingly for even individual students thereby reflecting a contradictory logic of identity formation.

A Class-based Western Identity: Looking in from the Dominant Culture

As noted, from the early 1970s through to 1988, Western High went through a rapid transition in terms of student population such that the largely white working class student population was altered as immigrants and students of colour including Asians, Native Americans, Pacific Islanders, Latinos and African Americans (who all were also working class) increased, making up a larger percentage of the student body. Teachers who talked about the time when the school was all white and working class, glow when speaking of the students who gave them respect, behaved in appropriate ways, reflected 'appropriate' values and were hard-working. In fact, several teachers referred to this era at Western, from the 1930s to the 1950s, as the 'golden age'.

In the later 1960s, as the area around Western switched from working class industrial manufacturing firms to family-owned service industries just trying to get by, and the student population became much more racially diverse, the principal at Western made a bold move. Instead of hiring teachers from the local area, and from the dominant religion in the area, he specifically started hiring a different sort of teacher. Many of the newcomers were not from the dominant religion. Additionally, several teachers were from out of state and were politically liberal in contrast to the overtly conservative teachers who taught during the golden age. The new teachers were not diverse in terms of race or class: most were white and middle class (there was a gender balance between male and female teachers). In terms of their cultural habits, however, they were different from the dominant population of teachers found in this local area and the state (many used alcohol, drank coffee or smoked, behaviours that were forbidden by the dominant religion).

The new Western teachers also seemed to have a certain sense of comfort or excitement about teaching working class students. When asked why teachers during this period accepted a job at Western, one stated that:

There wasn't a lot of uppity rich kids just mostly poor children. At the time there were only three kids who owned cars. I really looked forward to working with this group.

In some ways, it was not just that the school becoming diverse in terms of the race of its students; the teachers too were increasing in diversity, although in ways that did not centre on race. What is interesting about this diversity is that for both students and teachers it was referential to the local community and state. For students, this meant they were *different from* (reflected diversity) students in other schools in the area because they were predominantly working class, immigrants and students of colour, and a smaller percentage practised the dominant religion. For teachers, this meant they were *different from* (reflected diversity) teachers in other schools in the area who were overwhelmingly from the local community and the dominant religion and were conservative. From 1975 to 1988, both teachers and students were positioned as having a 'Western' identity in comparison with dominant norms in the local community and the state. (This is not *the* identity of teachers and students; only an identity that was largely formed when the point of view was from the dominant local culture to those living, working, and occupying the classrooms at Western High). Furthermore, the explicit rationale for employing these non-normative 'Western' teachers was that they were able to work with a 'non-normative' student population:

Western had a broad demographic. It's an immigrant school and there were people from many backgrounds. The principal thought it would nice to hire a staff that reflected that. Everyone was not from here [local area institutions of higher education].

In this sense, one over-riding form of segregation was a segregation between teachers and students in the state in general, on the one hand, and those at Western High, on the other. This segregation seemed to produce a Western identity, as indicated by this teacher's comment:

I do believe there was a perception that these were poorer kids. They always (even after the school closed) maintained that identification of being a Western High kid.

This segregation and school identity led to some caring practices that might not have been found in a school that was less unified in its opposition to the dominant culture of the area. We now turn to examine those caring practices and relationships.

The Effects of a Class-based Western High Identity

After Western closed in 1988, Western-identified teachers who went to other schools were discriminated against in that they were seen as less able teachers, in large measure because they had taught a particular student population and were viewed as outsiders themselves. They recall that, while still teaching at Western, they also developed a collective sense of identity: a 'we'– an identity based on being *different from* other teachers in the local community. As one commented:

I think there was a lot of loyalty to Western High. I have not taught with a stronger faculty, with a more cohesive faculty, where everyone liked each other. I thought it had a great spirit more so than [other eastside schools]. It really was a unique place so diverse and so open. Look at how diverse the faculty was, the students were. It was really unique. ... Many of us would gather in one of the teachers lounges where smoking was allowed and we would smoke, drink coffee, and compare notes. It was a very liberal group.

The cohesion was openly and comparatively linked to the dominant eastside schools; Western was a unique place. Teachers' openness about their differences – including smoking, coffee drinking and liberalism in contrast with the non-smoking, non-coffee drinking, and conservatism of the dominant religion in the area and the state – contributed to a collective identity. This Western identity, this 'we' identity, in turn, also produced a great commitment and dedication to the school. Dedication to the school had tangible benefits for Western students, not the least of which was a community orientation to schooling where participation was requested and desired among teachers, as reflected in this statement:

For years and years way up through the end [the closing of Western] the musical was a big production. It was such a big production that one year we had a red carpet and the kids wore tuxes. The entire faculty had something to do with it. Unlike at XXX [eastside school] I wasn't asked to do anything, not even sell tickets. The musicals at Western were a community affair.

However, the most important influence on teacher commitment to the school was that Western teachers in general were less prone to judge students in terms of poverty given that they were often judged in terms of their own habits including drinking, smoking, and being liberal and therefore out of step politically. As one teacher observed:

[At Western] I don't think they [students] were judged. I think it was okay to be poor. It was okay not to have enough money to join the choir. It was okay to apply for student aid. So I think you [students] were more accepted. I don't think that you were judged as opposed to other more economically stable schools, where some of those things may not be accepted.

Western-identified teachers, as segregated from other teachers in the area, lived in a contradictory world where their *difference from* produced types of discrimination when they interacted with dominant groups. Yet this same segregation in the form of *difference from* also produced a connection to Western students such that they were less judgemental about issues of poverty (class status) and wanted to contribute to the school in ways that went beyond the standard curriculum.

One way teachers contributed to the school was through the vocational educational programme which allowed teachers to be responsive to the economic conditions of students and their families:

We fed them lunch and for some of the kids that was the only meal they got so I guess that was pretty positive and they could earn money because we rotated the waiting schedule and kids could earn 10–15 dollars an hour. We ran a fast food restaurant and at the end of the year we would go to a [water park]. It was a student run business. We incorporated the special education kids as well.

We want to be very careful here not to romanticise vocational education. Obviously, this programme also acted as a governor that lowered expectations or at least reinforced expectations about these students and did little to provide the foundation to move forward in an academic direction; it also trivialised the cultural background of these students (Kantor, 1988). And yet the vocational education programme was part of a larger school perspective that tried to build relationships. For example, within the 'alternative programme' found at Western (students that were struggling with the regular curriculum) teachers showed a tremendous sense of caring for students. Besides trying to build relationships, teachers at Western seemed sensitive to students' economic needs, as indicated in this observation:

You'd be surprised how much you can learn about a kid's cultural background when you're talking with them one-on-one. And we [Western teachers] worked right there with them. During the summer we were able to work with kids [Western students]. We would go to their homes; we would do nannying or other projects to help them earn money.

This vocationalism is open to all sorts of criticisms. It is also the case that because of the collective Western identification of both teachers and students, teachers at Western did much more than subsequent teachers at eastside schools (where most Western students went after the closure) to work with these students and integrate issues of poverty into the curriculum. In the final analysis, Western teachers tried to treat students as members of a common community or even a common family:

So it was very common to have a student show up at your door, new to the school, new to the city. We'd just put our arms around them in that sense brought them into the classroom, went to work, and tried to build relationships. We were very sensitive to cultural differences. See, if you look at demographics and the location of the school it was close to neighbors and neighborhoods. It was real connected.

And yet it wasn't simply the neighbour that you don't speak to; it was the neighbour you think deserves an equal opportunity. As one teacher commented:

We tried to eliminate discrimination. We have got to make sure that people make their grades in classes depending on performance. It can't have anything to do with race or color or creed or anything like that. We would try to make sure that every student had the same opportunity.

So yes, the casting of teacher and student as *different from* created some possibilities for students in terms of engagement and connection with cultural realities, not the least of which was an extremely high level of poverty in the Western community. Western High was in a sense a refuge, a place of comfort and engaged caring relations between students and teachers. If one of the main effects of a class representation and identity formation for students was a caring set of student–teacher relationships, what are we to make of the formation of racial projects?

The Effects of a Race-based Western High Identity

The unified 'we' identity discussed earlier became a race-based pejorative, uncaring identity for immigrants and students of colour who were viewed as having cultural deficits. For many teachers at Western, these deficits had their roots in the culture of the immigrant parents and parents of colour. Teachers complained that, besides lack of involvement, immigrant parents and parents of colour did not care enough about their children to know what they are doing. This perspective became clear when a teacher contrasted an eastside school with a vast majority of white students and Western which at this time comprised approximately 50% immigrants and students of colour:

> Western had worker parents that didn't have any empowerment, they were worker bees that did their job and wanted their kids to succeed or didn't know where their kids were. It was a totally different parental thing. At XXX [eastside school] the parents are on you all the time. They know what their kids are doing.

In the view of parents' lack of involvement both within school and outside, teachers viewed immigrant parents and parents of colour as having low expectations for their children. For example, one teacher commented:

> I really did notice a difference when I transferred to XXX [eastside school] in 1988. These kids were coming from families where a college education was not a luxury but an expectation. A lot of Western students were not thinking of going to college. That didn't mean they were not incredibly intelligent and motivated. It's just that they didn't have that kind of background in their families.

In addition to the children's supposed 'lack of background', in part Western teachers' perspective that immigrant parents and parents of colour had low expectations for their children was based on the way they 'covered' for their children who didn't accomplish a required task. Another form of segregation for Western students concerned differing attitudes about parents. Immigrant parents and parents of colour were seen as unsupportive of the goals of the school, were less or not involved, and when they tried to help they didn't have the background to do so. In contrast, white parents met with no criticism at all. In fact, when the school was entirely white and working class, the education offered was considered superior (the so-called golden years), especially concerning discipline. Some teachers also felt the school was superior when it was an all-white working class school, as expressed in terms of student leadership by a teacher whose tenure spanned the rapid change of student population:

> And so for me, there was much more student leadership then than I see now. We had some great student leaders and a pep club [that] was better and things were better. To me education has slid downhill and it has a lot to do with the attitudes of students.

Regardless of whether one focuses on culture, discipline or student leadership, lurking near the surface is a perspective of immigrants and students of colour as a problem to be overcome. There is a longing for the good old days when the school was entirely middle class or working class and white. Taken together, teachers associated immigrants and students of colour with the downfall of educational quality and viewed immigrant parents and parents of colour as contributing to this downward slide. When it came to the representation of race, Western splintered into a segregated hierarchy such that in contrast to white students, immigrants and students of colour and their parents were at the core of educational problems.

The representation of immigrant students and students of colour as a 'problem' to be overcome was strengthened by a race-based tracking system. Immigrants and students of colour dominated the regular education classes and some of the extra-curricular programmes, while the white students were found in disproportionate numbers in the Advanced Placement (AP) classes. An implication of racial tracking was that regular education had a very different curriculum when compared with the AP curriculum. One reason for this difference was class size. Because of the smaller AP classes, the regular education classes became so large as to limit what could be done educationally in those classes. One teacher acknowledged:

> Gosh, there were years when I faced 240 kids a day so you have to alter things and it waters things down. There is no question that it is impossible to read 240 essays, so you say we will do this less often and get back to it in two weeks.

But it wasn't only class size that put limitations on regular education classes. Another reason why the curriculum in the regular education classes became stagnant was that 'new' innovations seemed to be frequently required from the school district. After a while, teachers simply tuned those innovations out and kept their curriculum the same regardless of the student body composition. Taken together, the curriculum at Western became divided: the innovative, critical thinking orienttation of AP classes was lacking from the regular education classes. The differences in content between the AP curriculum and the regular education class provide a clear example of race-based expectations associated with AP and regular education classes. Speaking of an AP class, a teacher noted:

> In Florence, when the Renaissance was flourishing and looking at the way in which the people express their awaking interest in the human form and human relationships ... I would never let them say you know it's boring I can't read it, I won't read it because I won't expect that answer, if you are human you will find something in it to discover about yourself in something you are reading.

When this same teacher thinks through what she can do in an AP class and compares this with what can be done in a regular education class, the gap in curriculum becomes clear:

> Toni Morrison was something I should have risked for an AP class but I would never have done it in a regular class – that's for sure – way too difficult.

Further, unlike AP classes the regular education classes often didn't assign home-work. Teachers' comments highlight some of the differences between the regular education and the AP classes. In particular, the quality and content of regular education classes were diluted. Even the assessments within the regular education classes seemed to lack any sort of innovative flair or high expectations, as this teacher identifies:

> My assessments were mostly quiz things, multiple choice – true/false matching sorts of tests. The C student takes every test and turns in every assignment, the B student the same with an 80% pass rate. For an A you have to go beyond.

The extra-curricular classes were much the same but seemed to be used for pride rather than academic advancement or to promote educational opportunities:

> I think the music department did create a lot of excitement and pride for Western. I think the school musicals were really important. I think the athletic teams had their moments. I don't think there was a lot of academic sort of pride.

CONCEPTUAL EXTENSIONS

By looking at competing projects, in this section we are able to see that refuge and care, based on the representation of class status, are only one aspect of the formation and development of student identities at Western. A contrasting and contradictory project (Omni & Winant, 2005) is based on the representation of race. The effects of this form of representation and identity development include: viewing students of colour and immigrant students (as well as their parents) as a 'problem' to be overcome; and race-based tracking that left these disenfranchised students with an inferior curriculum that was insensitive to their needs. These race-based effects are suggestive of Derrida's (2003) view of *différance*, in that *différance* is relational and never fixed:

> Positions are defined in relation to each other as specific forms of raced, classed, gendered, sexed, regional, or national identities which in their complex interactions define the plane on which social relations are organized – but never in fixed terms. (In Bennett, 2003, p. 51)

Our findings do point to this changing/non-fixed, complex plane of social relations. However, what is not accounted for either in the above view of *différance* or in this study is how this type of social relation, this cultural turn, this form of competing representations is produced. We have used race and class and then exploded these categories by incorporating complex views of culture, competing projects of difference, and the importance of point of view. We have taken a cultural turn (Hall, 1997), but this turn seems to be self-contained – the social relations are somewhat opaque and difficult to explain. If we do not go back to Marx or some cultural Marxist position (because the findings really don't reflect the insights and understandings of those theories), how are we to explain these findings? One possibility that is worth exploring is Foucault's (2003) notion of governmentality:

> Where it refers to the distinctive apparatuses and programs of governing which working through regimes of truth aim to involve us actively in the government, management, and development of our selves. (In Bennett, 2003, p. 53)

The forms of representation found at Western and their influence on identity formation take shape in 'technical ensembles, institutions, in pedagogical forms that impose and maintain them' (Bennett, 2003, p. 54). This suggests that forms of representation, the competing forms we mention in this chapter, produce pedagogical and other technical structures, such as a race-based tracking system, that help maintain the representations and ultimately the governing, management and development of our selves. However, because these forms of representations are not fixed, new projects of difference, technical pedagogies or other apparatuses are produced over time in history which may conflict dramatically with previous projects, thereby creating only one constant: complex and likely contradictory representations and identities within institutions. Clearly the complexity and contradictory nature of identities found at Western extends our thinking on the study of schooling to include the need for theories that account for the formation of apparatuses, such as raced-based tracking, forms of hyper-segregation, and surveillance practices. Both governmentality and *différance* may be concepts that could use more consideration in trying to address race and class issues that do not fit comfortably in theories of resistance and reproduction that reflect a consistent, homogeneous view of culture.

Lessons Unlearned

Our initial question was why parents, teachers and community members fought so hard to keep Western open. We can now shed some light on this query. For all the significant problems and limitations we have identified about Western, it was still a refuge of sorts. When Western students went to other schools, they experienced the hyper-segregation and uncaring attitudes that immigrants and students of colour had experienced at Western. What they lost, in leaving Western, was a refuge, where being working class (at least that aspect of an individual's culture) was represented as a respected and valued aspect of their culture, and that galvanised teacher commitment and engagement in both the private and public sectors.

Passion for keeping Western open, however, should not hide the uncaring hyper-segregation that reflected a non-caring attitude toward immigrants and students of colour. One of the interesting aspects of this finding is that class status and race were contradictory in their directionality. Class was a positive motivating factor that helped form a linked public/private 'we-ness' or collectivity while race led to the politics of containment,[3] hyper-segregation and ultimately an extreme form of non-caring. So what are we to make of the contradictory directionality between race and class?

LOOKING BACK AT OUR DISCOURSE COMMUNITIES

To begin, it seems important that researchers and inquirers from all methodological persuasions use their findings to unlearn what has been taken for granted in their discourse communities. For this study, we both utilised critical theory and unlearned some of the boundaries that contain this discourse. In particular, although race and class (among others) are essential to the analysis of the politics of schooling within many critical theory perspectives, it is less common to use multiple perspectives (i.e. in our case looking within Western and between Western and the dominant discourse in the local community) that are informed by competing projects of difference. If this sort of focus became more commonplace, we might find out whether the contradictory nature of identity formation at Western is reflective of a time where schools typically produce the contradictory directionality of race and class, or these cultural categories commonly act together. The lesson unlearned is that we are unlikely to see directional contradictions unless we view cultural categories from multiple perspectives.

Understanding Culture

In trying to wrap up the lessons unlearned, the most difficult and confusing issue may be our understanding of culture. By using the categories of race and class, as is common within critical theory discourse, we suggested that these categories reflect a great deal of internal cultural commonality– race or class means this or that about those individuals within this category. On the other hand, by exploding these categories we started to push against the boundaries of critical theory discourse by suggesting that these categories reflect internal cultural inconsistency – race and class do not necessarily mean this and that about individuals within these categories. In the end, therefore, we skirted any articulated view of what is meant by culture. Is culture a pre-existing, largely unchanging deposit of a bounded set of knowledge, values, experiences and linguistic practices, or a more dynamic, productive and generative set of practices involved in the regulation of social conduct and behaviour (McCarthy, Giardina, Harewood & Park, 2005)?

As we think through this query about culture, our findings indicate that culture, especially racial culture, is central to understanding and challenging the ways schooling reproduces group hierarchies. White privilege is, in part, reproduced because aspects of the White student's culture (working class) were valued. We did find, however, that students of colour and immigrant students were 'split' in terms of how teachers represented them. Aspects of their culture (the working class aspects) were valued while other aspects led to the politics of containment. If race or class was thrown out as a category we would not see the hideous effects of racially based practices and forms of representation. On the other hand, without exploding these categories we would not see how an individual student can be split, represented in contradictory ways. Our findings suggest that it may be worth making a double move where we use cultural categories such as race and class but also look for inconsistencies (heterogeneity) within those categories that reflects a more dynamic view of culture. As others explore the issue of culture in ways that move beyond our thinking it may be helpful to remember Lorde's (1984) powerful words in thinking about what is meant by culture:

> Once when I walked into a room
> my eyes would seek out the one or two black faces
> for contact or reassurance or a sign
> I was not alone
> now I walk into rooms full of black faces
> that would destroy me for any difference
> where shall my eyes look?
> Once it was easy to know
> who were my people. (p. 139)

At the core of our lessons unlearned is the possibility of using a complex view of student representation and identity formation to challenge the politics of containment. We are hopeful that this complex story will provide new possibilities for school reform that build on representations and identity formations that value aspects of student culture and challenge those that embody a pejorative view of their culture. When cultural workers look back at their own conceptual lens and confront the inevitable boundaries, it is possible to move beyond the view that schools are good or bad based on a dominant standard of educational excellence. It is possible to envision educational experiences that reflect the view that all aspects of the culture every student brings to the class are a benefit to be enhanced. This valuing, in our view, should be the basis of educational excellence.

NOTES

[1] Following Omni and Winnant (1986) we view racial formation as 'a central axis of social relations which cannot be subsumed or reduced to some broader category of conception' (p. 63). We view class as the socioeconomic status of the students.

[2] We use the word refuge interchangeably with caring in part because it begins to express how the particular notion of caring was constructed at Western. Refuge suggests that caring at Western provided a safe haven from the pejorative and negative assumptions about class status voiced in the local dominant community.

[3] We use this term to reflect what is more commonly referred to in the sociology of education literature as a model of reproduction, where schooling acts to reproduce social relations and hierarchies (Apple, 1990).

REFERENCES

Agar, M. (1980). *The professional stranger: An informal introduction to ethnography*. New York: Academic Press.

Apple, M. (1990). *Ideology and curriculum* (2nd ed.). New York: Routledge, Chapman, and Hall.

Anderson, A. E. (1988). *South high school: A history: 1931–1988*. [Brochure]. (Available from South High Alumni, Salt Lake Community College South City Campus, 250 W 3900 S, Salt Lake City, UT 84107.)

Bennett, T. (2003). Culture and governmentality. In J. Bratich et al. (Eds.), *Foucault, cultural studies, and governmentality*. New York: SUNY Press.

Burawoy, M. et al. (1991). *Ethnography unbound: Power and resistance on the modern metropolis*. Berkeley, CA: University of California Press.

Davidson, A. L. (1996). *Making and molding identity in schools: Student narratives on race, gender, and academic engagement*. Albany, NY: State University of New York Press.

Fordham, S. (1996). *Blacked out: Dilemmas of race, identity, and success at capital high*. Chicago: University of Chicago Press.

Grant, C. A., & Sleeter, C. E. (1986). *After the school bell rings*. Philadelphia: Falmer Press.

Hall, S. (1997). The centrality of culture: Notes on the cultural revolutions of our time. In K. Thompson (Ed.), *Media and cultural regulation*. London: Sage Publishers.

Kantor, H. (1988). *Learning to earn: School work and vocational reform in California, 1880–1930*. Madison, WI: University of Wisconsin Press.

Kozol, J. (1991). *Savage inequalities*. New York: Crown Publishers.

Lorde, A. (1984). *Sister outsider*. New York: The Crossing Press.

McCarthy, C., Giardina, M., Harewood, & Park, J. (2005). Contesting culture: Identity and curriculum dilemmas in the age of globalization, postcolonialism, and multiplicity. In C. McCarthy et al. (Eds.), *Race, identity, and representation in education* (2nd ed.). New York: Routledge.

Noddings, N. (1992). *The challenge to care in schools: An alternative approach to education*. New York: Teachers College Press.

O'Connor, C., Lewis, A., & Mueller, J. (2007). Researching 'Black' educational experiences and outcomes: theoretical and methodological considerations. *Educational Researcher, 36*(9), 541–552.

Oakes, J. (1985). *Keeping track: How schools structure inequality*. New Haven, CT: Yale University Press.

Ogbu, J. (1974). *The next generation: An ethnography of education in an urban neighborhood*. Orlando, FL: Academic Press.

Omi, M., & Winant, H. (1986). *Racial formation in the United States: From the 1960's to the 1980's*. New York: Routledge and Kegan Paul.

Omi, M., & Winant, H. (2005). The theoretical status of the concept of race. In C. McCarthy et al. (Eds.), *Race, identity, and representation in education* (2nd ed.). New York: Routledge.

Oxaal, I. (1990). Closing a high school: Student activities in the temporary organization. (Doctoral dissertation, University of Utah, 1990.) *Dissertation Abstracts International, 51*(12), 3981A.

Paris, Y. G. (1980). *Chicano students at South High School*. Master's thesis, University of Utah, 1980.

Sorensen, L. (1988). *Principal's address: South High yearbook*. Salt Lake City, UT: South High. (Available from South High Alumni, Salt Lake Community College South City Campus, 250 W 3900 S, Salt Lake City, UT 84107.)

Valenzuela, A. (1999). *Subtractive schooling: U.S.–Mexican youth and the politics of caring*. Albany, NY: SUNY Press.

Weis, L. (1990). *Working class without work: High school students in a de-industrializing economy*. New York: Routledge.

Wilson, A. (1987, February 8). 'Big, Bad' notion of South High is mostly myth. *The Salt Lake Tribune*, pp. B1, B3, B4.

Wortham, S., Murillo, E. G., & Hamann, E. T. (2002). *Education in the new Latino diaspora: Policy and the politics of identity*. Westport, CT: Ablex Publishing.

Andrew Gitlin
University of Georgia

Frances McConaughy
University of Utah

CONVERSATIONAL INTERLUDE ONE.
HOPES, DREAMS AND SLIPPAGES

Hazel Lawson: ... [A]ctually it (policy) shouldn't be top down. It should be far more interactive and so if can you apply these general solutions to the localised problems in terms of social equity – can we do something the other way round as well and look at more localised solutions to these bigger general problems? I've included on the handout, the concluding paragraphs of the chapter which sums it up ... and I'll just read the last sentence. ... Summing up really, 'in a climate of proliferating identities, closer attention to the subjectivities of learners (and I think teachers and other participants too) and how they're constructed and construct themselves as different from one another, may provide policy-makers with a new venue to explore in a search for more equitable social provision'.
...

Jean McPhail: Thank you, Hazel, very much for that paper and actually I'll try and sort of pick up where you left off and probably contest your *(inaudible)* if I may. So 'in a climate of proliferating identities, closer attention to the subjectivities of learners and how they construct themselves as well as teachers etc., etc. ...', I'd like to tell you a story about a failure experience that I had in New Zealand that took that premise as the guiding principle and failed. Now you may be able to help me understand why it failed beyond what Annemarie and I have done in writing this chapter and my colleagues and I have done, but I no longer see schools as sites, as they're constructed, where these kinds of things can happen. So let me state the end and then move quickly through the story. The end is that after spending 40 years in schooling and education, I no longer believe in the humanitarian vision of schools as we've constructed it. That is, it's just an ideal and is rarely practised even with all the best of policies, it seems to me, although there are exceptions to that. And the reason I think that that happens is because I now see schools as complex sites of power ... I believed [in the] premise that schools are sites of social justice and humanitarianism and idealism etc., and I no longer believe that they can easily be that in spite of the fact that very well-intentioned people actually go into education with all of those very fond hopes and dreams.
...

Annemarie Palincsar: *(Pause)* We have some time now for reflections on these two papers. I don't know if you (Hazel) want to respond to Jean's point of where she veers from your position or we can open it up to questions you have of either of the sets of authors or comments? *(Pause)*

Vanessa Andreotti: Okay, what I hear in both stories, and I know the school, ... my perspective on how they [are] conceptualised [is] it is the neo-liberal consumer identity. So I think there are two pushes for education for difference. One is a neo-liberal push related to individualised learning and the notion of being

K. Quinlivan, R. Boyask and B. Kaur (eds.), *Educational Enactments in a Globalised World:*
Intercultural Conversations, 41–43.

individual with no awareness of power. It is much more based on the consumer identity. And there's another push coming from different pockets of movements like queer theory, critical theory, critical race theory, post-colonial theory, talking about something else. The ambiguity there opens a productive space where you can maybe re-signify that and reclaim the context or it just opens up a big tension and conflict that is very difficult to negotiate.

...

Ruth Boyask: You know the discourse of universalism that's occurring particularly in things like personalised learning within England; that neo-liberal identity is a very homogenised identity. It's a consumer across all contexts and so for me, that's the difference, Jean ... subjectivity is not just one thing and it's certain kinds of subjectivities that are being left out of a discourse that's what we're trying to get a bit closer to in some of the empirical work that we're doing.

Jean McPhail: If you have the emergence of individual subjectivities without a corresponding concept of power, that power is going to be negotiated, then you're still left, it seems to me, with a highly contestable site and for reasons I don't quite understand, never want that talked about in school. It's sort of the silent topic and yet it's pervasive.

...

Kathleen Quinlivan: I just think there might be something to consider too about, I guess it's the whole question about, what can be productive about failure and I think it is very hard to talk about failure. Like failure in my research ... I think there's actually something really significant about attending to failure 'cos I remember at the end of your chapter, one of the things you said, you said a thing about 'we have to learn to do something differently here' and I think it's very difficult within the current kind of neo-liberal environment as [a] researcher to actually engage with failure and talk about failure because everybody has to have such a deep investment in their success as researchers. We have to be successful to get funding you know and all those kind of things, so the environment that we're working in makes it difficult to actually talk about the very things we need to talk about the most.

...

Jean McPhail: Yeah, I think schools are, I think they're complex sites of varying subjectivities, and within those subjectivities are dreams and those dreams are hard to ascertain sometimes because people are not open and willing to talk about them and yet schools are embedded with dreams. Parents' dreams for their children, teachers' dreams for the success of the [children] and that's a highly emotional issue which I think doesn't get addressed well in terms of the discourses that we have and I would agree with you: those dreams function both in terms of the researcher who unknowingly and perhaps too proudly walks into a context as well as the response of those within that context. *(Pause)*

...

Julie Allan: *(Comment after the 2009 American Educational Research Symposium)* The discussion provided, to an extent, some opportunities for opinions to clash and what emerged for me was that the source of the clash was the different world views of particular actors. Some saw the tensions or contradictions (I'd call them, after Derrida, aporias), such as the generalising and the individualising discourses that Hazel outlined as a gulf, while others saw them as a productive space: a kind of epistemological version of the glass half-empty or half-full distinction.

The notion of failure, discussed by Jean and Kathleen in their papers, provoked some good discussion and seems to me an extremely lucrative avenue for inter-cultural conversations. The domination of the 'what works' mentality within education has made any discussion of educational failures seem transgressive and Jean and Kathleen did present themselves as somewhat wayward for talking about their losses. A comparative analysis of failure could, I think, be an extremely productive arena.

...

[Libby Cohen, acting on Annemarie's invitation to respond to both papers, picked up a theme spoken to by Hazel about the policy initiatives in the UK, Every Child Matters and Every Disabled Child Matters, along with the five outcomes of the former seen as universal ambitions for all children: to stay safe, to be healthy, to enjoy and achieve, to achieve economic well-being and to make a positive contribution.]

Libby Cohen: I'm coming from a South Asian perspective, from Singapore and just being in that neighbourhood of Southeast Asia it's really hard to relate to what you're saying because for many countries every child doesn't matter ... Enjoyment, achievement of happiness are not what schools are focused on.

Hazel Lawson: I'm not sure they are in England either ... that's the policy rhetoric. There was even a document produced called *Excellence and Enjoyment* and to actually put the word enjoyment in a government policy is ...

Baljit Kaur: In India they had a similar expression in a policy document about a decade ago ... Joyful Learning!

Libby Cohen: I think we're talking about different parts of the globe.

Sean Darmody: [With regard to the] paradox that you've mentioned in England ... I stopped working at the Institute of Education and spent four years in a special school in the East End of London ... We were able to enact a male and female teacher in every classroom for they became special needs children, originally called sub-normal and there was the severely sub-normal based on IQ testing. But the facilities we got, the happiness bit was one of the first things that made me very angry with some of the teachers. It was a Victorian philanthropic hang-up – 'so long as the kids are happy, don't worry about teaching them anything' ... 'it confuses them'. 'They're not going to be successful therefore, don't do it.' And of course their social deprivations are much, much more than anything to do with IQ tests. The paradox was, if we gave the same facilities to the inner-city deprived, normal kids, just think how well they could do, but it wasn't available for them because they weren't categorised!

HAZEL PHILLIPS

INTERSTICE ONE: MĀORI ASPIRATIONS IN CONTEMPORARY TIMES

Old Narratives, New Articulations, Uncertain Outcomes

INTRODUCTION

Nineteen eighty-two was a landmark year for Māori, the indigenous people of Āotearoa New Zealand, and their education. It was the year that Te Kōhanga Reo, a Māori-initiated early childhood programme, began. Three years later the first Kura Kaupapa (primary school) opened, and secondary and tertiary options soon followed. Known as kaupapa Māori initiatives – by Māori, for Māori and (mostly) in the Māori language – all these educational institutions were established outside of state provision of schooling. After 150 years of protesting against and resisting colonial domination and assimilation, Māori desire for change was finally being realised. The kaupapa Māori initiatives were not just about creating positive learning experiences leading to successful learning outcomes or the assertion of the importance of culture and language in learning; they were also highly political acts that spoke directly to the 'gut refusal to be subordinated' (Mansbridge, 2001). It was no coincidence that these initiatives were developing at the same time as marginalised groups and communities around the world were making gains and fulfilling their political, social and cultural aspirations. These localised developments marked a global shift in which intellectual and material spaces were opening up within the context of neoliberal economies and promising a raft of democratic possibilities, including social justice and human rights. Within the promissory spaces created, the transformation of people's lives was no longer the stuff of utopian dreams; change appeared imminent and education at least for Māori was the vehicle. This brief commentary, reflecting on the impact of globalised discourses on Māori experiences of and in education over the last 25 years, considers whether schooling in a neo-liberal regime can realistically fulfil Māori educational and development aspirations.

Initially I set out to recount victory narratives about how Māori have claimed spaces within education and asserted their cultural frames of references, practices and values to create an education that better fits and reflects their aspirations and sensibilities. I planned to share how kaupapa Māori initiatives are working and how Māori 'standard stories' (after McCreanor, 2005) of failure and underachievement are being overwritten with accounts of success. Indeed kaupapa Māori initiatives have made a difference and, along with developments within mainstream schooling,

K. Quinlivan, R. Boyask and B. Kaur (eds.), Educational Enactments in a Globalised World:
Intercultural Conversations, 45–50.

many young Māori are leaving school as educational success stories. But for each of those students who is successful there is one whose educational and life experiences tell a different story (Ministry of Education, 2009). That is not to say that these 'victory narratives' are unimportant (Phillips, 2003). They are vital to the collective anthology of Māori and we should hold them close to us, but when considering the state of Māori education in light of the promissory spaces opened up over the past two decades, standard stories remain prominent.

The education *of* Māori and the subsequent marginalisation of Māori students have a long history in Āotearoa New Zealand as do Māori aspirations for educational success. Right from the beginning of state provision of native schooling, Māori saw an opportunity for western knowledge to enhance their lives *as* Māori (Simon & Smith, 2001). However, despite wanting access to this body of knowledge, the reality was that access to learning was limited to learning to become compliant labourers. The ideological forces that underpinned the spread of imperialism were also about the subordination of the other to fit the needs of an emerging colonial nation state. One hundred and fifty years on and in an emerging global society those same forces, though manifesting in different ways, continue to buttress contemporary education policies and practices. So too do Māori continue to find ways to resist and challenge, and to articulate aspirations for equality and self-determination.

Within the context of contemporary globalised discourses three mutually reinforcing narratives have become dominant themes in Māori educational settings and communities. They arise out of the historical struggle for Māori economic, cultural and political survival which since colonial times has been expressed in multiple and diverse ways. Within the context of contemporary education I want to draw attention to three particular narratives. These narratives not only talk back (hooks, 1989) to Māori standard stories; they also 'talk forward' to traditional understandings and practices in overcoming the historical inequalities that Māori face. Although they are framed in the discourse of emancipatory struggle, they shadow the rhetorical themes of current educational and social policy and the promises they contain; situating Āotearoa New Zealand as a knowledge society in which knowledge, skills and technological innovation are the keys to success in the global economy. Even though talk of the marketplace has taken a back seat in recent times, it nevertheless remains the central mechanism through which prosperity, freedom and equity are promised.

HUI TAUMATA

Since 1858 Māori have expressed their resistance to colonial processes and their desire for change through Hui Taumata, summit meetings of tribal leaders. The intent of the first hui (gathering) was to bring together leaders to advance Māori through a united iwi (tribal) front. Discussed in this hui were aspirations for iwi participation in society, retention of tribal economic resources and the terms of the relationship between iwi Māori and the Crown (Durie, 2006). Although the essence

of these aspirations has remained the same over time, more recently the hui have extended and particularised Māori consensus to include:
– to live as Māori
– to actively participate as citizens of the world
– to enjoy good health and a high standard of living.

Since the first hui the focus has shifted from a collective iwi identity to a more individualised one that unambiguously points towards Māori as global citizens. Despite, perhaps ironically so, the articulation of a more individualised Māori identity, the primary conduit for the realisation of these aspirations continues to be the whānau (extended family), the principal social unit of Māori society. Education, the marketplace, and the wider world according to the Hui Taumata consensus are accessed and experienced through the whānau (Durie, 2006). The centrality of the whānau to a specifically Māori identity is shared by Māori educators and communities alike. Although this level of consensus speaks to a collective understanding of whānau, the reality is more complicated. Diverse realities mean that there is no longer, indeed if there ever was, a Māori consensus of identity and whānau given that the political organisational structures of Māori society are based on hapū (subtribe) and iwi. Although many Māori do have a sense of connection and belonging and share the aspirations articulated by Hui Taumata, the challenges to this consensus are Māori who do not identify with these aspirations or are disengaged and/or disenfranchised *as* Māori.

CHOICE AND KAUPAPA MĀORI EDUCATION INITIATIVES

I started this commentary by highlighting the significance of kaupapa Māori initiatives to Māori education. Kōhanga reo, kura kaupapa and wānanga along with other kaupapa Māori initiatives have become prominent markers of what successful Māori education looks like. Notwithstanding that these initiatives were born out of the gut refusal to be subordinated, their development was also enabled by the ideology of choice and the establishment of Āotearoa New Zealand's quasi-educational marketplace. Underpinning this ideology is the expectation that diverse (read cultural) communities would have a voice and provide the education marketplace with choices. Ironically the promissory space in which kaupapa Māori initiatives were established has both extended and limited Māori choices. While on the one hand kaupapa Māori initiatives have opened up choices, on the other their popularity has meant that demand quickly outstripped provision: there are simply not enough schools, teachers to teach in them or teaching resources to support Māori pedagogical practices. This has meant that only a small percentage of Māori students and their whānau are able to choose kaupapa Māori initiatives to fulfil their aspirations for an education that validates Māori language, knowledge and values and most importantly their identity *as* Māori. Notwithstanding the importance of kaupapa Māori initiatives in meeting the aspirations of some Māori, diverse realities make a single option insufficient to meet the aspirations of all Māori. Kaupapa Māori initiatives cannot and never have had the authority to speak for all students and their whānau.

For the majority of Māori students who attend mainstream schools the experience of choice is different and arguably more problematic. Prior to the late 1980s every student had the right to attend their local school, a reflection of the egalitarian ideal of equality of opportunity and the role of education in its realisation. The subsequent emphasis on quasi-educational markets and choice, while still retaining the egalitarian ideal, assumes that students and their whānau will make decisions based on their intrinsic self-interest. In this scenario schools would be compelled to provide quality education; if they do not, students and their whānau would vote with their feet and go elsewhere. Yet in practice, even if whānau wanted to exercise choice for their sons and daughters, many simply do not have the means to do so. Families who are able to make choices are those with educational and social capital. One of the consequences of this difference has been 'white flight' from schools that have high numbers of Māori and Pasifika students (Collins, 2006). Occurring mostly in poor communities, the 'browning' of schools has led already financially strapped schools to struggle to provide the kind of education that prepares young people to take their place in a knowledge society (Ladd & Fiske, 2001). Moreover, in this quasi-marketplace schools, in various ways, are choosing their students. Rather than opening up opportunities and democratic possibilities, choice in education has worked to reinforce exclusionary social practices (Reay, 2004).

MĀORI POTENTIAL: THE NEW MANTRA

Finally the third narrative is framed more overtly in the promissory language of Māori potential. The articulation of this rhetoric is lead by Te Puni Kōkiri, the Ministry of Māori Development, and echoed in policy documents of other ministries including the Ministry of Education's five year education strategy (Ministry of Education 2008). This approach has become the public policy direction for the government and focuses on the unique cultural identity of Māori and their potential contribution, given that uniqueness, to the well-being and enrichment not only of Māori society but also of Āotearoa New Zealand as a whole.

According to the framework, mātauranga (Māori knowledge) and its transmission are identified as key enablers of Māori physical, psychological, emotional and spiritual potential (Te Puni Kōkiri, 2008). The framework's rhetoric comes out of a desire to move away from deficit thinking to invoke specifically Māori solutions that will advance Māori development. This is perhaps ironic given that by the very language of potential it suggests that something is missing. Of more concern is that the rhetoric of potential is strongly underpinned by the ideas of human capital and the entrepreneurial self (Peters, 2001) and marks a subtle and contradictory shift from the collective notions of identity, struggle and self-determination, to the notion of autonomous individuals who are empowered to change their own lives. In this scenario schooling becomes more about the investment in skills of individuals rather than the pursuit of collective Māori aspirations or the development of well-rounded citizens in multicultural societies (Mitchell, 2003).

These three mutually reinforcing narratives indicate the alignment of traditional Māori knowledges, understandings and narratives to the dominant discourse of economic globalisation otherwise known as neo-liberalism. This move reflects global trends of legitimating and valuing indigenous peoples' cultural and intellectual property, especially in relation to the contribution that indigenous knowledge and practices are making to both local and global problems. For example at the local level indigenous educational practices are being held up as ways forward to increasing the success of not just indigenous students but all students. At the global level indigenous practices and knowledge developed over successive generations are being used to develop environmentally sustainable frameworks. However, despite these developments, indigenous peoples and their knowledges and practices remain vulnerable to commodification and exploitation (Awang, 2000). More importantly these rhetorical strategies signify the very real possibility of the spaces created by neo-liberalism not just enhancing success *as* Māori but creating new Māori identities altogether. Although this could be understood through Lear's (2006, p. 103) notion of radical hope that is 'directed toward a future goodness that transcends the current ability to understand what [that hope] is', we have to be very careful that the schooling and opportunities we provide for young Māori do not end up constructing them in the image of the neo-liberal master. It may already be too late to prevent such an outcome as research shows that young people who have grown up in Āotearoa New Zealand's neo-liberal political economy are 'imbued with a neoliberal rationality' (Nairn & Higgins, 2007).

Twenty-five years on, the promises remain illusory. Although democratic possibilities have opened up, the realities of 'predatory economic globalisation' at the very same time have worked to undercut them (Gaonkar, 2002, p. 3). It is perhaps, ironically so, the mark of an entrepreneurial spirit that Māori narratives of resistance, challenge and hope reflect the times within which they are articulated. I find it difficult to imagine how globalised discourses that promise so much can unproblematically, given their neo-liberal underbelly, reflect and benefit indigenous peoples. Social justice and human rights are at best unevenly realised, and at worst are unrealisable given the way in which the dynamic of capitalism works to maintain the status quo. Indigenous people and marginalised communities the world over are experiencing new forms of subordination and assimilation in the face of globalisation. It is with these experiences in mind that I question whether the spaces opened up will be able to fulfil Māori educational and development aspirations, especially as they are currently articulated.

REFERENCES

Awang, S. (2000). Indigenous nations and the human genome diversity project. In G. Sefa Dei, B. Hall & D. Goldin Rosenberg (Eds.), *Indigenous Knowledges in global contexts: Multiple readings of our world.* Toronto, ON: University of Toronto Press.

Collins, S. (2006). 'White flight' threatens school. *New Zealand Herald.* Retrieved April 5, 2009, from http://www.nzherald.co.nz/warriors-still/news/article.cfm?c_id=1501094&objectid=10392647

Durie, M. (2006). *Whānau, education and Māori potential.* Massey University, Secondary Futures Project, Families Commission. Retrieved April 3, 2009, from http://www.secondaryfutures.co.nz/matrix/2006/01/hui_event.php

Gaonkar, D. P. (2002). Toward new imaginaries: An introduction. *Public Culture, 14*(1), 1–19.

Hooks, B. (1989). *Talking back: Thinking feminist, thinking black.* Boston: South End Press.

Ladd, H., & Fiske, E. (2001). The uneven playing field of school choice: Evidence from New Zealand. *Journal of Policy Analysis and Management, 20*(1), 43–63.

Lear, J. (2006). *Radical hope: Ethics in the face of cultural devastation.* Cambridge, MA: Harvard University Press.

Mansbridge, J. (2001). Opposition consciousness. In J. Mansbridge & A. D. Morris (Eds.), *Oppositional consciousness: The subjective roots of social protest.* Chicago: Chicago Press.

McCreanor, T. (2005). 'Sticks and stones may break my bones …': Talking Pākehā identities. In J. Liu, T. McCreanor, T. Macintosh, & T. Teaiwa (Eds.), *New Zealand identities: Departures and destinations.* Wellington, NZ: Victoria University Press.

Ministry of Education. (2008). *Ka hikitia: Managing for success, Māori education strategy.* Wellington, NZ: Ministry of Education.

Ministry of Education. (2009). *Ngā Haeata Mātauranga: The annual report on Māori education, 2007/2008.* Wellington, NZ: Ministry of Education.

Mitchell, K. (2003). Educating the national citizen in neoliberal times: From the multicultural self to the strategic cosmopolitan. *Transactions – Institute of British Geographers, 28*(4), 387–403.

Nairn, K., & Higgins, J. (2007). New Zealand's neoliberal generation: Tracing discourses of economic rationality. *International Journal of Qualitative Studies in Education, 20*(3), 262–281.

Phillips, H. (2003). *Te reo karanga o ngā tauira Māori: Māori students: Their voices, their stories at the University of Canterbury 1996–1998.* Unpublished PhD thesis, University of Canterbury.

Peters, M. (2001). Education, enterprise culture and the entrepreneurial self: A Foucauldian perspective. *Journal of Educational Enquiry, 2*(2), 58–71.

Reay, D. (2004). Exclusivity, exclusion, and social class in urban education markets in the United Kingdom. *Urban Education, 39*(5), 537–560.

Simon, J., & Smith, L. T. (Eds.). (2001). *A civilising mission? Perceptions and representations of the Native Schools system.* Auckland, NZ: Auckland University Press.

Te Puni Kōkiri. (2008). *Māori potential approach.* Retrieved April 3, 2009, from http://www.tpk.govt.nz/en/about/mpa

Hazel Phillips
He Parekereke, Institute for Research and Development
in Māori and Pacific Education
Faculty of Education
Victoria University of Wellington

RICHARD MANNING

4. PLACE, POWER AND PEDAGOGY

The Potential that a Critical Pedagogy of Place May Hold
for Enhancing Cross-cultural Conversations in New Zealand

INTRODUCTION

This chapter draws upon doctoral research (Manning, 2008) to consider how the application of a critical pedagogy of place might enhance the quality of cross-cultural conversations currently being held in the Port Nicholson Block area (Wellington district, in the Southwestern corner of New Zealand's North Island). This exercise is prompted by some of my research findings which correspond with some conclusions drawn by the Waitangi Tribunal in relation to its research in the Gisborne area.[1] The tribunal, in its report on the Tūranganui a Kiwa (Gisborne) claims, called on all New Zealanders to develop a greater 'consciousness' of 'historical memory of place' and concluded that:

> We cannot help but think that the unsettled state of relations between Māori [the indigenous people of New Zealand] and Pākehā [non-Māori people] in this country is in part due to the fact that these stories are remembered only by tangata whenua [literally 'people of the land'; local tribe(s)] and a few historians who specialise in New Zealand history. While only one side remembers the suffering of the past, dialogue will always be difficult. One side commences the dialogue with anger and the other side has no idea why. Reconciliation cannot be achieved by this means. Thus it seems no more than common sense that if stories such as these from Tūranga were more widely known in the community, particularly local communities more directly affected, the need to heal the wounds of the past before moving forward would be better understood by all. (Waitangi Tribunal, 2004, p. 740)

I will begin this chapter by describing my research methodology and objectives in relation to the Waitangi Tribunal's research in the Port Nicholson Block area.[2] I will then discuss the tenets of a critical pedagogy of place. Next I will outline the benefits my research participants identified that might result from a potential partnership between the iwi (tribe) of Te Ātiawa and those secondary schools that participated in my research. A metaphor will then be used to illuminate the implications of my research.

K. Quinlivan, R. Boyask and B. Kaur (eds.), *Educational Enactments in a Globalised World:*
Intercultural Conversations, 51–64.

RESEARCH OBJECTIVES AND METHODOLOGY

My research was conducted following the release of the Waitangi Tribunal's (2003) *Te Whanganui a Tara me ōna Takiwā* report which investigated the Crown's role in the alienation of lands and other resources in the Port Nicholson Block area. It was not designed to critique the tribunal's report, or to comment on the role of the Wellington Tenths Trust in the presentation of claims central to that report.[3] In summary, my research explored how two groups of research participants viewed the teaching of local, Māori, environmental and New Zealand history; particularly in relation to their own life experiences of learning about past and place. Nine Te Ātiawa people selected from a pool of potential 'expert' interviewees (nominated by the Wellington Tenths Trust) and nine senior history teachers were invited to reflect upon the cultural continuities and discontinuities they experienced in relation to how history was taught to them in their familial and secondary school settings. They were also asked what they felt should be taught today in Port Nicholson Block secondary schools and to suggest teaching approaches. A survey was also developed to identify topics taught in Port Nicholson Block secondary schools (Manning 2008, pp. 81–82).

These results were then related to a survey conducted by the New Zealand History Teachers' Association (2005) so that I could compare Te Ātiawa interviewees' topics preferences with those of history teachers locally and nationally. In summary, I found (Manning, 2008, pp. 123–153) that Te Ātiawa interviewees held local Māori, environmental and New Zealand histories in high regard, whereas these topics were often avoided by local history and social studies teachers and their peers elsewhere. Te Ātiawa histories of place were largely invisible in Port Nicholson Block secondary schools for this reason: the teachers I encountered often felt afraid to deal with contentious issues and/or did not know how to engage or consult with local tribes (or know that these tribes still existed). I concluded that a critical pedagogy of place, like that envisioned by Te Ātiawa participants (and Gruenewald, 2003), might remedy the cross-cultural conversations occurring in the Port Nicholson Block area and elsewhere in New Zealand.

A CRITICAL PEDAGOGY OF PLACE

When examining the relationship between critical pedagogy and place-based education (PBE) Gruenewald (2003, p. 3) observed that:

> Unlike critical pedagogy, which evolves from the well-established discourse of critical theory (Aronowitz & Giroux, 1993; Burbules & Berk, 1999; Freire, 1970, 1995; Giroux, 1988, McLaren, 2003), place-based education lacks a specific theoretical tradition, though this is partly a matter of naming. Its practices and purposes can be connected to experiential learning, contextual learning, problem-based learning, constructivism, outdoor education, indigenous education, bioregional education, democratic education, multicultural education, community-based education, critical pedagogy itself, as well as other approaches

that are concerned with context and the value of learning from and nurturing specific places, communities, or regions.

He proposed (2003, p. 3) that critical pedagogies and place-based pedagogies are 'mutually supportive educational traditions' that have grown apart and need to be re-converged. Gruenewald drew attention to the fact that place-based education is now 'frequently discussed at a distance from the urban multicultural arena, territory most often emphasized by critical pedagogues'. This tendency is ironic, because as McLaren and Giroux (1990, p. 154) observed:

> While critical pedagogy in its early stages grew largely out of the efforts of Paulo Freire and his literary campaigns among peasants in rural areas of Brazil and other Third World [sic] countries, subsequent generations of North American teachers and cultural workers influenced by Freire's work have directed most of their attention to urban minority populations in major metropolitan centers. Very little writing exists that deals with critical pedagogy in the rural school classroom and community.

Thus exponents of these two pedagogical traditions often avoid having the sorts of theoretical conversations that might support oppressed peoples' quests for eco-justice. As Gruenewald (2003, p. 3) suggested:

> Despite clear areas of overlap between critical pedagogy and place-based education (such as the importance of situated context and the goal of social transformation), significant strands exist which do not always recognize the potential contributions of the other. On the one hand, critical pedagogy often betrays a sweeping disinterest in the fact that humanity has been, is, and always will be nested within ecological systems (Bowers 1997, 2001). In a parallel story of neglect, place-based education has developed an ecological and rural emphasis that is often insulated from the cultural conflicts inherent in dominant American culture. Additionally, in its focus on local, ecological experience, place-based approaches are sometimes hesitant to link ecological themes such as urbanization and the homogenization of culture under global capitalism (see Hay, 1996, Chap. 6). In short, both critical pedagogy and place-based education have through these silences missed opportunities to strengthen each respective tradition by borrowing from the other.

Gruenewald proposed that critical pedagogy and PBE can contribute to the sort of 'critical pedagogy of place' that, in my assessment, may help address my research findings and the conclusions of the Waitangi Tribunal (2004), outlined earlier. He reasoned (2003, p. 3) that whereas critical pedagogy 'offers an agenda of cultural decolonization, PBE leads the way towards ecological reinhabitation'. Because the term 'decolonization' may invoke stereotypical assumptions in some New Zealand cultural settings, it is important to understand Gruenewald's (2003, p. 9) description of the relationship that exists between the 'twin goals' of 'decolonization' and 'reinhabitation' that are central to a critical pedagogy of place:

In many ways decolonization describes the underside of reinhabitation; it may not be possible without decolonization. If reinhabitation involves learning to live well socially and ecologically in places that have been disrupted and injured, decolonization involves learning to recognize disruption and injury and to address their causes.[4] From an educational perspective, it means unlearning much of what dominant culture and schooling teaches, and learning more socially just and ecologically sustainable ways of being in the world.

As the next section suggests, Te Ātiawa participants saw great potential in the possibility of adopting critical pedagogies of place to 'unlearn' much of what the dominant Pākehā culture and schooling had taught (or not taught) them about the area in which they now lived.

THE POTENTIAL BENEFITS OF A CRITICAL PEDAGOGY OF PLACE

Te Ātiawa Interviewees' Perspectives

Te Ātiawa interviewees' general endorsement of a critical pedagogy of place added further weight to Smith's (1999, pp. 34–35) observation that:

Coming to know the past has been part of the critical pedagogy of decolonization. To hold alternative histories is to hold alternative knowledges. The pedagogical implication of this access to alternative knowledges is that they can form the basis for alternative ways of doing things. Transforming our colonized views of our own history … requires us to revisit, site by site, our history under Western eyes. This in turn requires a theory or approach which helps us to engage with, understand and then act upon history.

Te Ātiawa interviewees consistently advised that local natural environs and cultural/historical landmarks should be used as strategic learning sites to support the teaching of local Te Ātiawa histories of place and the teaching of New Zealand history in general. They also believed that the teaching of New Zealand history should involve an interdisciplinary or 'holistic' approach to the design, delivery, assessment and evaluation of what I would liken to social inquiry-based, integrated curriculum activities. They reasoned that an interdisciplinary approach would give students a wider range of authentic and meaningful learning experiences than the textbook-driven lessons they had encountered at school. Five of the nine Te Ātiawa interviewees identified anthropology as the academic discipline that history teachers should first turn to when planning to teach about local tribal, Māori or New Zealand histories.[5] As one Te Ātiawa interviewee suggested:

Students need to know what was happening, what was in the minds of people and this is the problem I've found with New Zealand history – it's difficult, but you've got to, at least to some extent, have access to the Māori minds or worldviews being studied. To do that, I think that history and anthropology have to cross-fertilise skills, somewhat. So in making sense of something, I think you need to analyse history with a wider range of disciplinary lens to better understand what was actually happening. (Manning, 2008, pp. 185–186)

Anthropology was not the only discipline identified by Te Ātiawa interviewees. They also saw great potential in merging the teaching of New Zealand geography and history. One of them said:

I think that by drawing upon their geography skills and participating in on-site excursions, to learn about historical geographies and aspects of [local] archaeology, students will broaden their understanding of history and their development as individuals. It's not all about going to the library and picking up a history book or going through the archives to pull out written primary resources. History is also about being, physically, on-site. It's about looking at the land, possibly having that textbook there with you, but looking at the sites and asking oneself, 'could these things really have been done here, or where this pā site is situated, like it says in this book, or has the landscape changed?' (Manning, 2008, p. 187)

Te Ātiawa interviewees recognised that it might prove difficult for local history teachers to adopt a holistic approach without appropriate professional development opportunities, or the support of local Te Ātiawa people and Crown agencies. The following comment typifies this stance:

To bring all those [subjects] together would require a fairly interesting curriculum development. But, I'm sure it can be done. Whether they, the Crown, would pay for something like that is another thing. I think it would be most beneficial to integrate all subject experiences. So, yeah, I think you should be able to represent all aspects of time and place so that every angle can be explored and assessed. (Manning, 2008, p. 187)

Despite the challenges, Te Ātiawa interviewees reiterated their shared belief that it is vital for students to learn to develop ecological literacy skills, outside their classrooms, that would enable them to critically draw links between people and land, sea, flora and fauna through time. This thinking, consequently, aligned loosely with Freire and Macedo's (1987) belief that teachers need to assist their students to read the word and the world. The arguments of Te Ātiawa interviewees also aligned with the work of Russell (1997), who urged historians to read land-scapes in order to better understand how human history may have impacted upon contemporary ecosystems and landscapes. Russell suggested that the ability to 'read landscapes' would, in turn, help historians to recognise how changing envi-ronments may have influenced human history. As one Te Ātiawa interviewee observed:

You can't divorce history from other subjects or from the natural environ-ment. That's one of the big problems with the teaching of history. History teachers are still saying things like 'this event happened in 1887, that event happened in 1900, that event happened in 1977.' It is too simplistic because you can't divorce those events from the natural environment that they took place in. For instance if I'm talking about the history of this place, I will talk about the Waiwhetū Stream and how we've lived here for a long time and how important that stream is to us because it represents the mauri [life force] of water and how essential that is to being alive. I'll talk about the history of things that happened around that stream over the time that we have been here and explain why that's important to us and why it's important for the future: because the stream's being contaminated. So, you shouldn't exclude from history those other aspects of living, like science, maths or spiritual things. (Manning, 2008, p. 125)

Thus his views on the need for an integrated curriculum approach to the teaching of history coincide with those of Orr (1992, p. 125), who commented that:

Places are laboratories of diversity and complexity, mixing social functions and natural processes ... The classroom and indoor laboratory are ideal environments in which to narrow reality in order to focus on bits and pieces. The study of place, by contrast, enables us to widen the focus to examine the interrelationships between disciplines and to lengthen our perception of time.

Te Ātiawa interviewees emphasised that teachers and their students need to acquire knowledge of te reo Māori (the Māori language) if they are to recognise the historical information visible in the place names surrounding them. One Te Ātiawa interviewee used the analogy of a GIS/GPS mapping exercise to explain why she felt teachers 'should' learn te reo Māori:

Having that knowledge of te reo Māori would be like adding another dimension to appreciating a series of historical layers on a [GIS] map ... By developing knowledge of te reo Māori, you're adding another level of analysis to the history of a place ... A sound knowledge of te reo Māori does give you another insight into something much deeper, something that happened, here, in this place, or that this other particular place was named after someone or something that had happened and that you may be in peril by being in that place. (Manning, 2008, pp. 191–192)

This analogy also illuminated the fact that all Te Ātiawa interviewees were more cognisant of the pedagogical opportunities afforded by GIS/GPS technologies than were all of their teacher counterparts.[6] For example, a Te Ātiawa interviewee explained how he felt teachers could use these technologies to read the historic landscape:

It would be very interesting for students who are looking at the Te Ātiawa migrations from Taranaki to Wellington in the 1820s to use GPS/GIS technologies. I say that because I'm familiar with GPS. We've used it primarily for waka ama [outrigger canoe] events in order to map our courses. The GPS system that we used showed us the different routes that we've taken, the depth of water we've travelled across and things like that. So, it would be really useful technology to have in recording the paths that our tūpuna [ancestors] took along the land and through the coastal areas, to record the key landmarks that they would have encountered such as the mountains, hills and so forth. Also, that would help students to get a much deeper appreciation for the physical and spiritual endurance of our tūpuna, who had to locate different natural resources in order to pass through the different landscapes. By using GPS and GIS technologies, they can also learn a lot about the types of tools and resources that the people would have required in order to make their journeys. (Manning, 2008, pp. 193–194)

All Te Ātiawa interviewees supported the idea of forming a critical PBE partnership, with local secondary schools, underpinned by the principles of 'partnership', 'active protection' and 'participation' implicit within the Treaty of Waitangi (1840); as accepted by the Crown since 1989 when the principles for Crown action on the Treaty of Waitangi were set out.[7] They believed that teachers should collaborate with their tribe in the design, delivery, assessment and evaluation of community mapping projects, or any other place-based learning activities that address local Te Ātiawa histories of place. Te Ātiawa interviewees also believed that local Te Ātiawa people should assist local history and social studies teachers to teach about events that involved their Te Ātiawa ancestors in other regions of New Zealand, particularly Taranaki.[8]

When Te Ātiawa interviewees were asked 'how' they would like to teach local history students about their local Te Ātiawa histories of place, they favoured traditional learning experiences, such as walking the land and having their own Te Ātiawa-nominated experts assisting teachers and students to conduct authentic research tasks. This was most evident when one interviewee explained how the Wellington Tenths Trust had recently taken Wellington City Councillors along the different reaches of the Waitangi Stream to explain how the history of that stream was related to the proposed naming of Waitangi Park.[9] He said:

> Consider why it's called 'Waitangi Park'. In doing that redevelopment [e.g. the 'day-lighting' of the lower reaches of the Waitangi stream] and naming it 'Waitangi Park' the history of human occupation of that area suddenly comes alive! That was a mahinga kai, a place to gather crops. People [Councillors] were also quite surprised to find that though there's no stream, because it's all in an underground pipe now, there's still a large quantity of eels living in the Waitangi stream. They hadn't learned the history of that stream [at school] or that that stream's now in a pipe. But, despite that pipe and other pipes, the eels still migrate up and down the pipes below the city. They travel up into the Newtown area of the city and heaven knows how they survive, but they do survive in that subterranean stream … I think that when those people understood those elements of that place's history you could just see it was one of those 'ohhhhhhh' moments for them. They said things like: 'I'd never even thought about the potential of looking at historical things that way before.' It's kind of like 'out of sight, out of mind' and, as a result, it's also a bit like how Māori culture is now. It's just like the stream that's piped underground so that we never have to think of it again! (Manning, 2008, p. 198–199)

The history teachers who participated in this research also identified a range of benefits that might arise from adopting a critical pedagogy of place.

The History Teachers' Perspectives

The history teachers' responses suggested they were willing to experiment with place-based pedagogies, but only with the support of their school management teams, Crown agencies and local Te Ātiawa people. They all felt that they would need professional development opportunities to change their pedagogical approaches. The first teacher I interviewed stated that participation in this study had made him much more aware of his own professional development needs. He, along with most of his eight peers who were interviewed, shared a view of history education that aligned with Barton and Levstik's (2004, pp. 91–109) description of a 'moral response stance'. When describing this stance, Barton and Levstik concluded (pp. 106–107) that responding morally forms a 'major component of history education'. Although teachers rarely phrase their pedagogical objectives in 'moral terms' they 'invariably expect students to admire some people or events and to condemn others'.

Another teacher felt that a critical PBE approach would encourage more 'critical thinking' amongst her mainly Pākehā students largely because it would challenge them to reflect upon how cultural assumptions had informed their own senses of place and how their personal constructs of New Zealand identity and citizenship were challenged by local tribal narratives of place. She commented that:

> I think it [a critical pedagogy of place] would really open my students' eyes. Everywhere they go they'd have to be looking out for things and thinking 'what does that mean, why is that there?' Even things like why places are named what they're named. For example, I go past places like *Te Rauparaha Park* [named after the famous Ngāti Toa leader], in Porirua [a city north of Wellington] and I'm thinking 'yeah I know about him', but then other people are saying things in public like; 'why is it called that? What's he [Te Rauparaha] got to do with anything?' Or 'who is that guy?' (Manning, 2008, p. 202)

Her comments align with McLaren and Giroux's (1990, p. 263) proposition that 'at the most general level … a critical pedagogy must be a pedagogy of place, that is, it must address the specificities of the experiences, problems, languages, and histories that communities rely upon to construct a narrative of collective identity and possible transformation'. Her comments also align with Gruenewald's (2003, pp. 8–9) proposition that:

> A critical pedagogy of place … embraces the link between the classroom and cultural politics, and further, it explicitly makes the limits and simulations of the classroom problematic. It insists that students and teachers actually experience and interrogate the places outside of school – as part of the school curriculum – that are the local contexts of shared cultural politics … A critical pedagogy of place, moreover, proposes two broad and interrelated objectives for the purpose of linking school and place-based experience to the larger landscape of cultural and ecological politics: decolonization and reinhabitation.

These themes broadly mirror the thematic emphases of critical pedagogy and ecological place-based education, respectively.

In relation to the goal of 'reinhabitation', central to a critical pedagogy of place, it was interesting to listen to another teacher state that she believed her Māori students in particular need to 'see', 'feel' and 'touch' history at their own significant cultural landmarks to critically reflect upon their personal constructs of identity:

> I don't know if I can put it into words. I had a Māori student who went on the recent field trip to Tauranga and though he's not a traditional, so-called 'academic' sort of historian, he is an historian and he's really keen to know his whakapapa (genealogy) and any evidence that can show him his whakapapa. By going on the trip to Tauranga he was actually entering one of his own tribal areas [where vast tracts of land had been confiscated by the Crown and local ecologies were subsequently altered].[10] He had never been up Mount Maunganui, before and when we walked up and got to the top of Mount Maunganui, he stood there and took in all the surroundings.[11] He just stood there, quietly and eventually I said 'Are you ok?' Well, he looked at me and he said, 'Yes Miss. This is where my Grandmother comes from.' For me, that was the historian in him saying 'this is the past, this is the present and this is what I'm all about.' That was the evidence that he, personally, needed to actually fill in the picture of who he is. (Manning, 2008, p. 204)

In terms of the goal of 'decolonization', another teacher stated that ecological literacy activities would challenge his 'privileged' Pākehā students to reflect upon the existence of pre-European histories in ways that would challenge their 'narrow' (anthropocentric and Euro-centric) constructs of national identity.[12] He said:

> I think one of the terrible dilemmas of teaching New Zealand history is having this prevailing tendency of construing it as the period of European contact onwards and compressing everything else. It's this idea that the only meaningful history happened post 1769 [after the arrival of the British explorer Captain James Cook]. So, yeah, 'reading the landscape' is a cool idea and it'd help us to include Māori people before 1769 and then there'd not be so much of that tokenism anymore. One of the big criticisms I do get from my [Pākehā] students about New Zealand history courses is that 'there's not very much New Zealand history, is there?', and you really have to confront that sort of thinking, you know, that New Zealand history only began in 1840. I think that sort of thinking is largely down to immaturity in our overall Pākehā conception of how the process of history can only be read as occurring within something resembling a colonial play. (Manning, 2008, pp. 204–205)

This comment typified the teachers' responses to questions about incorporating flora and fauna as pedagogical props. It also recalled Orr's (1992, p. 85) view that the failure of history teachers to develop students' 'ecological literacy' skills amounted to a 'sin of omission and commission'. The teachers agreed that their pre-service and in-service teacher training had poorly equipped them to enable their students to 'read' historical landscapes, let alone work in partnership with local tribes. Eight of the nine teachers originated from outside the Port Nicholson Block area and felt 'disconnected' from local tribes.[13] As one teacher put it:

> I don't know who to approach here in Wellington, mainly because I grew-up in white middle-class Christchurch. So, it's all very threatening to me. I don't speak any te reo Māori, though I've tried many times to go on courses. My brain just doesn't seem to function like that, I just have no aptitude, what-soever, for learning other languages … However, I still want my students to get out there and learn about it [local tribal histories of place], but I just don't know who to go to and I'm scared they'll [local tribe/s] be offended. So, I need to meet someone in a collegial environment where I can feel safe, even if I don't know anything about this or that [inter/intra tribal] issue. (Manning, 2008, p. 207)

Another teacher added:

> For me, what I know about the local Māori community comes from the ten minutes of Māori news on National Radio between 6.25 and 6.35pm, or it's whatever happens on TV3 News. Otherwise, I've got no contact with anyone, Māori, at all. Probably the only 'flesh and blood' Māori person that I've ever had any contact with, since arriving here in Wellington, was a colleague of my wife, who worked at the Ministry of Education. (Manning, 2008, p. 240)

When the teachers were asked to describe their visions of what an ideal peda-gogical partnership with local Te Ātiawa people might look like, they offered similar responses. They wanted local Te Ātiawa 'experts', with support from the New Zealand Ministry of Education, to appoint an iwi education adviser to help them to learn more about local Te Ātiawa histories of place. They also wanted assistance from local Te Ātiawa 'experts' to develop teaching resources for usage in school, community and natural environmental settings that aligned with official curriculum guidelines. However, the teachers were cautious about how far these cross-cultural conversations might go in terms of altering the official curriculum. One teacher typified the cautious stance of her peers when she said:

> There's major 'pros' and 'cons' because, number one, if a local iwi comes along and says at a senior [curriculum] level that 'you should be teaching this' and it's not part of the [official] curriculum, you can't do it. Then they [the local iwi] turn around and say 'well, we told you what we want you to teach!' But, if you are constrained by the curriculum then there's just no way that we can put that into place! However, if Te Ātiawa has an education officer that knows the 'whys' and 'wherefores' of the education system and can say 'look, we can work it this way' and 'here's what's happened there, in that place', well, then it could be done. (Manning, 2008, p. 207)

Though the teachers were generally positive about the possibility of developing a critical PBE partnership, they felt ill-equipped to do so. Te Ātiawa interviewees, in turn, suspected that local history teachers would hesitate to relinquish their control of curriculum design processes and struggle to develop a critical pedagogy of place without Te Ātiawa support or the assistance of Crown agencies.[14] Both groups, accordingly, felt trapped by a cross-cultural impasse that still prevents them from having the sorts of cross-cultural conversations they said they desired. The pedagogical approach they sought, generally speaking, was not too dissimilar in scope to the learning experience that recently prompted Wellington City councillors to uplift a lower reach of the Waitangi Stream at Waitangi Park in central Wellington City (the capital city of New Zealand).

THE WAITANGI STREAM: A CONCLUDING METAPHOR

Wood (2007), via a poster, described Waitangi Park as 'Wellington's newest, most exciting, urban park, covering some three hectares of waterfront'. She added that 'the park has won international and national landscape design and architecture awards that recognise it's sustainable, ecological and social attributes and its sophisticated design'. As she recognised, the Waitangi lagoon and swamp, fed by the Waitangi stream system, was once an important food source for Taranaki whānui (tribes, like Te Ātiawa, originating from Taranaki) who inhabited the Te Aro Pā (village) and area, in central Wellington; when the Treaty of Waitangi was signed by local rangatira (chiefs) at Port Nicholson on 29 April 1840. The lagoon largely disappeared from sight following a large earthquake (1855). The Waitangi swamp and stream system then began to disappear following the gradual development of an urban wastewater system from 1859 onwards, which piped the stream system underground.

Today the Waitangi Stream remains a heavily polluted and largely subterranean waterway. The general public know little about the tuna (eels) that migrate up the storm water outfall and through the subterranean pipes/culvert system of the Waitangi stream from the harbour. They remain out of sight and out of mind. Like these indomitable tuna, Te Ātiawa and other local iwi have endured major disruptions to their traditional ways of life as a result of the spread of British imperialism and the onset of globalisation. Just as the tuna of the Waitangi Stream have journeyed thousands of nautical miles across the increasingly polluted Pacific Ocean, before swimming upstream, through a maze of pipes below the busy streets of Wellington Central, Te Ātiawa and other local iwi have conducted their own remarkable heke (migration/s) over the centuries, overcoming many obstacles and threats to their continued existence.

These tribes' narratives of place and place names, in turn, often refer people back to these epic journeys and events. Some of the schools I studied now sit atop sites that were, and still are, of great cultural/historical significance to local (and other) iwi. The teachers I interviewed, however, were largely unaware of this and often expressed frustration about the institutional cultures that inhibited their ability to form PBE partnerships with local iwi. My research indicates, therefore, that Te Ātiawa (and other local iwi) are not effectively enabled to 'participate' in conversations about the curriculum design, delivery, assessment and evaluation procedures of local schools; as per the principles of 'partnership', 'active protection' and 'participation' implicit within both the Māori and English texts of the Treaty of Waitangi.

It might be argued, furthermore, that some (Pākehā) teachers' fear of the Māori 'other', coupled with inadequate pre-service and in-service professional development opportunities, results in the delivery of a not-so-well hidden curriculum, undermining the frequency and quality of cross-cultural conversations conducted locally and nationally. These findings hold international implications, including (at least prima facie) contravening the intent of the United Nation's (2007) *Declaration on the Rights of Indigenous Peoples*, particularly Articles 8, 13 & 15. Though the New Zealand Government did not ratify it, the vast majority of member nations voted in favour of the declaration. Given the inferences offered in my Waitangi Stream metaphor I will conclude this chapter with an appropriate whakatauki (proverb) that I hope will stimulate further cross-cultural conversations about the teaching of history and social studies in New Zealand secondary schools.

Whakatauki

Ka patua te whenua i te kino,

ka ngaro te mana me te wairua mō te iwi.

Violence against the land is as destructive to

the mana [authority] and wairua [spirit]

of the people of that land as it is to the land itself.

NOTES

[1] The New Zealand State Services Commission (2006, p. 20) advised that the Waitangi Tribunal is a 'formal, ongoing commission of inquiry to hear grievances against the Crown', run under the auspices of the New Zealand Ministry of Justice. It examines historical and contemporary breaches of the provisions of the (1840) Treaty of Waitangi which was signed by Crown representatives and over 500 rangatira (chiefs), at different places around New Zealand.

[2] My research sought to explore the status of local Te Ātiawa histories of place in Port Nicholson Block secondary schools and to explore the potential for the application of place-based education models in that area which might lead to an educational partnership between local Te Ātiawa people and the participating schools.

[3] The Waitangi Tribunal (2003, p. 8) reported that the Wellington Tenths Trust was established in 1985 and 'represents the interests of the beneficial owners and the beneficiaries (the families of the owners) of the Wellington Tenths [native] reserves'.

[4] For example, those neighbourhoods that border the 'injured' environs of the Awheto Stream in Lower Hutt, or the Waitangi Stream in Wellington City.

[5] Anthropology, however, is not a distinct subject within the New Zealand national curriculum. Though Te Ātiawa interviewees recognised this fact (they were aware of the existence of social studies), most felt that history and social studies teachers should study anthropology in conjunction with their pre-service/in-service professional development requirements.

[6] They had been exposed to these technologies in conjunction with the Waitangi Tribunal claims process and during recreational activities such as fishing and waka ama (outrigger canoe) races. However, it should not be assumed that all local Te Ātiawa people are familiar with GIS/GPS.

[7] For more information about the treaty principles, see Hayward (2009).

[8] Events like the heke (migration/s) of Taranaki people in the 1820s led to their ancestors moving between Taranaki and the Port Nicholson Block/Kapiti Coast areas during later upheavals in Taranaki from the 1850s onward.

[9] This subterranean stream has recently been raised back into to the original surface level ('day-lighted'). I will use this process to provide a metaphor to conclude this chapter.

[10] For example, see Belich (1986, pp. 177–202) and Tapsell (2003, pp. 278–279).

[11] Mount Maunganui, or Mauao, as it was originally named, features a massive terraced fortress built upon its slopes. Geologically speaking, Mauao/Mount Maunganui remains the dominant landmark of the western Bay of Plenty area.

[12] Te Ātiawa interviewees all agreed that the complexities and diversity of pre-European, early Polynesian/Māori historical experiences must be addressed in secondary school history classes (Manning 2008, pp. 124–136).

[13] Only one teacher had had any interaction with local Te Ātiawa people.

[14] Te Ātiawa interviewees frequently identified the Ministry of Education, Te Puni Kōkiri/Ministry of Māori Development and the Ministry of Culture and Heritage as agencies that should support a schools–iwi partnership initiative that can facilitate intergenerational, cross-cultural conversations.

REFERENCES

Barton, K. C., & Levstik, L. S. (2004). *Teaching history for the common good.* London: Lawrence Erlbaum Associates.

Belich, J. (1986). *The New Zealand Wars and the Victorian interpretation of racial conflict.* Auckland, NZ: Auckland University Press.

Freire, P., & Macedo, D. (1987). *Literacy: Reading the word and the world.* South Hadley, MA: Bergine and Garvey.

Gruenewald, D. A. (2003). The best of both worlds: A critical pedagogy of place. *Educational Researcher, 32*(4), 3–12.

Hayward, J. (2009). *The principles of the Treaty of Waitangi (Appendix).* Retrieved February 8, 2009, from http://www.waitangi-tribunal.govt.nz/doclibrary/public/Appendix(99).pdf

Manning, R. F. (2008). Place, power and pedagogy: A critical analysis of the status of Te Ātiawa histories of place in Port Nicholson Block secondary shcools and the possible application of place-based education models. A thesis submitted in fulfillment of the requirements of the degree of Doctor of Philosophy in Educaiton, Victoria University of Wellington, November 2008.

McLaren, P., & Giroux, H. (1990). Critical education and rural education: A challenge from Poland. *Peabody Journal of Education, 67*(4), 154–165.

New Zealand History Teachers' Association. (2005). *NZHTA Survey Results, May 2005.* Retrieved June 5, 2007, from http://www.teacherscouncil.govt.nz/ethics/code/stm

Orr, D. W. (1992). *Ecological literacy: Education and transition to a post-modern world.* Albany, NY: State University of New York Press.

Russell, W. B. (1997). *People and the land through time: Linking ecology and history.* New Haven, CT: Yale University Press.

Smith, L. T. (1999). *Decolonizing methodologies: Research and indigenous peoples.* Dunedin, NZ: University of Otago Press.

State Services Commission (New Zealand). (2006). Timeline of the Treaty. In *The Treaty of Waitangi* (a boxed-set of four public information booklets), Treaty of Waitangi Information Programme. Wellington, NZ: State Services Commission.

Tapsell, P. (2003). Papamoa Pā. In M. Kawharu (Ed.), W*henua: Managing our resources* (pp. 272–288). Auckland, NZ: Reed Publishing (NZ) Ltd.

United Nations Permanent Forum on Indigenous Issues (2007, 13 September). *Declaration on the Rights of Indigenous Peoples*. Adopted by the General Assembly of the United Nations. Retrieved September 15, 2007, from http://www.un.org.esa/socdev/unpfii/en/declaration.html

Waitangi, T. (2003). *Te Whanganui a Tara Me ōna Takiwā: Report on the Wellington District*. Wellington, NZ: Legislation Direct.

Waitangi, T. (2004). *Tūranganui Tangata, Tūranganui Whenua: The Report on the Tūranganui a Kiwa Claims*. Wellington, NZ: Legislation Direct.

Wood, N. J. (2007). *Practical as well as pretty: How Waitangi Park wetlands treat stormwater and protect the harbour*. A poster prepared for the New Zealand Water and Waste Association Annual Conference, Rotorua.

Richard Manning
College of Education
University of Canterbury

DIDI KHAYATT

5. PERSPECTIVES IN EQUITY

What Progress Have We Made?

INTRODUCTION

For the past 15 years I have been teaching in the Faculty of Education of York University in Toronto, Canada's largest city and home to its most multicultural population. Toronto was once a stalwart 'English'-dominated city, where the population took pride in the Queen's visits as well as the traditional 'Britishness' of its culture. This image has changed in the last quarter of a century as the city has become the most requested destination for new immigrants from Asia, Africa, the Middle East and the West Indies. York University sits in the hub of that urban diversity.

Toronto is also home to one the largest queer population in the country. It has its own 'gay ghetto', its Pride Day Parade is the second largest on the continent after San Francisco's, and its cultural scene promotes and encourages a diversity of queer theatre, dance, clubs and a robust literary scene.

York University similarly prides itself on the diversity of its student population. It sits smack in the middle of what Peter McLaren (1980), infamously called 'the Jane-Finch Corridor': a large area of public housing that is populated mostly by a diversity of recent immigrants living in poverty. Most of York's 50,000-plus student body (making it Canada's third-largest university) comprises students who are the first in their family to go to university. It is both racially and sexually diverse, and has a mission statement that calls attention to its commitment to social justice.

Since being hired at the university's Faculty of Education, I have been teaching foundational courses that allow me to deal with social issues that students are likely to encounter when they start teaching in the surrounding schools. My courses are theoretical and have evolved over the last decade and a half, and my commitment to issues of social justice remains constant. How I teach and how the students receive the information and engage with the material are in constant state of flux. Within a context of racial diversity coupled with diversity of gender, sexuality and disabilities, the classroom becomes a site of complex negotiations, inadvertent accommodations and challenging discourses.

In this chapter, I will address some of the changes and accommodations that have been necessary over the years as scholarship progressively recognises the scope of diversities in terms of race, class, gender, sexualities and disabilities. I take

K. Quinlivan, R. Boyask and B. Kaur (eds.), Educational Enactments in a Globalised World: Intercultural Conversations, 65–76.

seriously the editors' challenge to address how, over the years, I have had to 'negotiate the complex terrain between abstract notions of education and education as a subjective experience'. What are the hurdles and complexities that must be negotiated as one teaches teachers? How does one deal with intersections of perspectives? These questions might be read in the light of discourses of globalisation that speak to and conceptualise a global citizen (or, in this case, a global student) and yet negotiate the particularities of dealing with diversity within a classroom. My emphasis, however, will be on addressing the complexities and, occasionally, the antithesis of progression that I encounter in my everyday teaching.

EQUITY AND SOCIAL JUSTICE: CHANGES AND SILENCES

Intercultural conversations about issues of equity and social justice might reveal how geographic and cultural contexts would influence what is taught and how it is delivered, not to mention what is considered fair and what is taken-for-granted unfair but still perseveres. These conversations would also challenge those involved to 'look for productive possibilities of education in a global world', as the editors of this book phrased it. To quote Altman (2008, p. 24):

> Globalization is itself a much contested term, and its impact on sex extends far beyond the realm of the imaginary. As economic changes speed up population movements, both between and within countries, leading to an explosion of urban populations and uprooting of millions of people from their traditional homes and mores, so too sexual behaviour changes, and more people, especially young women, become dependent on survival sex. At the same time, the circulation of images and new forms of media make the identities and behaviours of the affluent West available to people across the globe and create both envy and hostility to what is increasingly regarded by many religious leaders as western decadence.

Most of all, these intercultural conversations would highlight reflections on one's own work in the classroom. I often ask myself whether the concepts of 'equity and social justice' are a western privilege. I am hardly claiming that they do not exist in other parts of the world; I am suggesting that when a people are at war, for instance, or in the throes of famine, when a people are living in poverty and hope is scarce, social justice is scarcely on top of the agenda. Consequently I ask: considering that we continue to have wars and famine around the world, can we ever reach a moment when equity and social justice are equally negotiated and possibly mitigated on the global scene?

Here in Canada, however, the last three or four decades have seen tumultuous changes in the area of equity and social justice in education, particularly race and sexuality as these are discussed in Canadian schools. Scholars had been working on these issues for centuries but what was different in this instance was that the discussions were seeping down to the general public. By the late 1970s schools were beginning to teach about gender, race and class (at least in Toronto; see McCaskell, 2005), and boards of education were changing curricula to reflect the climate of social justice. The work of critical theorists who explored social class and its ramifications on schooling (see, to name a few, Paulo Freire (1970), Paul Willis (1977), Roger Simon (1992), Henry Giroux & Peter McLaren (1994) was now being applied to classrooms. At the same time, feminists everywhere (early scholars in this field include Madeleine Arnot & Kathleen Weiler (1993), Valerie Walkerdine (1990), Madeleine Grumet (1988), Rosemary Deem (1980), Ruby Heap & Alison Prentice (1991), and Jane Gaskell (1991) were demanding that gender be a focus and that girls be given the same considerations in the classroom as boys had been given traditionally. Anti-racist education (for instance, hooks, 1989; James, 1994) was also being emphasised as Ontario schools accommodated more and more immigrants of colour. More recently Aboriginal education began to be taken seriously.

The one area of discussion that remained conspicuously quiet in Canada for a long time was sexuality in education. I started working on issues of sexuality in 1980, when I commenced my doctoral studies. A basic question I had at that stage was who else in the academic community was interested in and writing about sexuality and education. There were no personal computers at the time or when, in 1982, I began working on my dissertation on lesbian teachers. My immediate range for a literature search was limited to the collections of the various university libraries in Toronto. However, I was told that if I was willing to pay, the University of Toronto's Robarts Library would carry out a computer search with the aim of answering my question for me.

In discussions with my (doctoral student) peers, I learnt that many of them had done similar searches, some costing close to $200. They told me that, through this method, they got reams of references and some even showed me the wide pages, folded accordion-like with many possibilities. It took me several months to put together my $200, which I then took to the library with a request for a search: anything on lesbian teachers, sexuality and education, schooling and sexuality, homosexuality in schools, etc. After a couple of weeks while the search was being conducted, finally the telephone call came to alert me to its conclusion. Two hundred dollars in hand, I went to the Robarts reference desk. I was given one (very wide) computer page, containing exactly nine references. It cost me $8, and all but two of the references were ones I had already come across. Today, early in 2009, as I write, I executed a Google search for 'lesbian teachers' and got 582,000 hits and the whole search was accomplished in 0.08 seconds, a time span of less than one breath.

In looking back to that earlier time, there is a tendency to either say to oneself (often despite proof of the opposite) that nothing much has changed (*plus ça change, plus c'est la même chose*) or, to the contrary, to assert that so much has changed for the better that our world is unrecognisable. In a recent article commissioned by the journal *Sexualities* for its tenth anniversary, Jeffrey Weeks (2008) wrote that in reviewing what transpired in the area of sexuality in the last 10 years, one is bound to fall into one of three traps. The first is to think that the transformation was inevitable; that it was a journey from sexual repression to sexual liberation. The second trap is to see 'everything as a decline from a state of grace'

(p. 29). The third and final trap is to believe that, despite all that has happened, nothing much has changed (2008, pp. 28–29). That said, Weeks sums up his position as follows:

> I cannot deny that there are elements in all these positions that are at least plausible. None, however, convince me fully. The progressive myth all too readily forgets the contingencies to the present. The declinist myth celebrates a history that never was, a world that was not so much lost as nostalgically re-imagined to act as a counterpoint to the present. The continuists want to stress the recalcitrance of hidden structures, but in doing so forget the power of agency and the macroscopic impact of subtle changes in individual lives that make up the unfinished revolutions of our time. (Weeks 2008, p. 31)

He goes on to conclude that the 'world we have won has made possible ways of life that represent an advance not a decline in human relationships, and that have broken through the coils of power to enhance individual autonomy, freedom of choice and more egalitarian patterns of relationships' (p. 31).

There is no doubt that the overall picture has improved. But has it improved on all counts? And what does 'improved' mean? Is it a progression toward a goal? And who benefits from this improvement? Are the benefits equitably distributed? That said, as Dennis Altman (2008, p. 24) puts it, referring to sexuality in particular, 'there is a growing dichotomy between the sort of research engaged in by much of academia and the experience of most people outside the university whose lives are touched by the new politics of sexuality.' Because these are very difficult questions to address, for the purpose of this paper, I shall take my own praxis as a basis from which to focus the discussion.

QUESTIONS OF IDENTITY

I remember, for instance, that well into the 1980s, dealing with social issues, regardless of the perspective, meant talking about identity. Even when questions were being asked about multiple identities and even when discussions of contradiction and instability of identities proliferated – until post-structuralist scholars (such as Jennifer Gore and Carmen Luke (1992) in education) were adopting such theorists as Judith Butler (1990) and Eve Kosofsky Sedgwick (1990) and 'queer' theorists and scholars of education were taking up their respective work – I, like many others, was drowning in the quagmire of thinking about different identities. As Sedgwick (1990, p. 54) wrote at the time:

> … as I have been suggesting, the violently contradictory and volatile energies that every morning's newspapers proves to us are circulating even at this moment, in our society around the issues of homo/heterosexual definition show over and over again how preposterous is anybody's urbane pretense at having a clear, simple story to tell about the outlines and meaning of what and who are homosexual and heterosexual. To be gay, or to be potentially

classifiable as gay – that is to say, *to be sexed or gendered* – in this system is to come under the radically overlapping aegises of a universalizing discourse of acts or bonds and at the same time of a minoritizing discourse of kinds of person. Because of the double binds implicit in the space overlapped by universalizing and minoritizing models, the stakes in matters of definitional control are extremely high. [original italics]

Sometime in the early 1990s, I was home one evening, when my friend Marian McMahon dropped by. She had just gone to hear British AIDS activist and scholar Simon Watney (see, e.g., Watney 1997). She related some aspects of the talk, reproducing Watney's impassioned plea to the audience that AIDS was not a just a 'gay' disease. I had read Butler and Sedgwick by then, but it was the first time I asked myself, 'What does it mean to call oneself "gay" or "lesbian"?' – when these terms had been, at one time, so clear to me – and 'What does it mean in terms of sexuality when a man who is married, and therefore presumably heterosexual, engages in secret sexual encounters with other men, becomes infected with AIDS and consequently infects his wife?' It was then that I understood the meaning of 'shifting, unstable identities' and it was that evening that I began to call into question the whole notion of 'gay' and 'lesbian' and, consequently, began to formulate my study about 'lesbians in Egypt'.

As a result of those questions, I understood that all 'homosexual' identities (whether lesbian, gay, bisexual, queer, etc.) had a history as well as a geography that placed them in 'western' (and I use the word problematically) cultures. Back then, in the mid-1980s, when western scholars began to shift their gaze to the plight of 'international gays and lesbians', much of what was being published were books and articles that tried to 'find' (unproblematically) gays and lesbians in exotic places like Brazil, Israel and India (see, for instance, Penelope & Valentine, 1990). I had read that Arabic did not have an equivalent word for 'homosexuality' nor for 'heterosexuality' (Schmitt & Sofer, 1992). Further study in the area revealed that although Schmitt and Sofer's assertion was at best questionable, the 'homosexual identity' certainly did not exist in Egypt where I was born and raised. I came out when I was 19 and had several experiences there before I left for Canada in 1967, never returning to Egypt to live. But even when I lived in Egypt, I spoke and read and was educated in English and French, so was familiar with the various texts that existed when I was growing up, including Radcliffe Hall's (1928) *The Well of Loneliness* (which I read in London when I was 20), Frank S. Caprio (1955) and D.J. West (1955). I was, however, part of the 5% exception: educated and classed differently from the rest of the population.

On that fateful night, after speaking with Marian McMahon, I asked myself, 'If there are no exact terms, if the identities do not exist, can there be lesbians in Egypt?' It took me six funded (Social Science and Humanities Research Council) years and many hours of interviewing in Egypt to learn that, of course, the sexual practices (homosexuality, queer, gay, lesbian, etc.) existed, but that these practices were not tied to a (circumscribed) identity. Later, I suggested that this lack of a definable 'queer' identity is precisely one of the reasons why it is difficult in countries such as Egypt to have a cohesive or recognisable political movement.

Gone were the days where my teaching was reduced to the presentation of simple binaries such as 'homosexuality' and 'heterosexuality'. It was instead a case of recognising, as Schneider (2008, p. 91) suggests, that '... the notion of a unified homosexual subject is rejected in favor of fluid, multiple types and identities of homosexualities, and heterosexuality is rendered less monolithic and more multiple'.

By this stage my thinking, and consequently my teaching, had changed quite radically. Since I had begun working at York University, I had found ways to include sexuality in my work. Recently in a short piece (Khayatt, 2008) I described at length my original discomfort at teaching about 'sexual orientation' compared with my eventual and more recent ease when talking about the subject. Over the years I also could see differences in how students engage with the topic: from titillated giggles, to admissions of having a 'friend' who is gay or lesbian, to a normalising discussion where the topic is not perceived as a major concern. Yet, even now, some students who claim 'such practices' contravene their religious beliefs, have trouble with the topic and argue vociferously against, for instance, gay or lesbian teachers. Most of the students, however, answer their concerns, and generally I do not have to give my (mostly unconvincing to them) argument that the very same Bible they are quoting condoned slavery, so why could they not accept that there are necessary changes that come with different ages and places? All the same, given that many of the most vocal Bible-quoting students are Black, when I do proffer my argument it sometimes gives them pause. I often ask, particularly when giving workshops to teachers, 'Is there anyone here who is against social justice?' Of course no one owns up to it, but if anyone later refuses to discuss sexuality on religious grounds, it becomes easier to deal with as I can move on to the question, 'Are we then to pick and choose our social justice?'

Embracing that sexuality is fluid affected my whole understanding that there is no 'set identity', challenging a notion of an unchanging, perpetual self. I began to adopt a lack of constancy in all terrains of sociality. So, for instance, my educational foundation courses always begin with recognising on whose land we all live and work and that we are all immigrants regardless of when our ancestors came to this country. That last statement may be obvious to many, but it came as a surprise to me almost 15 years ago when I was telling my partner about an incident related in one of my articles (Khayatt, 1994). One of my professors in 1980 had asked the class what they wanted to discuss and when the consensus was 'immigrant women', the professor turned to me and said, 'We have an immigrant with us and we could ask her.' All eyes turned toward me and I, not recognising that I was 'an immigrant', turned to look behind me. Celia Haig-Brown, to whom I was relating the episode, quickly asked why was I considered an immigrant any more than any of the other students in class, unless they were First Nations. I was astounded. At first, I argued with her strongly, but then I thought about it and had to concede. When I retell this moment to my classes or to teachers in workshops, there continues to be one or two who argue that they are not immigrants because, first, their ancestors came here a couple of centuries ago and they could trace their genealogy and, second, as they cannot say they come from any other country (no, they are not British or Swedish, but Canadian) then it stands to reason they are not immigrants. I explain that each one of us has a relation to the land on which we live and work, that this relationship is one that connects us indubitably with those who have come before us, and there is no doubt in anyone's mind that First Nations People were here before any of us.

SOCIAL JUSTICE FOR WHOM?

I have produced considerable work on social justice and equity in education: I have taught and written about any number of topics in the area, I have given workshops, sat on panel discussions, and presented scholarly papers. Yet, despite this work, I continue to make mistakes. Can one ever escape having grown up in a sexist, able-ist, racist and homophobic culture(s)? For instance, about five years ago I presented my syllabus to my new class at the beginning of the year, a syllabus I had carefully organised and constructed over a number of years, each year tinkering with it until I thought it was perfect. That year I discovered that my 'perfect' syllabus was flawed. I had taken for granted that all my students were able-bodied. Each week, my syllabus included a short film that dealt with the topic at hand and formed the basis of a discussion. That year, I had a deaf student, who could hear neither the film dialogue nor the discussion. I was mortified. Disability is seldom discussed because it seems obvious. Of course, each school would have a ramp, blind students would be accommodated, and deaf and hard-of-hearing students would have American Sign Language interpreters, and so on. My student that year, however, did not understand or use Sign Language. She was the only one in her family who was deaf and, because she could read lips and had 15% hearing, she could muddle along with the help of some equipment that enhanced sound, although that did not always work for her. She was an exceptionally strong student, a very likable personality and someone who people generally wanted to 'help'. She excelled despite her disability because students rallied around her and made sure she understood what was being said. She could also speak intelligibly, which helped. Some of the films in my syllabus had closed captions, so I kept them; otherwise I had to find others, and I did. That student obtained her degree and went on to teach in a deaf and hard-of-hearing school in Australia. I was the one who failed to apply my own theories of social justice in the classroom. On another occasion, I watched a Black high-school student bury something in the school grounds and quickly concluded that it must be drugs. When the principal came to investigate it we found out that the student had carefully and lovingly buried a small dead sparrow. None of us is immune to such prejudice, none of us can escape periodically being sexist or racist or insensitive to disabilities. After all, as I remind my students, we all live in a sexist, classist, racist and able-ist society – and, now that I am getting older, I would add age-ist!

I have been teaching for over 20 years, each year attempting to improve on the previous one. When I began teaching, I found it very difficult to come out to my classes and have written at least four articles outlining why. The most salient reasons were twofold: first, I am older and came out to myself in the early 1960s, a time when people did not feel comfortable coming out because of the dangers of losing one's job and one's family. And that was the level of risk in the 'western' countries, to say nothing of the risks in Egypt when I came out to my friends and family there. Second, I worked as a secondary teacher before I obtained my doctorate at a time when anyone who was 'queer' (and that term was not used then except in pejorative ways) was perceived as 'preying' on teenagers, converting them from stalwart heterosexuals to depraved homosexuals. Or else these youngsters would be infected by contagion alone: our very presence in the schools would alter their sexuality. Whatever the fears of the time, coming out in the northern Ontario school where I was teaching was not a viable option. With my doctorate in hand, I taught at university but still the discomfort of coming out lingered, particularly when the situation called for coming out with a declarative statement: I am a lesbian. I still do not take that option. Mostly, from the beginning of the year in my courses, I speak as if everyone knows that my partner is female (as does the whole university, from the president to my union to my colleagues and graduate students).

The tides have turned. Where I could teach with impunity about issues of class, race and gender but had difficulty with sexualities, I now find that teaching about gender is the most difficult. It is especially so when I come out as feminist, and they get to know my sexuality. Most students and many of my colleagues assume that we are in a post-feminist era because gender has successfully been dealt with and that we now should be turning our attention to other oppressed subjects. No amount of talking about patriarchy being alive and well and still with us seems to convince my students, both male and female. They try to tell me, amongst other things, that now fathers have half the home responsibilities; that women work, are paid the same as men and successfully attain the highest positions of responsibility whether in government or private companies; and that affirmative action is a policy that should be abolished as no one discriminates against women any longer. In short, the feeling is that women do not need attention. Younger women claim that they feel safe, that they can take care of themselves and that no, they are not feminist.

York University is known for its School of Women's Studies and, because I am cross-listed and sometimes even teach a course for the school, I often am asked to supervise some of its graduate students. Two years ago, one such student came to me to ask if I would supervise her thesis and I agreed. She was interested in researching power differences in young heterosexual couples in strip bars. What had inspired her to do the work was that her boyfriend insisted on taking her to strip bars, which she admitted enjoying, but what she was seeing there was what distressed her: the strippers were calling on young women in the audience to go join them and to strip with them. If a young woman refused, she was booed, but mostly she was pressured into complying by her boyfriend and by the young men in the group with whom she came. What my student wanted was to interview these young women to see how they felt about such experiences. What she accomplished was an excellent piece of work, the conclusion of which was that, although many say that young women have similar sexual freedoms to young men, these same freedoms seem to turn against them often because of unforeseen pressures to perform various practices or behaviours that may go against their own wishes. The young women to whom she spoke were often angry and disillusioned, or else defiantly cynical.

Tejeda, Espinoza and Gutierrez (2003, p. 36) state:

> The discourses of equity, access, and democracy act as currency in the political economy of academia. The race, class, gender, and sexuality of those who traffic in these discourses weigh heavily on the development of these modes of thought. The question of social justice *by* whom begs us to ask the question: Social justice *for whom*? We move away from notions of social justice that seek to create social space for the poor, dark-skinned, and indigenous to be more like their oppressors. [original italics]

I would add: 'female' to their list of 'poor, dark-skinned, and indigenous'. Although it is true enough that women have made gains in the last three decades, there are also concurrent practices, behaviours and tensions that lead one to question, social justice for whom? Have the gains been worthwhile? But, most of all, are the gains on a progressive trajectory or do we also see a reappearance of gender power differentials in areas that are, perhaps, different from previous eras, but still just as oppressive? And, on a global level, has anything changed? Can I in good faith teach my students that women's lives have, in general, improved around the world, that we have done away with rape, sexual slavery, cliterodectomy, etc.? Considering the strength of the fundamentalist movements in all religious denominations in the world, I find it difficult to think or teach about social justice being addressed on a global scale. Here in Toronto, perhaps, but as some of the anecdotes I describe above demonstrate, all levels of oppressions have gained to some extent and there is also no doubt that there has been a certain resurgence of certain means of discriminating, even if somewhat more sophisticated in form, against the more vulnerable of our populations. That teacher candidates are aware of the complexities and tensions that exist when thinking about equity is perhaps a hope that is more optimistic than real. That I am still doing my best to develop this awareness through my teaching is certain.

CONCLUSIONS

As I reach my 65th year, with 42 years of living in Canada behind me, I maintain that I have a long and deep experience of equity and how it is both practised in schools and theorised in the academy. On a personal level, I have lived through the need for concealment of my lesbian identity (particularly as a teacher) to a celebrated 'queer' identity, fluid and joyful, where previous concealment was dark and bereft. So, on the surface, my own life has benefited from recent developments, and yet I look around me at younger women and wonder about the work we did in the feminist movement and if they feel any gains. In 1995, when Mike Harris, a right wing Conservative politician, took over from a socialist-leaning government (NDP) in Ontario (in Canada, education is provincial), his government immediately began dismantling human rights sectors of the government such as employment equity and the Ontario Anti-Racism Secretariat; slashed healthcare funding in half; grossly reduced grants to school boards, colleges and universities; and cut welfare by over 21.6% (McCaskell, 2005, p. 218). What was amazing to me at the time was that, at the same time as he was hacking at any organisation or institution that even smelt of equity and social justice, Mike Harris (who was to be soundly defeated in 2003) was stating that he was committed to equality, that his government recognised that equity laws were 'paternalistic', and that disadvantaged groups had gained and been empowered so much that there was no need for laws that protected equity. This doublespeak is symptomatic of what is in place today: when I look at younger women 'choosing' traditional roles in their family, preferring to distance themselves from any talk of feminism, I have to question how progressive this progress is. Angela McRobbie (2009) coined the term 'disarticulation' to describe these contradictory messages about gender. By dis-articulation she means 'a force which devalues, or negates and makes unthinkable the very basis of coming-together (even if to take part in disputation encounters), on the assumption widely promoted that there is no longer any need for such actions' (p. 26). McRobbie goes on to explicate how this works:

> The cultural forms which function according to this logic of substitution are also spectral re-workings of their feminist predecessors, now transplanted into a popular domain. They promote a highly conservative mode of feminine 'empowerment', the hallmark of which is the active connecting-up of young woman [sic] with notions of change, the right to work, and with new free-doms, particularly sexual freedoms. (Ibid, p. 27)

Are young women being 'disempowered through the very discourses of empowerment they are being offered as substitutes for feminism' (ibid, p. 49) as McRobbie maintains? If the young woman I mentioned above whose peers pole-danced with strippers at the 'request' (read 'coercion') of their boyfriends is any indication of the new 'freedom', I would argue that McRobbie is absolutely right. The neo-liberal climate of our schools and universities in Canada seems to substitute talk of freedom (mostly in the area of sexuality) at the expense of social justice. I state this with caution because I recognise that I am imposing my understanding of gender relations on the young women; I could be accused of denouncing their actions as a consequence of false consciousness.

Such contradictions proliferate in this 'post-feminist' era. Where our schools are replete with curricula filled with anti-racism and anti-homophobia sentiments, the academic performance of many Black boys is below acceptable standards. So in Toronto we now have Black-centred schools. Where homophobia is rampant in school hallways as students call each other 'gay' pejoratively, Toronto comes up with the Triangle Program, a haven for queer kids. Girls enjoy sexual freedom but cannot demand rights for fear of being perceived as 'lesbian' and some Canadian and US universities are closing down their women's studies departments.

Finally, in negotiating the complex terrain between abstract notions of education and practice, my experience as outlined in this paper leads me to conclude that on a subjective level, I find that there have been tremendous gains. There is no denying that there is more discursive noise about the topic of equity and social justice in our schools. At the same time, one has to wonder if this noise is not often, in Foucault's (1980, p. 33) words, 'an immense verbosity' and nothing else.

REFERENCES

Altman, D. (2008). Visions of sexual politics. *Sexualities: Studies and Culture and Society*, *11*(1/2), 24–27.

Arnot, M., & Weiler, K. (Eds.). (1993). *Feminism and social justice education: International perspectives*. London: The Falmer Press.

Butler, J. (1990). *Gender trouble: Feminism and the subversion of identity*. London and New York: Routledge.

Caprio, F. S. (1955). *Female homosexuality: A psychodynamic study of lesbianism*. London: Icon Books.

Deem, R. (Ed.). (1980). *Schooling for women's work*. London: Routledge and Kegan Paul.

Freire, P. (1970). *Pedagogy of the oppressed*. (M. B. Ramos, Trans.). New York: Continuum.

Foucault, M. (1980). *The history of sexuality. Volume I: An introduction*. New York: Vintage Books.

Gaskell, J., & McLaren, A. T. (Eds.). (1991). *Women and education: A Canadian perspective* (2nd ed.). Calgary, AB: Detselig Enterprises.

Giroux, H., & McLaren, P. (Eds.). (1994). *Between borders: Pedagogy and the politics of cultural studies*. New York and London: Routledge.

Grumet, M. (1988). *Bitter milk: Women and teaching*. Amherst, MA: The University of Massachusetts Press.

Hall, R. (1928). *The well of loneliness*. New York: Avon Books.

Heap, R., & Prentice, A. (Eds.). (1991). *Gender and education in Ontario*. Toronto, ON: Canadian Scholars' Press.

Hooks, B. (1989). *Talking back: Think feminist, thinking Black*. Boston: Southend Press.

James, C. (1994). *Talking about difference*. Toronto, ON: Between the Lines.

Khayatt, D. (1994). The boundaries of identity at the intersections of race, class and gender. *Canadian Women's Studies Journal*, *14*(2), (Spring) Special Issue: Racism and Gender, 6–12.

Khayatt, D. (2008). Perspectives: Teaching sexuality for three decades. *Journal of Curriculum and Pedagogy*, *41*(2), Spring, 133–144.

Luke, C., & Gore, J. (Eds.). (1992). *Feminisms and critical pedagogy*. New York and London: Routledge.

McCaskell, T. (2005). *Race to equity: Disrupting educational inequality*. Toronto, ON: Between the Lines.

McLaren, P. (1980). *Cries from the corridor: The new suburban ghettos*. Markham, ON: Paper-Jacks.

McRobbie, A. (2009). *The aftermath of feminism: Gender, culture and social change*. London and Los Angeles: Sage.

Penelope, J., & Valentine, S. (Eds.). (1990). *Finding the lesbians: Personal accounts from around the world*. Freedom, CA: The Crossing Press.

Schmitt, A., & Sofer, J. (Eds.). (1992). *Sexuality and eroticism among males in Moslem societies*. New York and London: Harrington Park Press.

Schneider, B. (2008). Arguments, citations, traces: Rich and Foucault and the problem of heterosexuality. *Sexualities: Studies and Culture and Society*, *11*(1/2), 86–93.

Sedgwick, E. K. (1990). *Epistemology of the closet*. Berkeley and Los Angeles: University of California Press.

Simon, R. (1992). *Teaching against the grain: Texts for a pedagogy of possibility*. Toronto, ON: OISE Press.

Tejeda, C., Espinoza, M., & Gutierrez, K. (2003). Toward a decolonizing pedagogy: Social justice reconsidered. In P. P. Trifonas (Ed.), *Pedagogies of difference: Rethinking education for social change*. New York and London: RoutledgeFalmer.

Walkerdine, V. (1990). *Schoolgirl fictions*. London and New York: Verso Press.

Watney, S. (1997). *Policing desire: Pornography, AIDS, and the media continuum*. International Publishing Group.

Weeks, J. (2008). Traps we set ourselves. *Sexualities: Studies and Culture and Society, 11*(1/2), 17–33.

West, D. J. (1955). *Homosexuality*. London: Penguin.

Willis, P. (1977). *Learning to labour*. Aldershot, Hampshire: Gower.

Didi Khayatt
Faculty of Education
York University

KATHLEEN QUINLIVAN

6. WHEN 'EVERYTHING COLLIDES IN A BIG BOOM!'

*Attending to Emotionality and Discomfort as Sites of Learning
in a High School Health Classroom*

INTRODUCTION

Let's face it. We're undone by each other. And if we're not, we're missing
something. (Butler, 2004, p. 23)

In response to an analysis of the way in which the TV programme *Queer Eye for
the Straight Guy* framed gay men as competent experts who assisted straight
men, Ryan, a 16-year-old student, turned to me in frustration and confusion, and
exclaimed, 'Everything collides in a big boom!' His exclamation drew my attention
to the emotionality and discomfort involved in calling into question normalising
understandings of sexualities and genders.

In this chapter I suggest that student interactions characterised by strong
emotionality can indicate issues to teachers that genuinely matter to students. In
attending more fully to students' emotional interactions, teachers may be able to
tap into strong motivations for student learning. In making a case for engaging
with students' emotional responses, I show what happened when queer notions of
'thinking otherwise' in relation to sexualities and genders were introduced into the
predominantly heteronormative peer and classroom cultures of a health classroom
as part of a research project funded by the New Zealand AIDS Foundation (Quinlivan,
2006). Within this context I explore the extent to which the students, their teacher
and myself as a researcher were emotionally 'undone by each other'; as Butler
suggests, as we struggled to construct the differing subjectivities we wished to
present to each other in the classroom, and also negotiated the ways in which we
were positioned by one another. I then go on to speculate that paying closer attention to emotionality over the duration of the project might have enabled the teacher
and myself as a researcher to probe more deeply into issues of significance to the
students' lives.

I will explore the intentions that drove the project, and provide the methodological context for the study. I then move on to explore the dynamics of a
conversation occurring within the project where the diverse subjectivities of the
participants engaged in dialogue in relation to discourses of sexual and gender
diversity within the enacted curriculum of the classroom. I show how the dominant
heteronormative and gender normative discourses characterising the public spheres

*K. Quinlivan, R. Boyask and B. Kaur (eds.), Educational Enactments in a Globalised World:
Intercultural Conversations, 77–89.*

of the classroom and school met discourses of gender and sexual diversity, and were engaged with from the differing perspectives of the research participants in emotionally combustible ways. In the final section of the chapter, I discuss the extent to which attending to emotionality and discomfort as sites of learning to a far greater extent within the research project might have enabled the students, their teacher and myself as a researcher to more deeply mine the pedagogical potential of emotional responses.

INTENTIONS AND METHODOLOGICAL CONTEXT OF THE RESEARCH PROJECT

This classroom ethnography explores what it means to draw on post-structural approaches to interrogate and widen understandings of sexual and gender diversity. It draws on post-structural methodologies (Stronach & Maclure, 1997) which explore the usefulness of the generation of rich and specific contextual data in order to generate and test theories. As I will explain in more detail shortly, I am particularly interested in the pedagogical enactment of post-structural and queer theoretical perspectives, and their implications.

Over the course of the one-year study I participated in a research project with Emma, a 40-year-old specialist health teacher, and sixteen Year 12 health option students, aged 16 and 17 years, in a decile 6 co-educational school situated within commuting distance of an urban centre in the South Island of New Zealand. Informed consent was gained from the six male and ten female students and from the teacher. A range of qualitative data collection methods was drawn on over the course of the project. Eight classroom sessions were audiotaped as the importance of documenting the lived student cultures within the classroom and instances of the hidden curriculum as significant venues for learning emerged in the middle of the study.

As part of their course, the students were undertaking a unit entitled Issues associated with Gender and Sexuality. In initial interviews, they drew on understandings of sexuality and gender as biological and fixed. Despite students noting that traditional representations of masculinity and femininity and heterosexuality appeared to hold a high status amongst their peers, several of them recognised that they did not conform to those stereotypes. Some young women drew my attention to double standards of femininity that encouraged some of them to appear and act in actively sexual ways while at the same time demeaning girls who were known to be actively sexual by labelling them as sluts. Verbal and physical harassment of female and male students presumed to be gay was common. Stereotypical understandings of gay male sexualities as being effeminate and lesbian female sexualities as 'male acting' were also noted by both male and female students. Words like gay, faggot and homo were common terms of abuse noted amongst students. No students were known to be openly gay at the school. Young women I talked to expressed an interest in wanting to understand why and how understandings of gender and sexualities operated and changed. Several male students also noted that this topic was not one they had really considered before, as they thought the understanding of gender and sexuality as biological and fixed was 'just the way things were' and as such was unable to be changed.

Emma, their specialist health teacher and in charge of health in the school, was keen to participate in the project because this was the first time that she had embarked on teaching the Gender and Sexuality unit. In the initial interview she drew on gender role theory to frame her understandings of gender and sexuality, suggesting that gender roles are socially provided scripts for individual behaviours first learned and then enacted. However, she expressed some confusion, acknowledging that she would like to learn more about these issues. Emma was also interested in addressing the widespread and gender-based harassment and homophobia that she saw as a norm in the school, hoping she could provide a role model to students in terms of addressing these issues.

I have an ongoing research interest in the theoretical and pedagogical usefulness of queer theoretical frameworks for framing and understanding gender and sexual diversity. I am interested in the potential queer theory holds for problematising the normalcy of heterosexuality, rather than reinforcing binary framings of gender and same sex desire as abnormal and 'at risk' in relation to heterosexual and gendered norms (Rasmussen, Talburt & Rofes, 2004). Destabilising notions of sexual and gendered normalcies have the potential to disrupt fixed biological notions of sexuality and gender, allowing for an exploration of sexual and gendered subjectivities as something more fluid and temporal (Rasmussen, 2006; Rosendale & Birnley, 2007). In that way it provides an opportunity not to foreclose ways of thinking about gender and sexual diversity (Britzman & Gilbert, 2004). An attention to context recognises that the discursive construction of genders and sexualities shifts and moves over time, allowing subjects to engage with understandings of gender and sexuality and exercise some agency in relation to them.

THEORISING EMOTIONALITY AS A SITE OF LEARNING

It has been widely documented that engaging in thinking and learning about difference (Boler, 1999; Boler & Zembylas, 2003), particularly in relation to issues of gender and sexual diversity (Boler, 1999; Quinlivan 2007), produces strong emotional reactions. However my interests here go beyond the negotiation of emotionality that will arise when 'thinking otherwise' is engaged with. Looking at the data in retrospect I am struck by the emotionality that characterised many of the participants' interchanges and feelings during the project. While Emma and I attempted to acknowledge the emotional responses that emerged, we experienced difficulty in attending more deeply to the transformational learning potential that they could have held for both the students and ourselves. I suggest that it may be useful for researchers and teachers alike to work more deeply with emotionality as a site of learning.

Psychoanalytic frameworks have proved useful to me in terms of understanding the emotional labour involved in engaging with notions of gender and sexual difference. I find it useful to draw on Felman's (1982) psychoanalytic notion of provocation to both use and trouble the implications of queer theoretical and pedagogical approaches within secondary school contexts. Felman suggests that in many cases, the process of engaging with texts (in her case, written texts) can provoke readers into an engagement with the self. This provocation, as she describes it, can hail both the thought and the un-thought, the possibilities of different ways of being, as well as the things that we cannot bear to know. Robertson (2006), in her exploration of the life and teaching of the New Zealand educationalist Sylvia Ashton-Warner, draws on Felman's (1982) notion to explore the potential of framing learning as provocation. Robertson (2006) suggests that understanding learning as a site of disturbance, turbulence and disequilibrium, rather than that of stasis and composure, can help understand why and how emotional responses to different ways of thinking can emerge.

The notion of education as provocation (Felman, 1997) speaks to the often difficult and dangerous labour involved in what it means to learn and to teach. It resonates with the possibilities inherent in considering framing learning selves as 'not in compliance, but in transition and motion towards previously unknown ways of thinking and being in the world' (Ellsworth, 2005, p. 16). Cultivating such dispositions, Ellsworth and others (Britzman, 1998; Salvio, 2006; Taubman, 2006) suggest, may enable learners to call into question ways of knowing that they find difficult and dangerous. Ellsworth (2005) acknowledges that exploring notions of cultivating learning selves on the way to thinking differently involves the often painful emotional labour of letting go of a part of yourself in the process:

> In their process of emergence ... someone ... is in the process of losing something of who she thought she was. Upon encountering something outside herself and her own ways of thinking, she is giving up thoughts she previously held as known, and as a consequence she is parting with a bit of her known self. (p. 16)

Attending to a range of participants' emotional responses occurring within the research project provides a venue to explore the emotional effects of putting queer, post-structural and psychoanalytic theories to work (Alaimo & Hekman, 2008; Lather, 2007). It allows an exploration of the ways in which discursive constructions of genders and sexualities are engaged with from differing student, teacher and researcher positionalities, and the effects of the interchanges and feelings on the research participants. While recognising the emotionality that emerged as part of our discussions at the time, in retrospect, Emma and I tended to frame the activities we engaged in primarily as intellectual endeavours. As a researcher I had an awareness of the ways in which destabilising representations of gender and sexuality provokes strong emotional reactions (Berlak, 2004; Boler, 1999; Quinlivan, 2007), and the ways in which engaging in new ways of knowing through reform processes can destabilise both teachers (Zembylas & Barker, 2007) and researchers. However, both Emma and I were unprepared for the visceral force of the emotional responses that occurred in the classroom, and the extent to which they destabilised our sense of ourselves as teachers and researchers. I return to speculate as to why this may have been the case later in the chapter.

QUEER PROVOCATION: NORMALISING CONSTRUCTIONS OF FEMININITIES,
SEXUALITIES AND CLASS

The emphasis in working with students over the course of the research project
centred on exploring the ways in which gendered and sexualised discourses were
produced within the student peer culture and in a range of popular cultural texts,
and their implications (Rosendale & Birnley, 2007; Willis, 2003). Drawing on
deconstruction and discourse analysis we considered the effects of constructions of
sexuality and gender occurring in advertisements, music videos, films and TV programmes such as *Queer Eye for the Straight Guy*. Part of the process included
introducing ways of framing understandings of genders and sexualities that moved
beyond biological essentialism, and the implications the differing approaches had for
exercising agency and creating social change.

It appeared that the analysis we engaged in enabled the students, in many
instances, to challenge normative constructions of masculinity and heterosexuality
amongst their peers. One group of female students in the class noted that framing
understandings of sexualities and genders as socially constructed created the possibility of challenging the understandings. As Maree comments, the frameworks
make exercising agency and challenging normative discourses a possibility:

> Maree: Yeah I thought it was really cool that we went back to the beginning
> and to identify that they *are* socially constructed and that way you can
> challenge them and stuff and they're not really [fixed] – they're just what
> everybody else thinks. What it's meant for their life. I enjoyed that how –
> kind of like you can challenge it if you really want to. (Follow-up Interview
> with Molly, Jessica, Maree, Mary and Christine, 26 July 2004)

Many of the students were able to act agentically within their peer cultures outside
the classroom. Several male students drew on social constructionist frameworks to
challenge normative constructions of masculinity and heterosexuality amongst
their peers. One male student took action against gender-based bullying. After
clarifying an incident of gender-based harassment with their teacher Emma,
two young women in the class also made a complaint. Ironically, despite the widespread nature of the gender-based harassment at the school, the school systems
designed to support students to challenge such harassment did not support Sally
and Fiona in making the complaint. As Emma noted:

> Sally and Fiona came to me [and] asked me if I thought it was sexual
> harassment that a boy from Year 13 yelled out across the road, 'Where are
> you two blonde bitches going?' … as they were walking down the street at
> lunchtime. I said yes I would report it if it was me. They reported it. [The]
> Year 13 Dean … had a talk to them and said they shouldn't have reported it,
> they should've come to him. Protecting his Year 13 student, I suppose … The
> girls told me about this, and were confused with the mixed messages. From
> what I found out the boy said he didn't say that and also that they said
> something to him … I believe Sally and Fiona … there is a lot of this kind of
> sexual harassment at our school. After talking again with the girls, they were

pleased they reported it and they see it was wrong what the boy said. They also said to me they would stand up for themselves again. (Emma, Teacher Research Journal entry, 19 July 2004)

Despite the ways in which students challenged normative constructions of gender and sexuality outside the classroom, it became apparent that high degrees of emotionality were being generated amongst several groups of students in response to the areas, issues and frameworks we were exploring within the classroom. Engaging with understandings of masculinities, femininities, sexualities and desires, traditionally framed as private subjects within the public sphere of the classroom (Gilbert, 2004; Quinlivan, 2007) understandably proved challenging for some students. Peer policing and regulation of hegemonic forms of gender and sexuality emerged as a pervasive feature of the hidden peer curriculum within the class, both within and amongst differing groups of male as well as female students. The hidden peer curriculum proved to be a powerful learning site in relation to understandings of gender and sexuality (Nuthall, 2001; Quinlivan, 2005). The incidents largely revolved around male students, who had a deep investment in normative constructions of sexuality and gender, subtly policing male and female students who, they perceived, embodied derogated masculinities, femininities and sexualities (Martino & Pallotta-Chiarolli, 2005; Quinlivan, under review; Robinson, 2005). The high emotionality that characterised the students' intercultural dialogues proved difficult for both Emma and I to fully analyse and understand the pedagogical significance of when it arose. I will return later to consider the reasons for this, and some implications that may be useful to think about as a result.

The following incident arose within the context of a class discussion which focused on understandings of masculinities, femininities, and sexual desire and intimacy. Emma, their teacher, was reading aloud from an article that was discussing the ways in which socially constructed representations of feminine desirability shifted and changed over time. The text described how feminine curviness was once considered more sexually desirable than it is currently. Justin, a male student who overtly displayed his hegemonic heterosexuality in class, affirmed the argument put forward by the text when he exclaimed that he thought size 14 was huge. Sharon, a student on the outside of the popular heterosexual girls' group, and perceived as working class by several of the middle class young women that Justin was often keen to impress, contested his association of desirable femininities with thinness. In response, Justin tried to defuse the situation by passing it off as a joke:

Emma: *[Reading aloud from a text]* … 'The current western norm identifies female attractiveness with slender, well-toned bodies and aquiline facial features. Gone is the curviness of the pop-up – the pin-up girls of the 1940s and 1950s. Remember Marilyn Monroe. She was a size 14.'

Kathleen: A curvy little number.

Emma: A curvy little number. That was *really* attractive.

Justin: That's *huge. [Loudly and exaggeratedly]*

Kathleen: Size 14?

Sharon: Fourteen's huge? That's not very nice. *[Angrily]*

Justin: I'm joking. Calm down! *[Patronisingly and disparagingly while laughing]*

Emma: *[Nervous laughter]*

Kathleen: These things are very deeply …

Emma: *(Sighs)* Yeah, deeply engrained aren't they.

Sharon: You wouldn't fit a size 14! *[Scathingly]*

Justin: Na, I wouldn't want to! *[Laughs, and sneers at Sharon]* (Classroom Transcript, 27 May 2004).

Behind Justin's demand for Sharon to 'Calm down!' was the insinuation that Sharon had got carried away and lost control in her critique. Sharon and Justin's comments actually spoke powerfully to the shifting constructions of femininity and masculinity we were interested in exploring. My interruption in Emma's reading shows the extent to which we were at that stage of the project virtually team-teaching the class, and frequently discussing and evaluating both our own and the students' responses. However, as is apparent from the transcript, there was a nervousness about the degree of emotional intensity that characterised the students' interaction and their refusal to back down. While both Emma and I noted the high degree of emotionality generated in the interaction, it did not occur to either of us at the time that the anger and sarcasm that characterised Justin and Sharon's interchange were an indicator of an issue that really did matter to students, and that to engage with students' feelings and their responses might have proven productive in exploring the issues we were focused on. Emma's nervous laughter provides some indication perhaps of the extent to which the classroom is an environment that privileges notions of intellectual rationality and control, making it difficult for teachers (and researchers) to address and engage more closely with emotional and highly charged feelings (Taubman, 2006). In retrospect, the emotionality that characterised these interchange could have provided an impetus to explore socially constructed understandings of desirable femininities and their material effects on young women of all sizes.

Over the course of the next half hour we went on to discuss issues affecting gendered constructions of (heterosexual) desirability and the way in which they can affect young people's lives. In particular Justin spoke to why he considered emotional intimacy did not sit well with hegemonic constructions of masculinity, suggesting that some young men, in seeking to align themselves positively with hegemonic masculinities, actually missed out in terms of emotional intimacy with young women (Allen, 2004). Sharon again contested Justin's points, suggesting that dominant hegemonic masculinities resulted in young men pressuring young women for sex. Justin then alluded to the pressure that was on both young men and young women to be actively sexual.

After this particularly heated discussion, in which Justin, Sharon and their peers had engaged thoughtfully with some of the implications of intertwined constructions of hegemonic masculinities and femininities with sexual desirability, Sharon was asked a question by Emma. Sharon freely acknowledged that she had not been listening to the discussion while talking to her neighbour. At that point Justin referred to Sharon as a wastrel. She challenged him again, as she had earlier. As the transcript shows, Emma's response to the highly charged interchange between Justin and Sharon is procedural in terms of turn-taking. However, in retrospect perhaps both Emma and I failed to tap into the extent to which Justin had moved out of his comfort zone in questioning constructions of masculinity – in which he had earlier displayed a deep investment – leaving him feeling unusually exposed and vulnerable (Quinlivan, under review):

Justin: I think it's a desirable form of masculinity and femininity … to have sex …

Kathleen: That it's a desirable form of masculinity and femininity to be sexual – sexually active?

Justin: Oh, yeah.

Emma: Girls you wanted to say something? *[Pointedly drawing their attention to the fact that they were talking amongst themselves]*

Maree: No. Not now.

Sharon: Forgot what we were talking about actually … *[Casually and distractedly]*

Justin: You wastrels! … *[Angrily]*

Sharon: I don't like being called that, Justin. So get over it. *[Coldly and sarcastically]*

Justin: You're a wastrel! *[Insultingly]*

Abby: What's up with that? *[Flauntingly]*

Emma: I'm sorry I didn't see. Sometimes I see you chatting but I don't realise that you are wanting to talk to the class. Okay. So maybe put your hand up.

Maree: But no one else put his or their hand up …

Fiona: He's one person out of the whole class.

Emma: Yeah. I'll have a bit more awareness over there. I'm sorry. So identify at least 3 key messages *you* get about the connection about love and sex. Please write those down for yourself now. Not as a group … (Classroom Transcript, 27 May 2004)

As several students noted, there were other people apart from Justin talking, none of whom had raised their hands. However, in response to that incident Emma demanded that Justin apologise to Sharon in front of the class, which he found humiliating, especially in terms of being made to articulate the reasons for his reaction. From Emma's perspective, Justin failed to comply in demonstrating a genuinely sincere apology, which was required in the situation:

> Emma: ... Right, Justin's just got something to say.
>
> Justin: Sorry for what happened...
>
> Emma: For what? *[Perfunctorily]*
>
> Justin: I say sorry.
>
> Peter: What's he sorry for?
>
> Emma: Maybe you need to explain.
>
> Justin: I did explain.
>
> Emma: What's he saying sorry for? Sharon, do you feel that's an apology?
>
> Sharon: For calling me a wastrel and saying size 14 girls are big when there's a couple of people in this class that are bigger than size 14.
>
> Emma: Okay. So I'm asking Justin to say sorry for calling Sharon a name. You've got to mean it, mate.
>
> Justin: Sorry.
>
> Emma: 'Cos otherwise it's a waste of time saying it.
>
> Justin: Sorry ... (Classroom Transcript, 27 May 2004)

Although I am not disputing that Justin owed Sharon a sincere apology for his remarks, the cultural rituals of a public apology overshadowed any possible opportunities for extending students' learning in relation to the incident that occurred. Both Emma and I had been concerned for some time about the extent to which Justin's actions and behaviours were shutting down opportunities for dialogue and silencing both male and female students in the class, particularly those who were seen to be more closely aligned with derogatory representations of masculinity, femininity and sexuality (Quinlivan, in press). The fact that several students had complained about his actions and their effects on their peers and themselves exacerbated our concerns. However, the effects of the above exchange on Justin and the rest of the class are also important to consider.

Following the usual school trajectory of disciplinary procedures for disruptive students, eventually Justin was excluded from the class and sent to the counsellor to address his aggression. The exclusion resulted in him feeling even more anger. As several students commented to me in later interviews, Justin's rich engagement with the lived complexities of shifting constructions of genders and sexualities was no longer present as a 'provocation' (Felman, 1982) within the class. While the

85

classroom environment was certainly less combustible, it also became considerably less thought- provoking. Looking back, I cannot help but wonder that if Emma and I had been more attuned to attending to the emotionality that emerged in the interchange I describe, there might have been a way to work with the underlying constructions that emerged. I wondered (perhaps, optimistically?) that such processes might have even led to valuing Justin's contribution and insights and integrating him back into the classroom culture. Privately, he admitted to me later, that he sorely needed such integration with his peers and would benefit from it.

Although both Emma and I went some way to acknowledging the emotionality that proved to be a strong feature of the project, looking back it appeared challenging for us to work more productively with this aspect. In the final section I would like to suggest some reasons for this, and suggest some possible ways to proceed.

TOWARDS A CLOSER ENGAGEMENT WITH EMOTIONALITY AS A SITE OF LEARNING?

Authors such as Berlak (2004), Boler (1999) and Zembylas (2005) draw attention to the extent to which the Cartesian mind–body binary has lead to a subsequent privileging of intellectual as opposed to emotional and embodied knowledge. The differing values of these knowledges have led to a devaluation of emotional knowing as feminine and lower in status. The situation has been exacerbated both historically and in the current context, with the ongoing dominance of discourses of instrumental rationality which privilege the role that often narrow conceptualisations of evidence play in addressing the persistent failures besetting schooling (Atkinson, 2000; Kennedy, 2005; Powell & Barber, 2006; Tyack & Cuban, 1995).

Recognising the perceived 'irrationality' that is seen to characterise emotional and embodied ways of knowing, psychoanalytic and psycho-social frameworks draw attention to the anxiety-producing emotional labour involved in what it means to learn. As Britzman (2003) suggests, what is educative makes us anxious. Both Emma and I were aware of the emotionality generated in exploring issues such as sexuality and gender, and the importance of developing trusting relationships with students to enable issues to be raised and addressed. Despite providing a venue for those conversations to occur, the emotional intensity that characterised them proved challenging to deal with in the heat of the moment. As I have shown in the case of Justin, behaviour management systems and the approach of 'zero tolerance' adopted by the school fail to address the ambiguity, complexity and high emotion-ality that characterise the power relationships struggled over in the classroom (Taubman, 2006). The rationality that characterises pedagogical approaches informed by instrumentalism fails to take account of issues of love, aggression and control in the classroom.

Foregrounding emotionality as a site of learning in classrooms may be helpful in terms of acknowledging the extent to which learning is a profoundly destabilising process that cannot be engaged in without experiencing conflict and loss of equi-librium (Redman, 2005; Salvio, 2006). Recognising that the role of anxiety is fundamental to learning may also provide a venue for enabling teachers and students alike to learn to acknowledge anxiety, given the psyche's capacity to harness and manage anxiety increases as you learn to work with it (Powell & Barber, 2006). At times in the research project, both Emma and I felt anxious about the high emotionality that emerged in the classroom, and the resulting loss of control. The emotionality and anxiety generated through destabilising heteronormative and gender normative constructions in the classroom appeared to generate tensions with notions of teacher subjectivities that are heavily invested in maintaining authority and control in the classroom (Taubman, 2006).

Attending more closely to emotionality as a site of learning over the course of the research project may have enabled Emma and me to acknowledge that engaging in teaching and learning and attending to the students' and our own intersubjectivities is troubling and anxiety-producing work. Acknowledging teaching and learning as emotional labour may be more akin to what Phelan (1995, cited in Ellsworth, 1997) describes as standing over an abyss on a rackety bridge. Such an approach suggests the importance of attending to what happens within classrooms when things fall apart, break down, and feel uncomfortable and out of control. Attending to emotionality and discomfort as sites of learning could provide the possibilities for understanding and pedagogically working with the dynamics in the classroom in order to more closely engage with issues that genuinely matter to students.

REFERENCES

Alaimo, S., & Hekman, S. (2008). Introduction: Emerging models of materiality in feminist theory. In S. Alaimo & S. Hekman (Eds.), *Material feminisms*. Bloomington, IN: Indiana University Press.

Allen, L. (2004). 'Getting off and going out': Young people's conceptions of (hetero)sexual relationships. *Culture, Health and Sexuality, 6*(6), 463–481.

Atkinson, E. (2000). In defence of ideas, or why 'what works' is not enough. *British Journal of Sociology of Education, 21*(3), 317–330.

Berlak, A. (2004). Confrontation and pedagogy: cultural secrets, trauma and emotion. In M. Boler (Ed.), *Antioppressive pedagogies. Democratic dialogue in education: Troubling speech, disturbing silence*. New York: Peter Lang.

Boler, M. (1999). *Feeling power*. New York: Routledge.

Boler, M., & Zembylas, M. (2003). Discomforting truths: The emotional terrain of understanding difference. In P. Trifonas (Ed.), *Pedagogies of difference: Rethinking education for social change*. New York: Routledge Falmer.

Britzman, D. (1998). *Lost subjects, contested objects: Towards a psychoanalytic inquiry of learning*. New York: State University of New York Press.

Britzman, D. (2003). *After-education: Anna Freud, Melanie Klein and psychoanalytic histories of learning*. Albany, NY: State University of New York Press.

Britzman, D., & Gilbert, J. (2004). What will have been said about gayness in teacher education. *Teaching Education, 15*(1), 81–96.

Butler, J. (2004). *Precarious life. The powers of mourning and violence*. New York: Verso.

Ellsworth, E. (1997). *Teaching positions: Difference, pedagogy and the power of address*. New York: Teachers College Press.

Ellsworth, E. (2005). *Places of learning. Media, architecture, pedagogy*. New York: Routledge Falmer.

Felman, S. (1982). *Literature and psychoanalysis: The question of reading otherwise*. Baltimore: Johns Hopkins University Press.

Gilbert, J. (2004). Between sexuality and narrative: On the language of sex education. In M. Rasmussen, E. Rofes, & S. Talburt (Eds.), *Youth and sexualities: Pleasure, subversion, and insubordination in and out of schools*. New York: Palgrave Macmillan.

Kennedy, M. (2005). *Inside teaching: How classroom life undermines reform*. Cambridge, MA: Harvard University Press.

Lather, P. (2007). *Getting lost. Feminist efforts towards a double(d) science*. New York: SUNY Press.

Martino, W., & Pallotta-Chiarolli, M. (2005). *Being normal is the only way to be: Adolescent perspectives on gender and school*. Sydney, New S Wales: University of New South Wales Press.

Nuthall, G. (2001). The cultural myths and the realities of teaching and learning. In I. Livingstone (Ed.), *New Zealand Annual Review of Education: Te Arotake a Tau o Te Ao o Te Matauranga i Aotearoa* (Vol. 11). Wellington, NZ: School of Education, Victoria University of Wellington.

Powell, L. C., & Barber, M. (2006). Savage inequalities indeed. irrationality and urban school reform. In G. M. Boldt & P. M. Salvio (Eds.), *Love's return. Psychoanalytic essays on childhood, teaching and learning*. London: Routledge.

Quinlivan, K. (2005). Opening Pandora's box: Working towards addressing intersections of gender/diversity and learning/teaching in the secondary school classroom. *Delta 57*. 193–210.

Quinlivan, K. (2006). Building a partnership with students and their teacher to work towards affirming gender and sexual diversity with students and their teacher in a Year 12 health classroom. *Report to the New Zealand AIDS Foundation*.

Quinlivan, K. (2007). Twist and shout! Working with teachers towards affirming sexual diversity in a New Zealand girls secondary school. *Tidskrift Journal of Research in Teacher Education, 3*(14), 39–68.

Quinlivan, K. (Under review). Emotional provocations: attending to the materiality of queer pedagogies in a high school classroom. In (Eds.) *Queer Pedagogies, Theories, Practice, Politics. New York: Teachers College Press*.

Rasmussen, M. (2006). Play school, melancholia and the politics of recognition. *British Journal of Sociology of Education, 27*(4), 473–487.

Rasmussen, M., Talburt, S., & Rofes, E. (2004). Introduction. In M. Rasmussen, S. Talburt, & E. Rofes (Eds.), *Youth and sexualities: Pleasure, subversion and insubordination in and out of schools*. New York: Palgrave Macmillan.

Redman, P. (2005). Who cares about the psycho-social? Masculinities, schooling and the unconscious. *Gender and Education, 17*(5), 531–538.

Robinson, K. (2005). Reinforcing hegemonic masculinities through sexual harassment: issues of identity, power and popularity in secondary schools. *Gender and Education, 17*(1), 19–37.

Rosendale, G. B., & Birnley, K. (2007). Reconfiguring differences: Radicalising popular culture pedagogy. In T. Peele (Ed.) *Queer popular culture. Literature, media, film and television*. New York: Palgrave Macmillan.

Robertson, P. (2006). Recovering education as provocation: keeping countenance with Sylvia Ashton-Warner. In J. Simon & K. McConachie (Eds.), *Provocations: Sylvia Ashton- Warner and excitability in education*. New York: Peter Lang.

Salvio, P. (2006). Mother love's education. In G. M. Boldt & P. M. Salvio (Eds.), *Love's return. Psychoanalytic essays on childhood, teaching and learning*. London: Routledge.

Stronach, I., & MacLure, M. (1997). *Educational research undone: The postmodern embrace*. Buckingham: Open University Press.

Taubman, P. (2006). I love them to death. In G. M. Boldt & P. M. Salvio (Eds.), *Love's return. Psychoanalytic essays on childhood, teaching and learning*. London: Routledge.

Tyack, D. B., & Cuban, L. (1995). *Tinkering toward utopia: A century of public school reform*. Cambridge, MA: Harvard University Press.

Willis, P. (2003). Foot soldiers of modernity: The dialectics of cultural consumption and the 21st-century school. *Harvard Educational Review, 73*(3), 390–341.

Zembylas, M. (2005). *Teaching with emotion: A postmodern enactment.* Greenwich, CT: Information Age Publishing.

Zembylas, M., & Barker, H. (2007). Teachers' spaces for coping with change in the context of a reform effort. *Journal of Educational Change, 8*(3), 235–256.

Kathleen Quinlivan
School of Educational Studies and Human Development
College of Education
University of Canterbury

CONVERSATIONAL INTERLUDE TWO:
EMOTIONALITY AND LEARNING?

Kathleen Quinlivan: The first thing is that even though I have this immense allure for post-structuralism and problematising normalcy and to try and work in areas where I can actually enact that stuff, I still can't undo my rational self in that process and I realise that … the teacher's rational self and my rational self came into that context and it came from some place that wasn't even in my rational knowing … So there was me as an academic in there with all these 16-year-old kids and their health teacher in the classroom. Now that is a weird intercultural conversation [to] have to negotiate but [an] even more [significant realisation] than that was that there was deeply emotional stuff happening in a context that privileges rational, intellectual thinking.

Annemarie Palincsar: I missed that. Say that once more – that privileges?

Kathleen Quinlivan: That privileges rationality and the intellect … [W]e divorce those off from each other and we don't see emotionality as a productive site of learning … [W]e see the classroom as a site of intellectual engagement; when emotional stuff happens we all kind of freak out. We don't know how to manage that stuff and I think that we probably need to pay more attention to kind of embodied emotions as they are played out, and it's very counter-intuitive. It doesn't feel good to do that stuff. It feels like going into a really scary zone … I'm kind of still deeply interested in that idea of Elizabeth Ellsworth's of cultivating the learning self that's on the way to thinking differently. But what I really realise about, I mean I love these ideas, … but enacting this stuff, when you are actually engaged in these processes [is] really hard yet actually the enactment of it can teach you so much …

…

Jean McPhail: Sorry could you ask that question again?

Annemarie Palincsar: I asked if she would do the project again.

Kathleen Quinlivan: I probably would because I'm deeply interested in how kids understand and see the world and we had such an amazing time … Like it was just magic sometimes but it was really scary at the same time. We went into all these places that as a researcher and as a teacher I've never experienced, that level of ability to take these huge kind of risks and the kids took amazing risks too, like they came out and talked about their transgendered mothers and their lesbian friends and all the rest of it, but everybody came from such different places in terms of where their heads were at. By the end of the project the most homophobic boy in the class told me that rather than actually beating another boy up for being gay, that now he would just stand on the sidelines and not get involved. For him that was a huge distance for that to travel, but it also speaks to the pervasive heteronormativity in the school. The most homophobic boy in the class was my

K. Quinlivan, R. Boyask and B. Kaur (eds.), Educational Enactments in a Globalised World:
Intercultural Conversations, 91–93.
© *2009 Sense Publishers. All rights reserved.*

favourite person actually. He was the most insightful person because he was kind of up for asking and doing all these difficult things. And it was his homophobic actions in trying to normalise the other kids that led to the most interesting findings of the project. And talking about kids and popular culture and stuff, I just love doing that. So yes I would, I would, I would.

Sean Darmody: I have one question on top of that. If you had to change two very important things, what would you do differently?

Annemarie Palincsar: Good question.

Kathleen Quinlivan: I'm interested in this kind of pedagogy of discomfort and all of those kind of ideas and how you might help. I'd like to think if I was in that situation again working with that teacher again that we might be able to play it differently knowing all this stuff that I've thought about and talked about since. So that would be one thing but I'd like to think, actually I don't know whether I could undo my rational self. You know that terrible feeling? I mean I'm an ex-high school teacher and when the whole thing starts to slide and you know you're losing them? And there's a part of you that wants to get the control back. But actually I would like to think that I won't do that but it's a very hard thing to undo because actually a lot of this stuff is subconscious. The other thing I'd really like is more people to talk about some of the psychoanalytic frameworks around what it means to learn and the difficulty of learning … I'd like to hear more people talking about emotionality and the dangerous thing of what it means to learn and how terrifying it is, and how out of your comfort zone you are and how you cry when you do your PhD but that seems to be like a kind of weakness, because we all have to be so rational and intellectual and we divorce ourselves. We don't talk enough about what you said, Vanessa, what we bring to the table. We don't even know what some people bring to the table.

Ruth Boyask: It's interesting this whole issue of emotionality that keeps coming up again and again in relation to some of the work that we've been doing and I think it extends to the way that we rationalise difference in terms of categories and you alluded to that earlier, Andrew. The empirical work that Hazel mentioned briefly where we've been trying to talk to 18 to 20 year-olds about their experience of difference at school has raised hugely emotional responses about their experiences of difference. And *emotion*, not categories, has been the key frame for how they talk about schooling and their position within schooling.

Hazel Lawson: But it is interesting because we sat there and there're people in tears and we're thinking, 'God, research ethics!' It's, 'We've got these participants in tears and …you know we can't leave them and what do we do? And have we made this too emotional?' Those sort of things …

Vanessa Andreotti: Kathleen, that goes back to what Jean was saying, that doing that in an institution is not easy. We're institutionalised to be able to have control over everything and we can't, because there are no guarantees. You would do it again and other problems would come up and you don't know if you would be able to deal with those problems. You would have to see.

Kathleen Quinlivan: I'd be up for it though. I mean, what more can you say? Think of that class that you had with all those troubles. You know, you have to be up for it.

Vanessa Andreotti: But my rational self is saying, 'Leave New Zealand, go somewhere else'... But that's the rational self because I'm accountable to an institution that requires certain standards to be met and if the students are not exactly at this point, why do I have to do a teaching survey? And all the students say that I'm an awful teacher! What is meant to happen to my promotion? What is meant to happen to my job?

Andrew Gitlin: ... [Y]ou probably know this but it's new to me, relatively new to me ... this book ... by Martha Nussbaum, it's called *Poetic Justice* ... [S]he's working with judges ... and what she's doing is trying to expand the notion of rationality ... in particular she talks about imaginative compassion. And I think this notion, it's better, it's less dangerous, it's more rational; if we take the emotional out it's kind of still problematic ... Like John Dewey always gets around this concept. He wants emotion but he mostly wants growth. So he's not going to tell you what kind of emotion it is. As long as they grow, everything's fine. What I like about Martha Nussbaum – she's definitely a feminist and a literary person if you don't know her background – is that she argues over and over again, for not only emotionality but she says the judges will judge better ... if they're not only emotional but if they're compassionate. So when I talk to my students they all say, 'Oh well that means you're against law and order'. In this state of Georgia that I'm in, the students all go, 'Oh that means you're going to give into the, you know, you're just going to do whatever, anything goes'. So they have a totally screwed up view of what is compassion ... That would be part of what I would say but I want to correct one thing that I think I left an impression is that its not a matter of giving up rationality, it's being in, like Martha Nussbaum, in those spaces between rationality and something else so that you can look back. Like you have obviously Kathleen and said to yourself, 'I can see myself falling into a rational discourse'. As far as I can see, that's a success because you're ahead of most of us who don't even have a clue about that. Then on the other hand we have to create the space where we can also create that same opportunity for students – I guess in this case, health education students. Because what probably happened is they didn't get an opportunity because we don't often do that. We shut it down before that, for them to do the same thing. So they come out, you've learnt and I think you're a success by the way, but the irony is that the students, you don't give them a chance to be a success in the same way.

GILL VALENTINE

INTERSTICE TWO.
GLOBALISATION AND LANGUAGE DIVERSITY

Implications for the Enactment of Identities and Intercultural Relations

INTRODUCTION

Contemporary processes of globalisation have provoked social scientists to reflect critically on how mobility, identities and belonging are related as the global economy has accelerated patterns of migration, dramatically intensifying the connections among different peoples, cultures and spaces (Massey & Jess, 1995). One aspect of these new migration flows that has profound implications for the enactment of identities and development of intercultural relations is language use. Increased flows of people have facilitated the mobility of language, both transforming localities with the arrival of migrants raised in different linguistic communities and creating diasporas with multiple linguistic allegiances and perceptions of belonging that are no longer identified purely with territory. It is estimated that approximately 10% of pupils in English state schools are learning English as a second, third or even fourth language, and that over 300 languages are now spoken by pupils in the United Kingdom (Multiverse, 2004).

In this chapter I explore the role of language in the enactment of identities at school, focusing on its role in connecting or disconnecting young people from others and on the possibility that language can change the way that educational spaces are ordered. I am *not* concerned with linguistics – how words, dialects and the structure of language change when people speaking different languages come together. Rather my focus is on the role that language plays in how young people can enact their identities and make sense of their affiliations (cf. Hewitt, 1986; Rampton, 2006) within the context of the school. In doing so, I draw on evidence from research with Somali refugee and asylum seekers, aged 11 to 18, who now live in Sheffield, United Kingdom (Valentine, Sporton & Nielsen, 2008).

In adopting this approach, I understand language not as constructing identity, nor identity as determining language, but rather I recognise the two as mutually constituted. Butler (1990) theorised gender – one particular identity – as performative, arguing that gender emerges through a set of repeated acts that take place within a regulatory framework and that congeal over time to give the appearance of naturalness. Language or talk is one such element of performance (Cameron, 1998). Cameron (1998, p. 272) argues that 'people are who they are because of (among other things) the way they talk'. Individuals' verbal repertoires contribute to the

K. Quinlivan, R. Boyask and B. Kaur (eds.), Educational Enactments in a Globalised World:
Intercultural Conversations, 95–101.
© 2009 Sense Publishers. All rights reserved.

definition of the self and, as such, languages open up possibilities for different enactments of the self in different regulatory frameworks. The interactional nature of language means that it is a joint and negotiated performance rooted in what Wenger (1998) might dub 'communities of practice', produced in and through particular spaces. Languages are seen to be 'situated accomplishments', performed in and through different spaces (such as the home, the nation and the transnational diaspora), such that language may be used to define identities in specific spatial contexts and particular language practices may become salient or irrelevant in particular spaces. Here I think of space in geographical terms: it does not contain the social but is folded into social relations through practical activities. Space is both formed and transformed through endless practices and performances; yet at the same time space is not infinitely fluid – rather 'certain forms of space tend to recur, their repetition a sign of the power that saturates the social' (Rose, 1999).

Notably, language is one of the taken-for-granted norms that structure the everyday space of the school, in that educational environments have norms or rules about communicative behaviour that affect what children/adults can or cannot say or do, legitimising the enactment of some forms of behaviour and identities while constraining others. At the same time, minority communities can create themselves around practices such as language, building in effect particular solidarities, giving meaning to particular spaces and impacting on individuals' self-identities and rela-tionships with others (cf. Valentine & Skelton, 2007). It is apparent that language, space and identities are being constituted constantly and mutually. Language contact, then, as a form of intercultural relationship, might facilitate the production of a more progressive sense of space in schools. By focusing on the construction and enactment of subjectivities through language, this chapter poses questions and raises challenges for educational practice and theory in regard to language rights, cultural connectivity and intercultural citizenship.

EDUCATION FOR ALL? MANAGING LINGUISTIC DIVERSITY IN SCHOOLS

It may seem unremarkable to observe that English state schools are spaces produced through the English language. Yet in 1985 a UK government report *Education for All* was published into linguistic and ethnic diversity in national schools (Department for Education and Science, 1985). The Swann Report set out an educational strategy to overcome the linguistic and cultural disadvantages minority groups faced through the teaching of English as a second language (ESL). It argued that ESL and any additional language needs of minority ethnic children should be met within mainstream classrooms rather than developed through specialist linguistic resources that might unintentionally produce ethnic segregation within the state schooling system. (Comparable education policies were also developed in the USA, Canada and Australia.)

This policy remains largely in place today despite the fact that the Swann Report was primarily concerned with relatively stable, established working class ethnic communities (particularly those of Caribbean and South Asian descent) that were a product of post-war labour migration, whereas the contemporary twin forces of globalisation and neo-liberal market capitalism have subsequently produced major changes in the nature (official and unofficial), scale and patterns of migration and consequently the ethnic and linguistic diversity of UK pupils (Rampton, 2006). Technological change has also facilitated migrants' ability to maintain instantaneous links with other places and to manage diasporic identities in ways that Swann, who was largely dismissive of any connections minority groups may seek to maintain with other parts of the world, could not have anticipated. As such, there is an awkward disconnect between the dated educational strategy in place to deal with minority ethnic pupils and the contemporary realities of multilingualism in UK schools.

Indeed, the reality of mainstreaming ESL, and lack of provision of specialist linguistic resources, is that newly arrived migrants are placed into mainstream classrooms before they have the English language skills necessary to engage with the lessons. The superficial assumption is that exposure to English in this way, with some support from bilingual classroom assistants (who are usually low-paid and not qualified as teachers) will enable new arrivals to integrate (Bourne, 2001). Yet in practice the production of the school through the specific hegemonic language of English means that minority language speakers are defined as 'out of place' in the classroom which affects their sense of identification and belonging: leaving them feeling isolated 'outsiders'.

The school is made up of two spaces: the formal adult-controlled space of the classroom; and the informal peer spaces outside of lesson time (Valentine, 2000). Within the formal monolingual space of an English classroom, migrant children's multilingualism is rarely recognised as a skill or a resource. In contrast, the emphasis on English effectively dis-ables them because they are unable to express themselves effectively, and they may misunderstand important information and struggle with mundane tasks that they could complete in other linguistic environ-ments. Language competence, then, is not about skill or potential per se, but rather about positioning in space. For example, a young migrant starting at an English school may not be able to communicate effectively with the teacher because he/she has not yet become fluent in English and so will probably be assumed to lack academic ability. Yet the child may speak other languages fluently while the teacher may only speak English. Because language is a situated practice, the communi-cation difficulty between the child and the teacher is read in terms of the child's rather than the teacher's lack of linguistic competence. Yet, in a different place/time their relative competencies might be read differently as the space of language contact changes (Blommaert, Collins & Slembrouck, 2005, p. 211).

Several studies (e.g. Elbers & de Haan, 2004) suggest that differences between languages spoken at home and the majority language of the school may contribute to the relative underachievement of children from minority ethnic backgrounds. In particular, the language patterns within white middle class families are similar to literacy practices in the classroom thus facilitating the performance of middle class white children at school. In contrast, for Somali children, for example, the emphasis placed on speaking Somali within the home means that their English language skills are not developed within the family and there is also a disjuncture between their literacy practices at school and at home. Literacy in Somali is not widespread among Somali speakers in the UK given that an agreed Somali script was only introduced in the 1970s and that the formal education system in Somalia has been severely disrupted by civil war (Arthur, 2004). Somali children have been consistently at the bottom of achievement tables suggesting potential problems of integration in the education system (Education Data Services, Sheffield, personal communication, February 10th, 2009).

Despite the obvious frustrations that Somali children encounter in the formal space of their UK classrooms they are not necessarily passive or compliant in the face of English hegemony. Rather, they take up different positions mobilising their linguistic abilities (many have arrived in the UK after living in other countries en route from Somalia and so are multi-lingual) in both positive and oppositional ways. Some of the children do not just switch into their preferred language (e.g. Somali or Dutch or Danish) for off-task chat but also draw on this language as part of everyday learning to seek help from peers or to advance their understanding; others describe 'slipping' unintentionally into thinking and writing in their first language.

Such language switching can be interpreted differently by different teachers according to the specific spatial contexts of particular classes. Some teachers can use such moments to open up an intercultural dialogue with the pupils about difference. However, many teachers regard such practices as conspiratorial or as a threat to their own fragile authority in the classroom.

LANGUAGE CONTACT: MAKING AND BREAKING BOUNDARIES

In informal peer group spaces beyond the classroom, language contact plays an important role in both making and breaking boundaries between different groups of pupils. As Somali households are concentrated in particular city neighbourhoods the catchment areas of the schools in which Somali children are placed commonly include significant numbers of Somalis as well as other minority ethnic pupils. Not surprisingly children tend to form friendship groups based on shared languages (e.g. Somali or Dutch), sometimes using these strategically to exclude or gain an advantage over monolingual children.

Yet peer groups are not always linguistically exclusive and can operate bilingually (e.g. English and Somali) or even trilingually (e.g. English, Somali and a third language such as Dutch). These communication practices in turn can lead to the creative blending of languages (and identities) with little regard for grammatical and syntactical order. There are some parallels with Hewitt's (1986) study of the role of language as a medium in the relationship between white British young people and black British young people of Afro-Caribbean descent in London, which found that white young people adopted elements of creole speech used by their black friends.

Although monolingual societies like the UK tend to assume that monolingualism is a natural state of affairs, and to stigmatise second language users and to perceive bilingualism as exotic or unusual, young people appear to perceive language diversity as a normal part of everyday life (Bourne, 2001). These everyday practices hint at the potential for a future globalisation of language to emerge in which communication might no longer be necessarily embedded in national languages but rather in multiple practices composed of mixed codes, words and simultaneous communicative frames (Appadurai, 1996).

CONCLUSION: LANGUAGE MATTERS

Talking is central to the production of most everyday spaces yet despite this pivotal position of language it has received relatively little academic consideration beyond linguistics. The importance of language in socio-spatial relations is, however, likely to become progressively more apparent as contemporary processes of globalisation intensify cultural contact such that linguistic diversity increasingly characterises both local and global contexts. This both challenges traditional assumptions about the relationships among linguistic uniformity, cultural homogeneity and national identities, and impacts on self-identities (Appadurai, 1996).

Kloss (1971 and 1977) identifies a difference between tolerance-oriented and promotion-oriented language rights. Tolerance-oriented rights are the protections afforded to individuals against government interference in what language they choose to use at home or in other 'private' associations such as within their own communities. Promotion-oriented rights are the rights that individuals have to use a particular language in public institutions (e.g. school). In the latter context, Kymlicka (2003) makes a further distinction between limited and more constructive ways of accommodating speakers of particular languages in public institutions. One approach is to provide an interpreter or make other such special provision for those who lack the proficiency to use the dominant language. This norm-and-accommodation model may facilitate communication by enabling individuals to communicate with(in) public institutions, such as schools, and so to access benefits and rights to which they are entitled. However, it does not give speakers of minority languages more profound rights in terms of the recognition of their cultural identities (Kymlicka, 2003). To achieve such recognition, a second kind of approach is needed, involving designating a language as an official language and giving its users rights that provide a degree of equality with the dominant/other official languages regardless of their cultural proficiency in the majority language. In other words, this approach involves recognising the cultural identity of those who use the minority language within public institutions.

Most nation states, however, are reluctant to recognise bilingualism or multilingualism as rights, regarding them instead as pragmatic accommodations (Kymlicka, 2003). For a state to officially recognise a language it must also acknowledge and accept that it is a multicultural state. It must recognise that the state is not just the possession of the dominant group but belongs equally to all citizens (Kymlicka, 2003). If it is to attain this point of view, a state must acknowledge historical injustices to different cultural groups, examine public policies and institutions for bias/discrimination and address the way that different linguistic and cultural groups relate to the state. Kymlicka (2003) argues that a truly multicultural state must accept that 'individuals should be able to access state institutions and act as full and equal citizens without having to deny their own identities'. The evidence from the Somali research indicates that some children may intuitively recognise the importance of language diversity in moving beyond accommodating difference through the ways in which they blend languages in their everyday practices in the informal spaces of the school and in the process enact new forms of identification and create new intercultural affiliations.

The children's everyday practices demonstrate the need for language to take centre stage in debates about cultural connectivity in schools. To develop 'intercultural citizens' (Kymlicka, 2003) who, far from being fearful or resentful of other cultures, have positive attitudes to diversity, we need to reconsider education policy in the light of the contemporary realities of globalisation and population mobility. Appropriate policy might include the promotion of intercultural knowledge and skills through the recognition of minority languages within the education system and the provision of more opportunities and incentives for schools to: broaden the curriculum to incorporate more non-European language teaching; develop the monolingual skills of teachers; recognise the increasingly diverse range of linguistic needs and competencies of their pupils and parents/families; and promote multilingualism. Through fostering a more diverse range of language practices as part of wider social and economic processes of cultural hybridity, we might also, over time, produce a more progressive sense of national identity and belonging.

ACKNOWLEDGEMENTS

The argument in this essay was developed through collaborative research with Deborah Sporton on the experiences of Somali children who are refugees and asylum seekers. I wish to acknowledge the support of the Economic and Social Research Council in funding this research. Elements of this essay have previously been published in Valentine, Sporton and Nielsen (2008).

REFERENCES

Appadurai, A. (1996). *Modernity at large*. Minneapolis: University of Minnesota Press.

Arthur, J. (2004). Language at the margins, *Language Problems and Language Planning, 28*, 217–240.

Blommaert, J., Collins, J., & Slembrouck, S. (2005). Spaces of multilingualism. *Language & Communication, 25*, 197–216.

Bourne, J. (2001). Discourses and identities in a multi-lingual primary classroom. *Oxford Review of Education, 27*, 103–114.

Butler, J. (1990). *Gender trouble: Feminism and the subversion of identity*. London: Routledge.

Cameron, D. (1998). Performing gender identity: young men's talk and the construction of heterosexual of masculinity. In J. Coates (Ed.), *Language and gender: A reader*. Oxford: Blackwell.

Department for Education and Science. (1985). *Education for all: The report of the Committee of Inquiry into the Education of Children from Ethnic Minority Groups* (the Swann report). London: HMSO.

Elbers, E., & de Haan, M. (2004). Dialogic learning in the multi-ethnic classroom: cultural resources and modes of collaboration. In J. Van der Linden & P. Renshaw (eds.) *Dialogical perspectives on learning, teaching and instruction*. Dordrecht: Kluwer Academic Publishers.

Hewitt, R. (1986). *White talk, black talk: Interracial friendship and communication amongst adolescents.* Cambridge: Cambridge University Press.

Kloss, H. (1971). Language rights of immigrant groups. *International Migration Review, 5,* 250–268.

Kloss, H. (1977). *The American bilingual tradition.* Rowley MA: Newbury House.

Kymlicka, W. (2003). Multicultural states and intercultural citizens. *Theory and Research in Education, 1,* 147–169.

Massey, D., & Jess, P. (1995). Places and cultures in an uneven world. In D. Massey and P. Jess (Eds.) *A place in the world? Places, cultures and globalization.* Milton Keynes: Open University Press.

Multiverse. (2004). English as an additional language. Retrieved 12 May 2009 from www.multiverse.ac.uk/viewarticle2.aspx?contentId=381

Rampton, B. (2006). *Language in late modernity.* Cambridge: Cambridge University Press.

Rose, G. (1999). Performing space. In D. Massey, J. Allen & P. Sarre (Eds.), *Human Geography Today,* Cambridge: Polity.

Valentine, G. (2000). Exploring children and young people's narrative of identity. *Geoforum, 31,* 257–267.

Valentine, G., & Skelton, T. (2007). The right to be heard: citizenship and language. *Political Geography, 26,* 121–140.

Valentine, G., Sporton, D., & Nielsen, K.B. (2008). Language use of the move: sites of encounter, identities and belonging. *Transactions of the Institute of British Geographers, 33,* 376–387.

Wenger, E. (1998). *Communities of practice: Learning, meaning and identity.* Cambridge: Cambridge University Press.

Gill Valentine
School of Geography
University of Leeds

MARY LOU RASMUSSEN AND LOU PRESTON

7. JOURNEYING ON THE FRINJ
OF OUTDOOR EDUCATION

INTRODUCTION

In this chapter we offer a conceptualisation of the construction of the pedagogical relationship between people and place. This conceptualisation considers pedagogical experiences that might prompt students to think differently about relations between people and places of learning often utilised within outdoor education. We see ourselves as journeying on the frinj of outdoor education in so far as we are arguing for a reconceptualisation of what constitutes good 'pedagogical' practice within this field of inquiry. This observation is based on what we believe is a troubling perception that distinguishes between outdoor activities as a site for the refinement of practical knowledge, and the classroom as a space for the 'theoretical study of environmental history, ecology and the social studies of human-nature relationships' (Victorian Curriculum and Assessment Authority, 2005, p. 7). Our objective is to argue for the value of a pedagogical approach that situates study of these theoretical issues while journeying in the outdoors.

THE NATI FRINJ

Natimuk is a small rural town in northwestern Victoria, Australia; it also happens to be the closest community to Mt Arapiles, a world-renowned climbing site. Since 2001 the town has been irregularly hosting the Nati Frinj. It began as a fringe event to nearby Horsham's art festival with 'a curry and chilli contest, chalk drawing, a sculpture exhibition, and a musicians' jam'.[1] The second Nati Frinj was presented in 2002 by the Arapiles Community Theatre, in association with Y Space and the Melbourne-based Next Wave Festival. The festival drew 2000 people for the Colony performance on the silo: 'a combination of aerial dance and projection … with the theme of a vigil for tolerance'.[2]

In 2003 the Nati Frinj included a Space and Place show, Gillian Pearce's performance project. The project used a collection of poetic images to tell 'stories and experiences of drought, floods, dust storms, mouse plagues, fires, and huge thunder and lightning storms…a performance that explores the relationship to land and space, and what gives us our sense of place' (Pilkington, 2004). According to Pilkington (2004), who wrote a review of the Nati Frinj for ArtsHub, the event brought together a number of local artists including musicians, a dance company, puppeteers, and, an animator. Participants in Frinj performances also included

K. Quinlivan, R. Boyask and B. Kaur (eds.), Educational Enactments in a Globalised World: Intercultural Conversations, 103–113.
© 2009 Sense Publishers. All rights reserved.

members of the local Indigenous community, the country fire brigade, school children and senior residents of the town.

The festival also includes a street parade – the Hay and Thespian Mardi Gras. Festival director Shiree Pilkinton uses the parade to:

> get everybody involved ... to combine the art and agricultural community... That event ... [which] brought 1500 to Natimuk's main street in 2005 featured kids on tractors alongside artists in bathtubs, and was key in engaging the broader community, she says, bridging gaps between farmers and artists (Marino, 2005).

The festival has also included an Art Trail, a film festival (the Golden Silos), a market and a café and cabaret venue.[3]

OUTDOOR EDUCATION IN AUSTRALIA: A CONTEMPORARY SNAPSHOT

While we acknowledge the diverse purposes and practices of outdoor education in Australia (McRae, 1990), in this chapter the term 'outdoor education' is used to describe theory and practice congruent with the recent environmental aims of a Victorian school curriculum area. Outdoor education in Victoria is a discrete subject with course advice available for P-10 (formerly through the Curriculum Standards Framework) and upper secondary (years 11 and 12) through the Victorian Certificate of Education (VCE). Recently the merger of environmental studies with outdoor education at the VCE level created the new subject, outdoor and environmental studies (Board of Studies, 2000) and, as the most recent study design explains, it is 'a study of the ways humans interact with and relate to natural environments' (Victorian Curriculum and Assessment Authority, 2005, p. 7). Similarly there was a strong environmental focus in the curriculum document (CSF) for P-10 outdoor education which described the goal of outdoor education as 'the creation and maintenance of healthy, positive, sustainable relationships between people and the natural environment' (Directorate of School Education, 2005, G1). We accept that personal and social development aims are still a common focus in secondary school outdoor education in Victoria (Lugg & Martin, 2001); however, for the purposes of this chapter, we are more interested in, and support, outdoor education that puts self in relation with others and cultural/natural places.

Concomitant with, and perhaps because of, this new direction in outdoor education there has been some recent questioning (in the outdoor education literature) of traditional/habitual practices and dominant discourses in outdoor education. In particular, there has been a suggestion that the activity basis of outdoor education is underscrutinised (Brookes, 2002; Lugg, 2004; Payne, 2002; Zink, 2005). Payne (2002) argues that the traditional core activities, such as rock climbing, kayaking and cross-country skiing, have not received the critical examination vis-à-vis their appropriateness to meeting the recent social and environmental aims. Lugg (2004), draws on Payne and others' critiques (for example, Brookes, 2002; Nicol, 2002; Wurdinger, 1997) to interrogate the common practice of using adventure activities such as those listed above and questions their relevance to the Australian landscape and current educational imperatives. She points out that 'Australian outdoor education programs ... may be based on assumptions and activities that were developed in other times and places ..." (p. 6). This is apparent, she argues, in the focus in Australia on 'imported' activities (from Europe and North America) that may not have relevance to a mainly hot, dry, flat continent with modest amounts of snow, a limited number of fast-flowing rivers and relatively low mountains. She also points to the cultural and historical shaping of outdoor education practice through influences such as the British adventure education model with roots in military training, 'character' building and the development of leadership and self-reliance (Lugg, 2004, p. 6). The 'traditional' outdoor adventure model, she contends, is also perpetuated by the tendency in Australia to link outdoor education to physical education and competency-based training.

These borrowed traditions and historical alliances that continue to be largely (and uncritically) accepted in Australian (Victorian) outdoor education have resulted, some have argued, in a mismatch between theory and practice. Payne (2002, p. 6), for example, suggests that, in relation to its critical and environmental aims, outdoor education theory 'appears to be moving faster than (actual) "practice"'. In the same vein, Preston (2004) notes the dissonance between current rhetoric on improving human–nature relationships and outdoor education practice, and is critical of a propensity in outdoor education practice to treat the place/ 'natural' environment as a backdrop to the activity. Brookes (2002), in a critical reading of outdoor education discourse in Victoria, further contends that there is a neo-colonialist tendency to treat particular places visited in outdoor education as empty sites. He argues that outdoor education curriculum discourse has been dominated by 'universalist and decontextualized understandings of outdoor education' (p. 405) and calls for 'a sustained academic inquiry centred on curriculum, place and experience' (p. 413).

This chapter continues the task of imagining an alternative theorisation of this relationship of curriculum, place and experience, influenced by others who have called attention to the unproblematic use of the term 'experience' in the outdoor literature (see, for example, Bell, 1993; Hovelynck, 2001; Payne, 2002; Zink, 2005). Yet, as Zink (2005) notes, tacit agreements in outdoor education on 'what counts as experience and how it comes to count as experience' are rarely contested and 'experience appears as if it were something abstract' (p. 16). Using the work of Foucault, Zink highlights some of the complexities and contradictions inherent in experience and critiques the notion that students construct their own meaning from experiences. This latter point is also taken up by Brown (2004) who is sceptical of supposed self-learning through practices of reflection or 'processing' in the facilitation of experiences.

The above provides a brief glimpse into several recent attempts to interrupt some of the stable/core/habitual understandings and practices of outdoor education. Although the authors cited present a general challenge to lessen the hold on particular activities and taken-for-granted or 'formulaic' (Payne, 2002) ways of 'doing' outdoor education, there is scant evidence of major shifts in pedagogical practice within the field. A recent literature search aiming to find examples of other ways of 'doing' and conceiving outdoor education, particularly in relation to using community arts projects, revealed a proliferation of creative pedagogical tools but little that attempts to reconceptualise what constitutes a valuable pedagogical experience in the outdoors. In the next section we briefly elaborate on a theoretical framework that aims to better understand the relationships among pedagogy, place, sensation and subjectivity.

ELLSWORTH'S ANOMALOUS PLACES OF LEARNING

At first glance, Ellsworth's text *Places of learning: Media, architecture, pedagogy* (2005) might seem an odd point of departure in a chapter that is theorising differently about outdoor education. However, we contend that Ellsworth might be a useful interlocutor for those within this field of inquiry because of her attempts to grapple with the relationship between experience and pedagogy.

For Ellsworth, understanding the relationship between experience and pedagogy does not commence with an ethnographer's impulse to better understand 'individuals' personal or subjective experience of schools or of teaching strategies' (2005, p. 2) through a process of careful observation. Rather, she thinks of pedagogy 'in relation to knowledge in the making rather than to knowledge as a thing made'. This is an important distinction, in that it is critical of pedagogy that 'orbits around curricular goals and objectives, as well as measurable, verifiable educational outcomes' (p. 5). This is not to say that there are no intersections between this understanding of experience and 'traditional' educational outcomes, but it is a refusal to think about pedagogy as something already made. This process of theorising pedagogy prompts a focus on 'the various qualities and design elements that seem to constitute the pedagogical force of each place of learning' (p. 6).

This understanding of pedagogy is underpinned by an understanding of experience that involves bodies that have affective somatic responses arising out of an assemblage of other bodies, spaces, surfaces, sounds, temperatures in which they are situated (Ellsworth, 2005, p. 4). Such a theorisation is implicit within the field of 'outdoor education' where being out of doors provides opportunities for generating different understandings of self, other and environment. But how does one discern between assemblages of experience? Are all assemblages equally valuable pedagogically? What constitutes a pedagogical experience that might 'become a catalyst for generating new thought about pedagogy and its force in the experience of the learning self' (p. 5)? What pedagogical experiences that might fit under the rubric of outdoor education incorporate pedagogical elements and qualities that provoke us to think or imagine in new ways (p. 5)?

In order to answer these questions, it is first necessary to examine more closely some of the qualities that might be found in what Ellsworth describes as 'anomalous places of learning'. These places don't endeavour to provide the ultimate 'experience' in which somebody might participate; but rather, these are places that are influential in making participants think differently about themselves and their surroundings. In terms of outdoor education, one way this might happen is by conceptualising places of learning that interweave:

... different people, practices, and disciplines ... The will to teach then becomes thinkable in terms of a distributed emergent desire to innovate, design, and stage materials of expression and conditions of learning in which something new may arise. Teaching becomes not a 'medium' for communicating the personal expression of a particular teacher's 'artful' instructional skills or educational imagination, because that would make pedagogy a code or language for a pre-existent subject, agent, or public. (Ellsworth, 2005, p. 28)

In imagining anomalous spaces of learning, Ellsworth focuses on events that bring together diverse people and practices, disciplines and places. This theory of pedagogy decentres the significance of the teacher in the production of pedagogical events. It does not hold that the teacher is redundant, but it recognises the limitations of any one individual in constructing pedagogical events that can provoke different ways of becoming. There is recognition of the possibilities that emerge in pedagogical spaces that involve varied mediums and ways of communicating. For Ellsworth the challenge is not to produce 'better' teachers, but to develop teachers with an eye for creating and participating in places of learning that 'depart from the dominant perception of learning as the acquisition of knowledge' (2005, p. 28).

In contemplating anomalous spaces of learning Ellsworth is also interested in places that challenge binary modes of thinking: inside/outside, self/other, subject/object (2005, p. 33). She is interested in pedagogical events situated in transitional spaces; spaces that rupture our understandings of inside/outside, self/other, subject/object. Developing a transitional space, entering a transitional space or recognising yourself as a part of a transitional space may result in 'strange constructs' brought about by the sensations evoked through participating in such a space. Such a process involves thinking of pedagogy 'as an address to a self who is in the process of withdrawing from that self, someone who is in a dissolve out of what she or he is just ceasing to be and into what she or he will already have become by the time she or he registers something has happened' (p. 34). In such a configuration a specific pedagogical outcome is not the object of participation; rather participation in something anomalous is key, and the outcome of that participation remains unknown, unpredictable and unforeseeable.

The objective is to create and/or participate in an event that prompts 'new ways of knowing that also transform knowledge, self-experience, awareness, understanding, appreciation, memory, social relations and the future' (Ellsworth, 2005, p. 37). However, in *Places of learning* the location of such events is decidedly urban. Museums, art galleries, housing estates, sports stadiums, public buildings, monuments and memorials are prominent in Ellsworth's imagining of anomalous spaces of learning. In this chapter we ask how might the events created outdoors and indoors in urban spaces extend our understanding of what constitutes the 'place' of outdoor education? How might one imagine different ways of journeying through and relating to the outdoors? We explore these questions in order to provoke some different ways of perceiving the future of outdoor education.

We also consider how traditional sites of outdoor education might be reconceived as anomalous spaces of learning. What types of interdisciplinary learning might transform knowledge, understanding and appreciation of such sites? What types of events might prompt new ways of knowing about objects and places that are not part of the built environment? How might such events play a part in determining what is intrinsic to outdoor education?

ANOMALOUS PLACES OF LEARNING IN THE OUTDOORS

Our theorisation of places of learning is, we argue, especially apposite in the field of outdoor education because this is an area of knowledge that values experience and the process of thinking about alternative spaces of learning away from traditional classroom environments. But we wonder how this field of outdoor education might become more experimental, blurring the boundaries between what constitutes indoors/outdoors and inside/outside in a material and affective sense. How is it possible to enable people to think differently about themselves and their surroundings by creating experiences of learning that place inner thoughts, feelings and desires in relation to buildings, rock formations, history, culture, landscape and weather?

In the context of this chapter, Ellsworth's theorisation of anomalous places of learning prompts us to inquire into what sort of events might encourage new ways of knowing about places we often visit in the name of outdoor education. How might interdisciplinary spaces of learning be better utilised not just to evaluate an experience in the 'outdoors', but to create different forms of relation with familiar places; relations that can be informed by the input of diverse people, practices and memories? In contemplating the Nati Frinj as one such anomalous place of learning we are not offering a blueprint. Such a task would clearly be against the spirit of what we are proposing. Rather, we are striving to gesture towards linkages and alignments that can be 'carried over into other sites, opportunities and problems. Carried over, that is, with the clear imperative 'not to imitate but to return a difference' (Ellsworth, 2005, p. 115).

As indicated above, the location of this pedagogical experience was the town of Natimuk, Victoria, population 500. The centrepiece of the Frinj is the sound and light shows performed on wheat silos which are the most prominent physical feature of the town. We are interested in the processes used to create the projections, and in tertiary outdoor education students' experience of viewing the 2004 performance of Space and Place. First we will consider how the event was staged and then turn to students' perceptions of the event.

In contemplating the role of media in pedagogy Ellsworth argues:

> The power of the media thus lies not only in their encodings of meaning and representations of reality, but also in their abilities to 'move events' and create 'event potentials' in new spaces and unanticipated contexts ... media give body to relationality as they keep potentiality and difference in circulation and motion. They put diverse and occasionally warring ideas, identities, sensibilities, traditions – and people – into relation with each other, actually or imaginatively. Media thus are imbued with the potential for catalysing new

forms of corporeality, new embodiments, new ways of knowing and being human. (2005, p. 126)

Analysing the Space and Place performance in terms of meaning and representation, it is possible to see that the themes involved in the performance were selected to draw specifically on the landscape and weather of the Wimmera region, and to consider people's stories regarding these everyday occurrences. Such a theme lends itself to a diverse audience; the vagaries of flood, fire and drought affect all who live in the community. The theme also supports the participation of performers of all ages and backgrounds (school children, senior citizens, local Aboriginal people, members of the Country Fire Authority, rock climbers and artists).

Together, these people participated in making fleeting histories of the town. Histories in the form of such events are transitory; such projections disappear without leaving a trace. They cannot be written down and in this respect they refuse easy answers. The style of performance also refuses narrative authority; aerial gymnastics, shadow puppetry, a giant animated tractor and Indigenous dance combine to dazzle and disrupt any predictable story of this space and place. Although we are engaged by Ellsworth's refusal to rely on authorised educational enactments, we also foresee potential limitations in her constant invocation of the 'new'. As Alison Jones recently argued in her discussion of 'getting lost' in educational research (2008), Indigenous students and scholars have underscored the significance of memory and dis/continuity in working against the colonisation/ commodification of their stories of place. Jones goes on to note that for Indigenous students 'the pose of certainty and the language of certainty become an emotional and strategic necessity' (Jones, 2008, n.p.). For us, events such as Natimuk might tell a story and 'put difference in motion', but those producing such events might also be mindful of the strategic and emotional value of retelling stories and staging certainties.

Another element of the Space and Place performance that particularly engaged us was its powerful affective dimension. Staged against the backdrop of 30-metre-high wheat silos, the crowd gathers in a paddock at dusk. The silos, a traditional meeting point within rural communities, take on a new dimension as they form the stage for an intricate aerial dance performed utilising sophisticated rock-climbing skills on a contoured concrete surface. The paddock is framed by long queues of people lining up to buy food, a tent housing a band, and a black sky ceiling. Participants sit on the earth, looking up at the stars, feeling the cold night air, the dew on the ground, and sounds of the night interweaving with staged sights and sounds.

Bringing together such a band of performers also has the effect of drawing together a large and varied crowd, potentially 'catalysing new forms of corporeality' (Ellsworth, 2005, p. 126) for participants and audience alike. At the very least, the story told through Space and Place offered those present an opportunity to listen to and experience different renditions of life in the Wimmera region. The structure of the event encourages new ways of knowing oneself, one's place and one's neighbours. Altogether, the pedagogy of the event keeps the space open for each participant's own feelings and interpretations – not presuming to know the audience, nor one story the audience should hear, nor how the stories should be received or experienced.

Lou Preston attended the event with a group of tertiary outdoor education students in 2004 as part of a rock-climbing field trip to Mt Arapiles. The climbing trip was not organised around the festival; the timing coincided by chance. Students were given the option of participating in the Space and Place event and the whole group chose to attend the performance. Some of these students were later interviewed by Preston as part of a broader study, a longitudinal investigation of the formation of environmental ethics among tertiary students undertaking the course in outdoor education (Preston, 2008). A key aspect of this study considered the implications for the teaching of outdoor education, especially in relation to the importance of 'place' and the spatial dimensions of pedagogy.

In deciding to take the students to such an event Preston might be construed as bucking a tendency within this discipline. Rather than taking students into the 'wilderness' and away from groups of people and the built environment, this activity sought to integrate both the townsfolk and the built environment with the field experience of outdoor education. Below, we consider the students' thoughts (pseudonyms used) on incorporating such events within outdoor education curricula.[4]

As a group the students were unanimous on two counts: the activity was a positive addition to the outdoor education curriculum, and it was personally enjoyable. 'Awesome', 'amazing', 'clever' were words used to describe the event (Preston, 2008). One student commented further that the event encouraged:

> ... connecting with a place and understanding its historical background and you can't always get that from practical experiences ... I don't think that outdoor ed should be something that you can just go out and walk and canoe or whatever – you've sort of got to respect and understand why you are in that place and where that place has come from and – I guess I see it as not a completely practical thing. (Michelle, interview, Preston, 2008).

Another student, Kelly, noted that through participation in the event 'you kind of felt a little bit more part of that area' (interview, Preston, 2008). Sue perceived it as a way of forming a stronger connection with the town of Natimuk: 'I drive past those silos from now on going "Oh that's where we went and saw the –"' (interview, Preston, 2008).

In the above quotations, we concede the responses might have been tailored in part to what the participants anticipated would please the interviewer, Preston, who was also their trip leader and teacher at the time. But we also perceive an openness to a form of outdoor education that focuses less on 'skills and stuff and we kind of take a step back and look at the bigger picture' (Kelly, interview, Preston, 2008). The 'bigger picture' may consist of being in the space and place in which those skills are developed. In this sense, attending the event meant that, at least for some students, it provided a space where things were undone – in this instance there was an undoing of preconceptions that Arapiles is just a place you go to climb.

Participation in the event also prompted students to consider themselves as more than 'a group that comes in and uses the facilities and leaves – by going to that and supporting it you've now given back to that community' (Kristy, interview, Preston, 2008). It also enabled 'learning a little bit about that [place] and seeing them go to an event, seeing an event that happens in their area and participate – by seeing it we were participating in it' (Kristy, interview, Preston, 2008). At the same time as these quotations confirm the insider/outsider relation between those who 'use the facilities' and those who live in the community, they also suggest a blurring of such relations. Attendance at the event gives students an opportunity to play a part in community building, and it also offered them 'something different and it was great to see things from someone else's perspective ...' (Michelle, interview, Preston, 2008). In terms of tertiary curriculum, the Space and Place performance allowed students to access different understandings of a place with which they were familiar but had never really got to know.

In terms of outdoor education, attendance at the event might also inspire different understandings of what constitutes the content and purpose of this discipline area. By putting self into relation with 'cultural' and 'natural' landscape in such a setting, the limits and possibilities of both realms flow into one another. Similarly, using the skills of climbing in performance, as well as using climbers as performers, this performance constructs anomalous notions of what climbing is for, where one should climb and how others might be incorporated in the event of climbing. Such an event may inspire these future teachers to play a part in staging such under the rubric of this discipline area or as an interdisciplinary project, further complicating their own students' understanding of relationships between self/other, place/community and nature/culture.

The success of this experience in terms of the possibilities listed above is difficult to measure. In keeping with Ellsworth, there were no predetermined curricular outcomes that Preston sought to achieve by taking students to this event. Hence, she did not facilitate the customary debrief at the end of the experience to 'uncover' learning. Apart from the students' supportive comments discussed above, there is no evidence to suggest that these people, now teachers, have sought to incorporate similar experiences into their outdoor education programmes. It is unlikely that all participants would see the possibilities we could see and it is probable that for some the Space and Place event would appear as a distraction from the 'real' business of rock climbing. Another limitation is the uniqueness of the experience. It was a one-off event – the limitations of university schedules have not permitted repeated attendance – and we acknowledge the need for further experimentation with anomalous places of learning that incorporate different disciplines and media to encourage different ways of thinking about interactions among people, place and space.

CONCLUSION

Through this journey with Ellsworth to anomalous places of learning, we have gone to the frinj of outdoor education and challenged traditional conceptions of what counts as outdoor activity. Through this activity we sought to integrate community- the people and the built environment, with the field of outdoor education. Thus covering different terrain, perhaps less familiar to those accustomed to traditional activity-based practices of outdoor education. We went without any specific curriculum objective in mind or knowing the outcome of the participation.

As suggested above, the leader was not the 'facilitator' of the experience – there was no attempt to excavate predetermined student learning/outcomes. Students were able to experience/critique the event without any expectations of what they should derive from such an experience, which is not to say that it was not pedagogical or that certain curriculum objectives were not met.

We have attempted to show the productive possibilities of an outdoor education that transcends some of the boundaries of the discipline. By taking students to a community event employing an interdisciplinary pedagogical approach using visual art, abseiling, storytelling and music, we hope students might be prompted to imagine different forms of outdoor education. We imagine that this event might inform their own educational enactments, bringing outdoor education into urban and/or rural places, as well as bringing together people who might not usually perceive themselves as participants in the 'outdoors'.

Rather than advocating that this type of event replace traditional practice, we propose that it may be used to complement or extend what gets 'done' in the name of outdoor education. In this sense our understanding of pedagogy is reminiscent of that articulated by the editors of this collection. In short, we envisage an outdoor education that works against instrumentalism and perceives education as ethical subjective experience.

NOTES

[1] See http://www.natimuk.com retrieved 10/06/06.
[2] See http://www.regionalarts.com.au/raa1/files/HeartWork/HEARTWOR-Sec1.pdf retrieved 11/06/06.
[3] For further details see the Nati Frinj website http://www.natimuk.com/html/fringe2000.html retrieved 10/06/06.
[4] The following citations are taken from interviews conducted for Preston's (2008) doctoral dissertation, *Becoming green: The formation of environmental ethics in outdoor education.*

REFERENCES

Bell, M. (1993). What constitutes experience? Rethinking theoretical assumptions. *Journal of Experiential Education, 16*(1), 19–24.

Board of Studies. (2000). *Outdoor and environmental studies: VCE study design.* Melbourne, Victoria: Board of Studies.

Brookes, A. (2002). Lost in the Australian bush: Outdoor education as curriculum. *Journal of Curriculum Studies, 34*(4), 405–425.

Brown, M. (2004). 'Let's go round the circle.' How verbal facilitation can function as a means of direct instruction. *Journal of Experiential Education, 27*(2), 161–175.

Directorate of School Education. (2005). *Curriculum standards framework: Outdoor education course advice.* Melbourne, Victoria: Directorate of School Education.

Ellsworth, E. (2005). *Places of learning: Media, architecture, pedagogy.* New York: Routledge.

Hovelynck, J. (2001). Beyond didactics: A reconnaissance of experiential learning. *Australian Journal of Outdoor Education, 6*(1), 4–14.

Jones, A. (2008, April). *The dangerous desire for 'getting lost' in educational research.* Paper presented at Annual Conference of the American Educational Research Association, New York.

Lugg, A. (2004). Outdoor adventure in Australian outdoor education: Is it a case of roast for Christmas dinner? *Australian Journal of Outdoor Education, 8*(1), 4–11.

Lugg, A., & Martin, P. (2001). The nature and scope of outdoor education in Victorian schools. *Australian Journal of Outdoor Education, 5*(2), 42–48.

Marino, M. (2005). A matter of scale. Retrieved June 10, 2007, from http://www.theage.com.au/news/Arts/A-matter-of-scale/2005/01/10/1105206048297.html#

McRae, K. (Ed.). (1990). *Outdoor and environmental education: Diverse purposes and practices.* South Melbourne, Victoria: MacMillan.

Nicol, R. (2002). Outdoor education: Research topic or universal value? Part Two. *Journal of Adventure Education and Outdoor Learning, 2*(2), 85–99.

Payne, P. (2002). On the construction, deconstruction and reconstruction of experience in 'critical' outdoor education. *Australian Journal of Outdoor Education, 6*(2), 4–21.

Pilkington, S. (2004). Meeting place—A new installment, Retrieved June 10, 2007, from http://www.artshub.com.au/au/news.asp?sType=feature&catId=1069&sc=&sId=62638

Preston, L. (2004). Making connections with nature: Bridging the theory–practice gap in outdoor education. *Australian Journal of Outdoor Education, 8*(1), 12–19.

Preston, M. (2008). *Becoming green: The formation of environmental ethics in outdoor education.* Unpublished doctoral dissertation. University of Melbourne, Melbourne.

Victorian Curriculum and Assessment Authority. (2005). *Outdoor and environmental studies: Victorian certificate of education study design.* East Melbourne, Victoria: Victorian Curriculum and Assessment Authority.

Wurdinger, S. (1997). *Philosophical issues in adventure education.* Dubuque, Iowa: Kendall/Hunt.

Zink, R. (2005). Maybe what they say is what they experience: Taking students words seriously. *Australian Journal of Outdoor Education, 9*(2), 14–20.

Mary Lou Rasmussen
Faculty of Education
Monash University

Lou Preston
School of Human Movement and School Sciences
University of Ballarat

RUTH BOYASK, REBECCA CARTER, HAZEL LAWSON
AND SUE WAITE

8. CHANGING CONCEPTS OF DIVERSITY

Relationships between Policy and Identity in English Schools

INTRODUCTION

In the 21st century world, discourses of globalisation that imply universality pervade our consciousness and social structures, yet one of the paradoxical outcomes of globalisation is a greater awareness of and attention to diversity. In this chapter we investigate policies that intend to address social equity for school-aged learners in England through acknowledgement of their diversity. We explore the dynamics that underpin these policies and their substantive claims so that we may better understand their interactions and intersections with learners' identities, the ways learners construct themselves and how they are constructed by others.

Many democratic nations have made significant efforts to enact social inclusion through recent public legislation (such as the No Child Left Behind Act 2001 in the USA and the Children Act 2004 in England and Wales). However, these policies have been subject to critical scrutiny and comment on the extent to which they genuinely represent the complex identities of learners in the 21st century (Roche & Tucker, 2007; Ryan, 2004). In addition to the contested status of the policies, further complications arise because they are enacted unevenly and their general nature comes into conflict with the prevailing cultures of specific educational settings (Boyask, Quinlivan & Goulter, 2007; Kaur, Boyask, Quinlivan & McPhail, 2008; Stein, 2004).

Although there is a clear recognition of diversity in recent discussions on furthering social cohesion, there is also evidence to suggest that our current attention to diversity is heightened by social conflict, as different interests compete for public goods such as education (see Ainscow, Conteh, Dyson & Gallanaugh, 2007). Rationales of social justice and participation have underpinned the allocation of public funds to education in England, beginning with the United Kingdom government's involvement in schooling in the 19th century (Brancaccio, 2000). However, debate and discussion on what constitutes fair provision of education are construed differently in different times and by different stakeholders. Currently the debate seems to be centred largely on the complex make-up of learners' identities and how their specific differences can be accommodated through general social provision. Our analysis of the recent history of policy initiatives in English education reveals a general movement towards recognition of increasingly specific and diverse

K. Quinlivan, R. Boyask and B. Kaur (eds.), Educational Enactments in a Globalised World:
Intercultural Conversations, 115–127.

identities. For example, in recent years acknowledgement of racial and ethnic diversity has expanded to include awareness of cultural differences at a regional level. It is also increasingly recognised that different forms of diversity intersect and impact upon learning outcomes, for example the combination of ethnicity and gender in the achievement of boys (see Department for Education and Skills [DfES], 2007b). At the same time, however, greater specificity and complexity have raised problems for effective social provision. How can society fairly distribute public goods in recognition of complex and unique identities? Recent policy initiatives that are concerned with learner diversity, such as personalised learning, Every Child Matters and the Citizenship Curriculum (Department for Education and Employment and Qualifications and Curriculum Authority, 1999; DfES, 2004, 2006) are some of the government's responses to this problem. Emerging research and evaluative literature associated with their implementation indicate discrepancies between conceptualisations of diversity in policy and the practices of schooling (Campbell, Robinson, Neelands, Hewston & Mazzoli, 2007; Maylor & Read with Mendick, Ross & Rollock, 2007). Such discrepancies suggest to us that their implementation may result in further complications rather than assisting provision for diverse learners through schooling.

This chapter is situated within the authors' larger project concerned with conceptualisations of diversity and the effects they have on the social outcomes of young people. In the wider study we are interested in three contexts: 1) teaching and learning relationships and other micro-level contexts; 2) institutional or meso contexts, such as relationships within school and local community; and 3) national policy, media and other macro-level influences. We examine conceptualisations of diversity within these contexts, and consider how they interact and intersect with the subjectivities of learners (see Waite, Boyask, Lawson & Carter, 2008). Although each context contributes to the establishment of learning, many contemporary understandings about learning, especially those derived from Vygotsky and Leontev's sociocultural theories of learning (see Lave & Wenger, 2001; Rogoff, 1990; Wertsch, 1991), regard interaction with others as most influential upon learning. We concur that the examination of primary and micro-level relationships, such as those between learner and teacher, is essential when developing theories of and interventions in learning (Luke & Hogan, 2006; Nuthall & Alton-Lee, 1998). However, we are also mindful that learner subjectivities are constructed in relation to social institutions, such as schools, and to their interactions with wider social impulses. Therefore it is important to examine how conceptualisations of diversity at these levels interact with learning within micro-level settings in order to influence learning promoted through the enactment of policy. We acknowledge that transporting conceptualisations between contexts is difficult, for example from policy through guidance to school teachers, given that conceptualisations are mediated by their social location (see Day, Kington, Stobart & Sammons, 2006). We also know that tacitly held beliefs about diversity can affect the quality of educational experiences of young people in schools.[1]

In this chapter we are largely concerned with the macro context of national policy and its proposed transference into the other two contexts through government guidance for schools. We examine tensions in macro-level policy arising through general provision and specific attention to diversity. We explore how policy is portrayed in government guidance as translation for implementation and how this is then received and enacted in practice within the local context. We argue that macro-level policy, made with the intention of impacting on an individual level, takes insufficient account of the process of translation into practice, assuming a straightforward transfer. In so doing we suggest that macro-level policies take insufficient account of the meso and micro contexts and ignore the complex, multi-faceted nature of individual learner subjectivities, the lived experience of diversity, and are therefore, too blunt an instrument to effect change in schools as intended. We consider whether policies could be designed so that they more readily inter-connect with the pre-existing conditions and cultures of schools, taking better account of the identities of teachers and learners; such that the enactment of policy is viewed as a more multi-directional and interactive process.

EXPLORING MACRO-LEVEL CONCEPTUALISATIONS OF DIVERSITY

In 1948 the General Assembly of the United Nations declared that all people were equal, behoving member states to disseminate this core value throughout public life and, in particular, schooling. Since that time, the recognition of rights has become an assumption that underpins the policies and practices of schooling within England. Recognition of equality of all people has extended to include a commitment to educational equality, enacted through a mass education system that, in some senses, is intended to provide for equal access to the opportunities that education is presumed to afford. The Universal Declaration of Human Rights (1948) pro-claimed equality for all and this value has become embedded within educational systems and institutions; yet through its enactment the underlying principle of 'sameness' has fragmented. This fragmentation is evident in debates about the nature of equality and how it is conceptualised, which according to Rassool and Morley (2000) were '... prevalent during the period of welfare interventionism during the 1960s and 1970s' (p. 238). Influential studies in the sociology of education pointed out that distributing education in the interests of social justice and equality also contributed to differentiation of social groups because of dif-ferences in opportunity, access and outcomes, reinforcing the cultural dominance of some groups and the curtailment of equity (Rassool & Morley, 2000). The recognition that universal and universalising principles of equality and their enactment can result in social injustices suggests that an alternative formulation is required. Daniels, Hey, Leonard and Smith (1999), citing Solstad, suggest that there are two referents for social equity: one is equality, which tends towards gene-ralisation; and the other is diversity. When principles of equity are referenced to diversity, they are realised through actions that take account of the particularity of contexts and subjectivities.

In England's current educational context, social justice is frequently seen in tandem with notions of difference and diversity, emphasising that solutions to problems of equity must be specific and tailored to individuals. Conceptualisations that emphasise diversity and individualisation represent a change in substantive understandings about achieving equity. Although the prevalence of such conceptualisations is growing in response to the challenges of achieving equity through equality, reference to diversity raises challenges of its own as decisions about provision from the limited resources of the public purse become much harder when recognised differences are proliferating to the extent of unique and individual differences. Furthermore, the language of universalism apparent in the United Nations document has not disappeared; the principle of equality and its application through generalisation are still at work in macro-level policy. We considered whether the use of dual referents (equality and diversity) within policies that intend to address equity mitigate the problems entailed in the other. In some cases it appears that the dynamic between making generalisations and attending to specificity furthers the pursuit of equity; in others it does not.

Dynamics of Generalisation and Specificity in Macro-level Policy

Since the United Nations' declaration we have witnessed greater *specificity* within the human rights discourse, with groups of people claiming recognition of their particular identities within its remit. The cohesive discourse of equal human rights threw up questions about whether a comprehensive approach to equality was sufficient to address inequalities, because equality did not necessarily equate with equity. In response to the civil rights and identity politics movements of the 1950s and 60s, social provision expanded to take account of different kinds of identities that were subject to inequality. Discriminatory practices were addressed through ground-breaking pieces of legislation such as the Sex Discrimination Act 1975 and the Race Relations Act 1976; these put a legal duty on public bodies and employers to attend to more particular kinds of inequalities. The gender and race equity movements opened spaces for the recognition of more specific differences. For example, the disability rights movement pioneered a campaign of 'nothing about us, without us', which sought to raise consciousness of the inequalities that disabled people were subject to (Campbell, 2008).

As this dynamic was transferred to the education arena, educational policy seemed to struggle between making general all-encompassing policy statements on the one hand, and attending to increased specificity in conceptualisations on the other. For example, in the area of special educational needs, the Warnock Report (Department for Education and Science, 1978) and its subsequent enshrinement in the Education Act 1981 introduced the concept and terminology of special educational needs, suggesting that a fifth of the school population could be expected to have special educational needs and that any child might experience special educational needs at some point in their school life. This conceptualisation was much broader than previous medical and deficit-orientated categories. Yet this same report and Act introduced new forms of categorisation based on 'learning difficulties'. Identification with one of these categories appeared to presume that difference equated with deficiency and required a compensatory approach to education, suggesting that these be renamed and normative generalisations about ability be made rather than productive and empowering responses to the diversity amongst children and young people.

More recently policy has recognised that the social context of children and young people can determine how they differ from one another. This change is evident in the social model of disability (Campbell & Oliver, 1996), which advocated the removal of practical and attitudinal barriers that prevented disabled people from participating in life's opportunities on an equitable basis with all others. Its application has extended across all social groups disadvantaged by gender, ethnicity, sexual orientation or other factors. For example, recognition of the context of school children emerged within the Education Reform Act 1988 and its associated enactment through the national curriculum. The national curriculum was intended to 'promote the spiritual, moral, cultural, mental and physical development of pupils at the school and of society' (Office of Public Sector Information [OPSI], 1988), and would apply to all including, with modifications, those with special educational needs. This Act put a duty on schools that all children would gather in a daily act of collective worship, in the Christian tradition. While no reference to religions other than Christianity was made, some recognition of the country's increasingly diverse make-up came with a duty on schools to give consideration to 'any circumstances relating to the family backgrounds of the pupils concerned which are relevant for determining the character of the collective worship which is appropriate in their case' (OPSI, 1988, 84(6)a).

Peters and Marshall (1996) suggest that within this era of change we are witnessing a shift in the conceptualisation of society, towards a prevalence of individualism and self-interest that competes with communitarian values such as social equity and justice. Within this context tensions emerge between individual and social good. In the latter part of the 20th century, scepticism of 'grand narratives'[2] and universal discourses began to unravel some of the social contracts formulated on the basis of equality and human rights throughout the earlier parts of the 20th century. In England this was evident through a neo-liberal agenda and resultant social fragmentation that started with Thatcherism. For example, Margaret Thatcher's Conservative government reintroduced and extended policies of selection for entry to secondary school. The Education Act 1979 repealed Labour's comprehensive school policies and the Education Act 1980 put selection on the basis of ability (through the 11 plus examination) into legislation (Chitty & Dunford, 1999). However, we contend that England is now immersed in a new kind of universalism that has occurred as the number, particularity and substance of differences that count have increased and become more complex.

Statistical evidence shows a diversifying school population; for example, by 2010 minority ethnic children will make up an estimated 20% of the United Kingdom's school population (DfES, 2007a, p. 17). These demographic changes in identities within the school population echo wider social trends linked to rapid global change in the late modern and postmodern eras and the 'disembedding of hitherto settled identities, at a personal and social level' (Rattansi & Phoenix, 2005, p. 99). In response to these changes, issues of difference and identity are now at the centre of debates on the effective provision of educational opportunities for young people and ways to improve their educational outcomes. Recent policies recognise not only that differences in the identities of children and young people should be accommodated within education policy, but that educational provision should be integrally connected with provision for other aspects of their lives. For example, by 2003 the government was pulling together plans for what it claimed was the most wide-reaching reform of children's services in modern times – the Every Child Matters agenda. This reform culminated in the Children Act 2004 which legislated for service configurations and systems that local authorities would have to put into place in order to meet the five Every Child Matters outcomes for *all* children in England (OPSI, 2004). The legislation represents a fundamental shift from the focus on difference and narrow categorisations to one of identifying and addressing children's needs in a holistic manner. A similar advocacy for a holistic and inclusive model to address the rights of diverse individuals is apparent amongst other key players in the equalities agenda for children and young people. The Equalities Act 2006 legislated for the dissolution of the Equal Opportunities Commission, the Commission for Racial Equality and the Disability Rights Commission, and the creation of the Equalities and Human Rights Commission (see Mcghee, 2006).

Within these holistic frameworks diversity is universalised, which we contend may hide the challenges of equitable social provision. If all kinds of difference count, then decisions about acting on the policy remit become more rather than less complicated. As a result the rights of particular marginalised groups can become lost in the complexity. So, for example, if national frameworks such as Every Child Matters are inclusive and relevant to all children, then why is there an emergence of campaigns such as Every Disabled Child Matters (National Children's Bureau, 2006), which highlight that diverse needs are not being adequately catered for by seemingly cohesive frameworks?

EFFECTS OF POLICY AND GUIDANCE ON PRACTICE

Recent policies, then, reveal an apparently deliberate homogenisation of difference. School-related policy initiatives such as Every Child Matters and personalised learning (DfES, 2006) are deliberate in defining *all* children as *different* from one another, as they respond to the increasingly specific and changing identities that evidently affect learning outcomes. Schools and teachers within the state sector have professional responsibilities to uphold national policy, and there are mechanisms for transporting policy into schools, for example, through guidance and continuing professional development. But the guidance issued to support such policies shifts the conceptualisations significantly from the holistic ones enshrined in policy, and tends to draw upon hitherto determined categories of difference. For example, the duty for schools to value diversity and promote 'community cohesion' (Department for Children, Schools and Families [DCSF], 2007) appears to contradict a model of difference apparent in the guidance that makes common use of terms such as 'social inequalities', 'marginalisation', 'vulnerability' and 'social exclusion' (see DCSF, 2007; Office of National Statistics, 2008), widely interpreted and enacted within schools as a discourse of deficiency. Similarly policy around inclusion and inclusive education has an holistic emphasis yet an increasing number of 'types' of learners are specifically identified – for example, children defined as 'gifted' and/ or 'talented' (DCSF, 2008a), Gypsy, Roma and Traveller learners (DCSF, 2008c) and children who are 'new arrivals' (DCSF, 2008b). The requirement for state schools to gather and analyse data using predefined categories (for example, age, gender, entitlement to free school meals, language status, ethnicity) and in relation to attainment leads teachers to attend to such conceptions of difference (Ainscow et al., 2007).

We contend that this dynamic heightens contradictions between generalisations within policies and how specific identities are provided for, and thus reinforces and normalises particular forms of difference within schooling even whilst policies claim to do otherwise. However, we also argue that even more important than showing discrepancies between conceptualisations of diversity within policy and guidance are considerations of how they interact and intersect with diversity as it is experienced within schooling.

Discerning a direct relationship between policies and the lived experience of social justice – that is, genuinely affecting classroom practice in accordance with policy guidelines – is notoriously problematic (see Kaur et al., 2008). Policies regarding schooling are enacted within contexts made complex by the multiple histories, allegiances and beliefs of the people who make them up. For example, consider the Maylor et al., (2007) review of research on diversity and citizenship in the national curriculum. Their key findings suggest that teacher knowledge and misconceptions about diversity are largely to blame for irregularities in curriculum implementation and reception. Other researchers suggest teachers' misconceptions about inclusion, for example interpreting inclusion as a form of assimilation, can be held directly responsible for children's experiences of exclusion within mainstream settings (Higgins, McArthur & Rietveld, 2006; Rietveld, 2005). Maylor et al., (2007) offer a solution to discrepancies in teacher knowledge is to transfer macro-level conceptualisations of diversity evident in the national curriculum to the meso- and micro-levels of schooling through initial teacher training and continuing professional development. The assumption is that policy guidance and its transference will effect pedagogical change within the micro-context of teaching and learning interactions (see Maylor et al., 2007, p. 7).

However, it appears to us that this problematic about discrepant teacher knowledge is largely a construction of looking at education from the top end and bringing about change through cascading and trickle down. There are problems with this approach. The tendency to holism at the macro-level is designed to acknowledge and account for a wider range of differences, yet in practice it obscures the privilege of some kinds of difference and excludes others. A discrepancy between intention and effect extends across many initiatives meant to further social justice through schooling. For example, investigations by Reay et al., (2008) into white middle class identities within comprehensive schooling found that some white middle class parents sent their children to comprehensive schools because their intentions were egalitarian, but they also found that there was '... more self-interest than altruism and a superficial endorsement of social mix rather than any actual commitment to social mixing' (p. 252).

We are aware that tensions arise simply because macro-contextual conceptualisations of diversity are necessarily general. While they create generic spaces, their distance from the material reality of children and young people's experiences in classrooms means their effects are inevitably blunt (Kaur et al., 2008). This lack of precision makes more difficult the task of institutions and individuals who are charged with acting in the interests of the public good. For example, the success of attending to personalised need through the multi-agency approaches advocated in Every Child Matters or the pedagogic practice of personalising learning is dependent upon the work of individual practitioners. These individuals are held accountable to the very general macro-level conceptualisations of diversity, whether officially defined through policy or debated and refined through the media.

Although it is intended that practitioners will 'learn how' to put these conceptualisations into practice through pre-service and in-service education, recent work on professional learning suggests that changing how practitioners operate is a much more complex endeavour than providing guidance from above through formal training opportunities (Day et al., 2006; Eraut, 2002; Hodkinson & Hodkinson, 2004). According to Eraut (2002), what teachers actually do in the classroom is more likely to reflect their implicit understandings, which are largely derived through professional practice. What Eraut has arrived at through observation of teachers' practice corresponds with theories about the complex nature of identity that underpins much recent work on diversity (see Clarke, 2006; Rattansi & Phoenix, 2005), and about how subjectivities are constructed through discourse and practice (Shotter, 1998; Wetherell, 2008; Wetherell, Lafleche & Berkeley, 2007). Implicit understandings are produced through a complex interaction between social structure and individual psychologies, suggesting that understanding and changing practice requires close investigation of the public and private world of the self (Wetherell, 2008). In light of the recognised imperfections of transferring knowledge from the top to the bottom and without significant understanding of the *processes* by which different conceptualisations of diversity become embedded within subjectivities, it is not surprising that researchers such as Maylor et al., (2007) find that teacher knowledge and practice is incongruent with policy.

Not acknowledging this imperfection of policy, and the resultant tensions between policy and practice, results in discourses that unjustly blame teachers for imperfections in the enactment of policy, and students for discrepancies in attainment. However, recognising the problem does not on its own provide a solution. As academics who are concerned with widening possibilities for school children and young people, and actively working with practitioners and policy-makers to achieve better learning outcomes, we are committed to finding better solutions. Currently we are considering the following proposition. If applying general solutions to localised problems is necessary for just social provision, but also results in conflict and disjuncture, might we mitigate problems by concurrently applying localised solutions to general problems? In the following section we explore how macro-level solutions may be strengthened by greater consideration of specific and localised responses to diversity and learning.

WHAT CAN THE GENERAL LEARN FROM THE SPECIFIC?

In a discussion about expanding the repertoire of evidence that policy-makers draw upon in the development of policy, Luke and Hogan (2006) praise responses that are localised and specific to cultural contexts. While they recognise that global economic impulses are driving education systems internationally, they advocate entering into global discourses and stretching them from within. We would go further to speculate that not only should macro-level responses or policies be altered through their interaction with local cultures (perhaps corresponding with our meso-level context); in the interests of social justice they should also take greater cognisance of the effects of educational interventions upon specific subjectivities.

Thus far, public policy responses to increased diversity have tended towards holism. However, categorisations of social identity and grouping still compete within these holistic frameworks. We argue that the resultant conflict between categorical and holistic representations of diversity can work against the intentions to recognise diversity, and end up homogenising the specific concerns of individuals. Our concern is that it is convenient in school guidance documents to categorise in order to fit with the system of accountability in education (we have ticked the boxes for dealing with the needs of child type X or Y), yet subjective identification '… does not follow any neat logic of group- and category-based identities' (Wetherell, 2008, p. 74). Doing justice to the complex phenomenon of identification:

> … demands a subtle account of the ways in which the social gets packaged in forms that people can turn into identity and make psychological. It also requires analyses of meaning-making (or discourse) in the very broadest sense, incorporating the physical, the visual and the tactile organisation of human conduct along with text and talk. (Ibid.)

Wetherell's description of the subtle and multifaceted ways that individuals construct themselves and are constructed as different from one another makes pigeonholing children and young people into discrete categories a rather clumsy response. We are aware that finding a satisfactory means to take account of specific effects within generalised policies is a difficult prospect in light of tensions between processes of normalisation and diversity. However, we remain hopeful that public policy informed by its enactment within meso- and micro-level settings may create deliberate rather than incidental dynamics between the opening and closing of possibilities for learners and learning.

Our own attempt to apply complex theories of identity to policy and social provision of education has led us back to the young people themselves. We are currently investigating the use of person-centred methodologies for eliciting rich and personally relevant information about the identities of young people (see Waite et al., 2008). Although our contention in this chapter remains within a theoretical and therefore speculative frame, our current empirical work is designed to explore the idea that young people themselves are a most valuable source of insight about their own learning identities and how policy might best provide for their differences. Recently we have embarked on a project that brings together our methodological, conceptual and substantive interests to compare 18-year-olds' subjective accounts of their experience of diversity, look for patterns in their conceptualisation of differences by qualitative and quantitative means, and provide leads for what a subjective approach to characterising young people's diversity offers general public policy.

CONCLUSIONS

Through an investigation of policies that intend to provide fairer educational participation and outcome, we have illuminated a changing dynamic in how the school population is categorised. In line with wider social impulses of individualism, globalisation and diversification, we have seen universal principles of equality applied to more specific categories of diversity. Specific identities acknowledged within education policy have proliferated, so that national policy must take into account a much wider range of differences between children and young people. While the number of acknowledged identities has increased, there is also further recognition of their complex construction within dynamic social relationships. As a result of these changing conceptualisations of diversity, there is a new, holistic response emerging at the level of state policy to an apparently diversifying demographic (Mcghee, 2006).

In this chapter we have drawn connections between recent national policy initiatives and their intended enactment through schooling (e.g. citizenship education and Every Child Matters) to show the intended directions for teacher development and practice in English schools. However, although such policy responses are underpinned by discourses of equality and human rights, and clearly intend to further social justice through school-based enactments, their realisation within schooling contexts is imperfect and there exist wide gulfs between intention and effect. Moreover, even though tensions between generalisation and diversity provide problems for social justice at the macro- and meso-levels of schooling (see Norwich, 2008), we also contend that this dynamic is at work within other contexts of schooling, such as inter-subjective relationships and production of the 'self'. In a climate of proliferating identities, closer attention to the subjectivities of learners and how they are constructed and construct themselves as different from one another may provide policy-makers with a new venue to explore in the search for more equitable social provision. Without this level of analysis, there are significant questions to be answered about the robustness of current conceptualisations of diversity in state schooling policy for genuinely addressing the lived experience of diversity.

NOTES

[1] Alison Jones's (1991) case studies of the experiences of girls in streamed classes provide an example of the negative effects on learning outcomes of tacitly held beliefs about differences between young people.

[2] See Lyotard (1979) for an explanation of the emerging scepticism of universalism and 'grand narratives' that he associates with the changing nature of knowledge within the postmodern condition.

REFERENCES

Ainscow, M., Conteh, J., Dyson, A., & Gallanaugh, F. (2007). *Children in primary education: Demography, culture, diversity and inclusion* (University Research Report No. 5/1). Cambridge, UK: University of Cambridge.

Boyask, R., Quinlivan, K., & Goulter, M. (2007). *Write-on! Investigations into the relationships between teacher learning and student achievement through writing: Final Report prepared for TLRI, Teaching and Learning Research Initiative.* Retrieved December 21, 2007, from http://www.tlri.org.nz/pdfs/9240_finalreport.pdf

Brancaccio, M. T. (2000). Educational hyperactivity: The historical emergence of a concept. *Intercultural Education, 11*(2), 165–177.

Campbell, J. (2008). *Fighting for a slice, or for a bigger cake?* St John's College, Cambridge, UK: Equality and Human Rights Commission.

Campbell, J., & Oliver, M. (1996). *Disability politics: Understanding our past, changing our future.* London: Routledge.

Campbell, R. J., Robinson, W., Neelands, J., Hewston, R., & Mazzoli, L. (2007). Personalised learning: Ambiguities in theory and practice. *British Journal of Educational Studies, 55*(2), 135–154.

Chitty, C., & Dunford, J. (Eds.). (1999). *State schools: New Labour and the Conservative legacy.* London: Woburn Press.

Clarke, S. (2006). Theory and practice: Psychoanalytic sociology as psycho-social studies. *Sociology, 40*(6), 1153–1169.

Daniels, H., Hey, V., Leonard, D., & Smith, M. (1999). Issues of equity in special needs education from a gender perspective. *British Journal of Special Education, 26*(4), 189–195.

Day, C. W., Kington, A., Stobart, G., & Sammons, P. (2006). The personal and professional selves of teachers: Stable and unstable identities. *British Educational Research Journal, 32*(4), 601–616.

Department for Children, Schools and Families. (2007). *Guidance on the duty to promote community cohesion.* Nottingham, UK: DCSF Publications.

Department for Children, Schools and Families. (2008a). *Effective provision for gifted and talented children in primary education.* Nottingham, UK: DCSF Publications.

Department for Children, Schools and Families. (2008b). *New arrivals excellence programme: Management guide.* Nottingham, UK: DCSF Publications.

Department for Children, Schools and Families. (2008c). *The inclusion of gypsy, roma and traveller children and young people.* Nottingham, UK: DCSF Publications.

Department for Education and Employment, & Qualifications and Curriculum Authority. (1999). *The national curriculum handbook for secondary teachers in England.* London: Department for Education and Employment.

Department for Education and Science. (1978). *Warnock committee report.* London: HMSO.

Department for Education and Skills. (2004). *Every child matters: Change for children in school.* Nottingham, UK: DfES Publications.

Department for Education and Skills. (2006). *2020 Vision: Report of the teaching and learning in 2020 review group* [Gilbert Report]. Retrieved December 21, 2007, from http://www.teachernet.gov.uk/_doc/ 10783/6856_DfES_Teaching_and_Learning.pdf

Department for Education and Skills. (2007a). *Curriculum review: Diversity and citizenship.* Nottingham, UK: DfES Publications.

Department for Education and Skills. (2007b). *Gender and education: The evidence on pupils in England.* Nottingham, UK: DfES Publications.

Eraut, M. (2002). Menus for choosy diners. *Teachers and Teaching, 8*(3/4), 371–380.

Higgins, N., MacArthur, J., & Rietveld, C. M. (2006). Higgledy-piggledy policy: Confusion about inclusion. *Childrenz Issues, 10*(1), 30–36.

Hodkinson, H., & Hodkinson, P. M. (2004). Rethinking the concept of community of practice in relation to schoolteachers' workplace learning. *International Journal of Training and Development, 8*(1), 21–31.

Jones, A. (1991). *At school I've got a chance: Culture/privilege: Pacific Islands and Pakeha girls at school.* Palmerston North, NZ: Dunmore Press.

Kaur, B., Boyask, R., Quinlivan, K., & McPhail, J. C. (2008). Searching for equity and social justice: Diverse learners in Aotearoa, New Zealand. In G. Wan (Ed.), *The education of diverse populations: A global perspective.* The Netherlands: Springer Science and Business Media.

Lave, J., & Wenger, E. (2001). *Situated learning: Legitimate peripheral participation.* Cambridge, UK: Cambridge University Press.

Luke, A., & Hogan, D. (2006). Redesigning what counts as evidence in educational policy: The Singapore model. In J. Ozga, T. Seddon, & T. Popkewitz (Eds.), *World yearbook of education: Educational research and policy: Steering the knowledge-based economy* (p. 170). London: Routledge.

Lyotard, J.-F. (1979). *The post-modern condition.* Manchester, UK: Manchester University Press.

Maylor, U., Read, B., Mendick, H., Ross, A., & Rollock, N. (2007). *Diversity and citizenship in the curriculum: Research review.* London: Department for Education and Skills.

Mcghee, D. (2006). The new commission for equality and human rights: Building community cohesion and revitalizing citizenship in contemporary Britain. *Ethnopolitics, 5*(2), 145–166.

National Children's Bureau. (2006). *Every disabled child matters: Off the radar – how local authority plans fail disabled children.* London: National Children's Bureau.

Norwich, B. (2008). *Dilemmas of difference, inclusion and disability: International perspectives and future directions.* London: Routledge.

Nuthall, G. A., & Alton-Lee, A. G. (1998). *Understanding learning in the classroom: Understanding learning and teaching project 3.* Report to the Ministry of Education. Wellington, NZ: Ministry of Education.

Office of National Statistics. (2008). *Focus on social inequalities.* Retrieved May 1, 2008, from http://www.statistics.gov.uk/focuson/socialinequalities/

Office of Public Sector Information. (1981). *Education Act 1981.* London: Her Majesty's Stationery Office.

Office of Public Sector Information. (1988). *Education Reform Act 1988.* London: Her Majesty's Stationery Office.

Office of Public Sector Information. (1989). *Children Act 1989.* London: Her Majesty's Stationery Office.

Office of Public Sector Information. (2004). *Children Act 2004.* London: Her Majesty's Stationery Office.

Peters, M., & Marshall, J. (1996). *Individualism and community: Education and social policy in the postmodern condition.* London: Falmer Press.

Rassool, N., & Morley, L. (2000). School effectiveness and the displacement of equity discourses in education. *Race Ethnicity and Education, 3*(3), 237–258.

Rattansi, A., & Phoenix, A. (2005). Rethinking youth identities: modernist and postmodernist frameworks. *Identity: An International Journal of Theory and Research, 5*(2), 97–123.

Reay, D., Crozier, G., James, D., Hollingworth, S., Williams, K., Jamieson, F., et al. (2008). Re-invigorating democracy? White middle class identities and comprehensive schooling. *The Sociological Review, 56*(2), 238–255.

Rietveld, C. M. (2005). Classroom learning experiences of mathematics by new entrant children with Down syndrome. *Journal of Intellectual and Developmental Disability, 30*(3), 127–138.

Roche, J., & Tucker, S. A. (2007). Every child matters: 'Tinkering' or 'reforming' – an analysis of the development of the Children Act (2004) from an educational perspective. *Education, 3–13, 35*(3), 213–223.

Rogoff, B. (1990). *Apprenticeship in thinking: Cognitive development in social context.* New York and Oxford, UK: Oxford University Press.

Ryan, J. E. (2004). The perverse incentives of the No Child Left Behind Act. *New York University Law Review*, 932–989.

Shotter, J. (1998). Social construction as social poetics: Olive Sacks and the case of Dr P. In B. M. Mayer & J. Shotter (Eds.), *Reconstructing the psychological subject: Bodies, practices and technologies.* London: Sage.

Stein, S. J. (2004). *The culture of education policy.* New York: Teachers College Press.

United Nations. (1948). *Universal declaration of human rights.* Retrieved September 11, 2008, from http://www.un.org/Overview/rights.html

Waite, S., Boyask, R., Lawson, H., & Carter, R. (2008). *Concepts of diversity in the UK: Person-centred methodological approaches to tracking identity formation within education.* Paper presented at Children's Identity and Citizenship in Europe 10th Conference, Istanbul University, 28–31 May 2008.

Wertsch, J. V. (1991). *Voices of the mind: A sociocultural approach to mediated action.* Cambridge, MA: Harvard University Press.

Wetherell, M. (2008). Subjectivity or psycho-discursive practices? Investigating complex intersectional identities. *Subjectivity, 22*, 73–81.

Wetherell, M., Lafleche, M., & Berkeley, R. (2007). *Identity, ethnic diversity and community cohesion.* London: Sage Publications.

Ruth Boyask
Faculty of Education
University of Plymouth

Rebecca Carter
Faculty of Education
University of Plymouth

Hazel Lawson
School of Education and Lifelong Learning
University of Exeter

Sue Waite
Faculty of Education
University of Plymouth

EVE COXON

INTERSTICE THREE: EDUCATIONAL ENACTMENTS AND THE 'NEW AID ERA'

Implications for the Pacific

INTRODUCTION

This chapter draws on the author's work in the most culturally diverse region in the world, and in particular her focus on the extent to which aid is used to promote equitable and sustainable education development in the small island states of the Pacific. For the critical researcher, participation in and reflection on the process of aid delivery provides a rich opportunity to explore the intersection of local and global. The notion of 'educational enactments' provides a particularly apt metaphor for considering the local impact of the most recent education policy blueprints devised by the international development community for implementation through-out the 'global south',[1] in which Pacific Islands countries (PICs) can be included. Critical questions are posed of the recently reshaped global aid agenda and the aid delivery mechanisms by which the avowed commitments to poverty reduction and social justice for marginalised groups worldwide are purported to be met. In responding to the book's core theme of the challenges to difference and diversity at the local/national level[2] in the face of the pervasive educational instrumentalism promoted through dominant global discourses, the chapter acknowledges the power of global 'education for development' discourses at the national/Pacific policy level. Also noted, however, is the extent to which local educational practices are enacted by Pacific education communities, teachers and learners. Although these may be embedded within the constraints of global educational forces, their first points of reference are the social relations that inform the contextually derived subjectivities and identities of those concerned.

GLOBALISATION AND DEVELOPMENT IN THE PACIFIC

It is maintained that neo-liberal globalisation has continued the 'modernisation' project, begun over 50 years ago when colonial empires were breaking up as the mechanism for integrating the newly emerging nation-states into the global economy (Coxon, 2004). Earlier modernisation theories predicted a global cultural convergence and eventual homogeneity as the cultural outcome of the modernisation/development processes undertaken by the emerging states. However, the cultural diversity that characterises the post-modern world is often taken to be

K. Quinlivan, R. Boyask and B. Kaur (eds.), Educational Enactments in a Globalised World:
Intercultural Conversations, 129–135.

testimony to the efficacy of local cultural agency in mediating the effects of globalisation processes. This is nowhere more the case than in the Pacific Islands region. A factor of considerable power contributing to the complexity of each PIC's development context is the extent to which indigenous cultural meanings and values continue to inform social relationships and everyday material practices. Although the distinct local traditions and cultural histories found throughout the region have been affected to an extent by global processes, many of these – and notably those related to land tenure and use – effectively predate colonialism. The neo-liberal economic model is still promoted by the international financial institutions (IFIs) and bilateral development agencies active in the region as the only effective approach to development. In the view of many Pacific commentators, this poses a serious threat to Pacific communities which, to varying degrees, are still characterised by sociocultural ethics of redistribution, reciprocity and inclusiveness (Coxon, 2004).

While these small Pacific states exhibit an unparalleled diversity of culture and language as well as great variation in physical and political characteristics, they share many economic and educational challenges. Pacific economies are small with limited private sectors and relatively large public and informal sectors. Remote from international markets, they are reliant on imports for many basic commodities and on a narrow base of exports for income. They are very prone to natural disasters and other causes of environmental degradation. Population growth in many of the countries is outstripping the capacity to provide adequate basic services such as education. The need to address perceived deficiencies in education is seen by Pacific governments and aid donors alike as an essential means of targeting poverty, nationally and regionally; aid to education is seen by all parties as having a crucial role in this process (Coxon & Munce, 2008).

THE IMPACT OF THE NEW AID ERA

Over the past few decades, shifting conceptualisations of 'development' goals and processes, and how aid contributes to them, have informed changes in understandings of the education–development relationship and education aid policies generally. Although the overarching development assumption that aid leads to a reduction in poverty has remained, understandings about how this should happen have shifted considerably over time (Coxon & Tolley, 2005). In brief, during the so-called 'development' decades of the 1950s–60s, governments of the new developing states were seen as responsible for the initiation of social and economic change aimed at transforming 'backward' economies into both producers and consumers on the world market. The role of aid was to provide the technical expertise, equipment and finance required to fill the gaps. It was expected that the benefits of the ensuing economic growth would 'trickle down' to the poor.

Two key events marked a significant but short-lived shift in international development policy and practice during the 1970s. One was the powerful critique of the modernisation model provided by Dependency and World Systems theorists. The other was the demands of developing countries within the United Nations (UN) for a new international economic order that could address the gap between rich and poor countries. The need for non-economic objectives to be included in the aid/development equation in order for poverty to be reduced was widely accepted and 'basic needs' and 'redistribution with growth' strategies became the focus of development agencies' attention. However, a slow-down of the world economy led to the abandonment of the new poverty-focused approach. During the 1980s the structural adjustment programmes (SAPs), described by Rist (2008, p. 226) as the 'harbingers of neoliberal globalisation' and imposed by the IFIs on the world's poorest states, increasingly became the mechanism for ensuring the global application of an economic policy formula aimed at market-led development. The concept of development became reduced to economic growth by means of the free market. Under the influence of the IFIs, aid donors increasingly used aid as a form of leverage to ensure recipient states' agreement to adjust their economies according to the SAP blueprint.

Despite these wider shifts, because of its perceived links to economic growth through the provision of human capital, education itself has always been awarded a central role as an agent of modernisation/development. The belief in education as an instrument of economic growth persisted even through the pessimism of the 1990s, when the political, social and economic consequences of the structural adjustment programmes led to an extensive questioning of the almost universal acceptance of the notion that development should be seen primarily in terms of economic growth, and that aid should be targeted towards market-led solutions to poverty alleviation. The critique led to both a decrease in aid volumes and an increase in political debates about the concept of 'development' itself and how aid could be more effectively deployed, including aid to education (Coxon & Tolley, 2005).

International conferences and meetings, convened by various UN organisations and other key development agencies, discussed all aspects of international aid policy, and led to what Glennie describes as the globally agreed 'Better Aid Agenda' of 'the New Aid Era' (2008, pp. 14; 21). The latter term was coined to describe the period beginning in 2000 with the UN Millennium Summit which produced a set of globally agreed Millennium Development Goals (MDGs)[3] – including the goal of universal primary education and gender equity in primary and secondary education by 2015. This gave rise to more optimism regarding the aid/development nexus by providing a global agenda with the possibility of 'combating poverty in its multiple dimensions' (Norrag, 2008, p. 88). Also in 2000 the second Education For All (EFA) conference produced a revised timeframe for the targets set by the first EFA conference in 1990.

A further aspect of the Better Aid Agenda arose from the 2003 aid harmonisation conference in Rome which focused on the effectiveness of aid delivery, in particular the need for donors to coordinate their aid contributions when working in the same recipient country and within the same sector, and to align these with the national sector plans of the country concerned. The focus on the sector-wide approach (SWAp) as a better aid modality than the predominant project approach was reaffirmed through the 2005 Paris Declaration on Aid Effectiveness to which over 100 governments signed up. Since 2005 'more and better aid has become a lexicon of development' (Glennie, 2008, p. 89), with the focus of the Paris principles and targets on aid quality as well as quantity. The faith in education as the means of addressing poverty through economic development is held to as fervently in the New Aid Era as it was in the 1950s.

Given the focus by the Better Aid Agenda on such concepts as 'partnership' and 'local ownership', it could be assumed that the educational policies and practices enacted within the New Aid Era would be characterised by a commitment to inter-cultural conversations across the aid relationship. One might expect that a concerted attempt to ensure the articulation of local and global educational thought in ways that recognise the role of local culture(s) in shaping and sustaining the development of education (Stephens, 2007) would be recognised as necessary to ensure the achievement of the very worthy educational goals and targets set by the MDGs and EFA.

However, many commentators view mechanisms such as the MDGs and revised EFA targets as being primarily intended to ensure the implementation of the World Bank's 'global blueprint' for education development (Mundy, 2002). They maintain that in shaping the dominant aid discourse within which these mechanisms are awarded the key role in education development, the World Bank seeks to marry a faith in the globalisation of markets with an espoused commitment to poverty elimination. Some argue that the poverty reduction focus, in explicitly privileging primary education, downplays the importance of secondary and higher education. As well as discouraging critical analysis of how education contributes to development, this leads to decreased investment in peripheral countries' tertiary education capacity, thus rendering such counties even more dependent on western development 'expertise'. According to Tomasevski (2003), who argues for a human rights approach to education development, EFA and the two educational MDGs are nothing more than bureaucratic accountability mechanisms for increasing access to what already exists. As such, they fail to take into account the complexity of social and cultural factors within which education is located, and substantive questions about the quality of educational structures and processes – issues about what is taught and how – are ignored. In other words, the instrumentalism of the early modernisation models of education, rejuvenated through the discourses of neo-liberal globalisation (Coxon & Tolley, 2005), continues in the New Aid Era through 'the implementation of universal "solutions" that take little if any account of cultural and contextual realities' (Stephens, 2007, p. 120).

Furthermore, experience to date of the actual workings of the 'partnerships' promoted in the last few years indicates that their main concern is to establish what the donors see as more efficient management structures and processes, rather than to address historically formed power differentials between aid donor and aid recipient. It seems clear too that the SWAp emphasis on donors 'speaking with one voice' introduces a strong possibility that such an approach could give donors added strength, thereby both reducing the space for 'partner' countries' own educational agenda, and stifling critique, debate and the search for alternatives in education development that might come through conversation with multiple donor voices.

ALTERNATIVE PACIFIC MODELS OF EDUCATION

Increasingly the indigenous peoples of the Pacific and elsewhere are expressing concern about their lack of control over the content and direction of their education systems. The limitations of yet another one-size-fits-all approach in meeting the diverse educational needs of Pacific Islands countries are clear when considering the varied educational contexts across the region. Although for some PICs the key MDG/EFA focus on access for all primary-aged children remains crucial, many other PICs – despite their limited resources, vulnerability to natural disasters, and the logistical difficulties of delivering education services to remote communities on tiny land areas surrounded by vast oceans – have already met or are well on track to meeting the set targets. Those with close to universal access to primary education (for example, Tonga, Cook Islands, Niue, Tokelau, Nauru, Samoa, Palau) see their key focus as raising the quality of education at all levels. Many Pacific education communities do not accept the narrow conceptualisation of the education–development relationship the global mechanisms imply, or what they consider to be useful knowledge. In general, Pacific educators identify the constraints imposed by their colonial legacies as a major barrier to quality improvements, which they see as best addressed with locally determined curricula and pedagogies that speak directly to indigenous knowledge systems, values and ways of relating (Helu-Thaman 1999; Sanga & Taufe'ulungaki, 2005; Taufe'ulungaki, 2002). They argue for a critical understanding of those traditions concerned with social relations, of their role as guardians of the sustainable use of natural resources and protectors of local biodiversity. Local cosmologies, social and economic systems, geography, history and the arts are all areas worthy of attention in Pacific education systems.

The need for recognition of the educational structures and processes of indigenous knowledge systems in order to enact transformative, empowering and culturally appropriate teaching–learning environments has been long argued by Pacific educationists. In the words of Helu-Thaman (1999, p. 69):

> Pacific peoples … have their own cultures and associated cultural identities that they perceive to be unique. Their worldviews are closely connected to their *vanua/ples/fonua* concepts which are inadequately translated to mean 'land' or 'place', but which embody social and spiritual as well as physical dimensions …. Formal education … continues to reflect the tensions between Western and indigenous knowledge, values, and understandings, creating challenges to educators as well as development planners.

Although the local determination of education is an ongoing struggle, Pacific peoples are active in upholding diversity in educational enactments across the region. One example of such agentive action is the 'Re-thinking Pacific Education Initiative', a collective of Pacific educators from across the region who have – in the face of the global education 'partnership' of the New Aid Era – undertaken research, held conferences and symposiums and produced publications aimed at interrogating all aspects of their education systems. These alliances emphasise the uniqueness of diverse Pacific cultural and educational contexts and the reassertion of their local ownership (see Sanga & Taufe'ulungaki, 2005). They do not accept 'culture' as just another variable to be factored into the global educational blueprint. Neither do they accept the possibility of equitable and sustainable educational development resulting from the application of a top-down, universally applied policy prescription. Rather, they point to the need for a bottom-up process that takes account of the local historical and cultural foundations of education. Such an approach recognises that the co-existence of local and global may enable the production of a critical response to the instrumentalism that has informed most educational policy thinking in the region to date.

CONCLUSION

Despite the lip-service paid in the so-called New Aid Era to the upholding of cultural diversity and the need for aid-funded education development to be locally led, the global education agenda continues the same instrumentalism and universalism as were prevalent in preceding eras. However, it is clear that the challenge from Pacific educators in their search for alternative educational development models, combined with the contextual realities of everyday educational practice, has offered a degree of resistance to the notion of global education convergence. The danger in the New Aid Era is that the strengthened donor voice that operates through mechanisms such as the sector-wide approach at the local level will direct educational funding in ways that stifle such resistance. The key problems for Pacific educators and learners in these social and historical times are as they have been throughout the 'developing' world for the past 50 years – externally imposed educational models and a serious lack of the resources that could enable the development of locally designed and improved education policies and practices.

NOTES

[1] This term refers to those regions and countries often labelled 'third world', 'developing' or 'underdeveloped'.

[2] My references to 'local' education policies in the PICs pertain to those of national systems.

[3] Worth mentioning is that the MDGs are only a slightly revised version of the International Development Targets set by an Organisation for Economic Co-operation and Development (OECD) Development Assistance Committee meeting in the mid 1990s at which there was *no* representation from non-OECD countries – the notion of 'globally agreed' should be treated with some cynicism.

REFERENCES

Coxon, E. (2004). Beyond economism: Globalization, development and culture. *International Journal of the Humanities, 1*, 741–751.

Coxon, E., & Munce, K. (2008). The Global education agenda and the delivery of aid to Pacific education. *Comparative Education, 44*(2), 147–166.

Coxon, E., & Tolley, H. (2005). Aid to Pacific education: An overview. In K. Sanga, C. Chu, C. Hall, & L. Crowl (Eds.), *Rethinking aid relationships in Pacific education*. Wellington, NZ and Suva: Victoria University & USP.

Glennie, J. (2008). *The trouble with aid: Why less could mean more for Africa*. London and New York: Zed Books.

Helu-Thaman, K. (1999). Different eyes: Schooling and indigenous education in Tonga. In F. Leach & A. Little (Eds.), *Education, cultures, and economics: Dilemmas for development.* New York and London: Falmer Press.

Mundy, K. (2002). Retrospect and prospect: Education in a reforming World Bank. *International Journal of Educational Development, 22*(5), 483–508.

Norrag. (2008). The new politics of partnership: peril or promise? *Norrag News, 41.* Retrieved May 26, 2009, from http://www.norrag.org/issue.php?id=41

Rist, G. (2008). *The history of development: From western origins to global faith* (3rd ed.). London and New York: Zed Books.

Sanga, K., & Taufe'ulungaki, 'A. (Eds.). (2005). *International aid impacts on Pacific education.* Wellington, NZ: Institute for Research and Development in Maori and Pacific Education, Victoria University.

Stephens, D. (2007). *Culture in education and development: Principles, practice and policy.* Oxford, UK: Symposium Books.

Taufe'ulungaki, 'A. (2002). *Pacific education – are there alternatives?* Suva: Institute of Education.

Tomasevski, K. (2003). *Education denied: Costs and remedies.* London: Zed Books.

Eve Coxon
Faculty of Education
University of Auckland

JEAN CLAIRE MCPHAIL AND ANNEMARIE S. PALINCSAR

9. DISCOVERY MEETS INQUIRY

A Cross-cultural Essay

INTRODUCTION

The lure of cross-cultural educational work is the anticipation of interacting with different conceptions of teaching and learning, and different arrangements of schooling to both inform one's culturally embedded views and expand one's repertoire of ideas towards enhancing education. In this sense, the educator who embarks on a cross-cultural educational adventure is less like a tourist who travels to see the known and more like an international traveller who commits to journey through uncharted experiences to discover the unknown. Journeying as a traveller, however, is a more complicated experience than travelling as a tourist in the sense that one is exposed not only to fresh and enriching uncharted experiences, but also to the risks and conundrums that lie beneath the surface. The latter can elicit feelings of disquiet and raise more questions than answers.

As two North American educationist travellers who worked in Horizons (a pseudonym adopted for this essay), a special character charter elementary school in New Zealand, we journeyed through a varied range of experiences. From the first blush of excitement at the freshness and promise of a new experiment in 21st century schooling, we moved on to the complications that emerged when our culturally assumed ideas of adult education and exemplary science teaching and learning were confronted by significantly different ones that were incommensurate with ours.

This experience left us with at least the following two choices. We could assume a view of cultural diversity that positions cultural views and attitudes as necessarily grounded in *specificity* that trumps older views of *universality*. Or we could challenge ourselves to examine more closely our shared and disparate knowledge and assumptions of quality teaching and learning. The latter seemed the wiser choice, given the world's need for citizens who are prepared for 21st century demands and the consequent responsibilities educators must assume to prepare children for productive membership and participation in our increasingly global world.

The following are some of the questions that we used as grist for the conversations we had in preparing this dialogic essay: *What are the critical understandings and tools that elementary children need to 'travel' well in the world? Do educational ideas – like economic ones – translate across cultures, or are educational ideas too*

K. Quinlivan, R. Boyask and B. Kaur (eds.), Educational Enactments in a Globalised World: Intercultural Conversations, 137–149.
© *2009 Sense Publishers. All rights reserved.*

culturally specific to travel easily around the globe? How can educationists talk within and across cultural contexts to effectively share ideas, create fertile alliances, and collectively enhance teaching and learning opportunities for students and teachers?

Before following up these questions, we pause to describe the context in which we conducted our work. Jean begins by describing her history of working in Horizons and then Annemarie describes her brief foray into teaching there.

CONTEXT OF OUR CROSS-CULTURAL WORK

Jean's Introduction

I, Jean, a North American educationist, left a position at the University of Michigan, USA to join the faculty of the University of Canterbury in Christchurch, New Zealand in 1999. I was enticed to migrate to New Zealand by the prospect of doing a longitudinal study of a new special character charter elementary school, Horizons, with an emphasis on student-driven interest-based learning, a topic that had been my primary research focus (Freeman, McPhail & Berndt, 2002; McPhail, Pierson, Freeman, Goodman & Ayappa, 2000; McPhail, Pierson & Goodman, 2004). Beginning in 2001 and extending until 2005 a team of researchers from the University of Canterbury – Ruth Boyask, Baljit Kaur, Kane O'Connell and I – launched our intensive teacher–parent–researcher project aimed at co-constructing a vision of quality interest-based learning and a related set of democratic educational practices (Boyask, MacDonald & McPhail, 2004; Boyask, McPhail, Kaur & O'Connell, 2008).

Horizons was conceptualised and presented to the public and to the Ministry of Education in New Zealand in 2000 as a *special character school* adapted to the new challenges of the 21st century. Like all experimental schools that have drawn their blueprint from a mixture of political, social and educational discourses of the time, Horizons' pedagogical vision drew from both neo-liberal thought, with its market-driven focus, and select progressive educational ideas. As such, it attracted much interest from a range of professional educators and laypeople who were critical of the 19th century model of schooling with its emphasis on central government control, within-school hierarchies and a conservative and formal curriculum that had not kept pace with the new knowledge and skills needed in typical 21st century communities and workplaces. Thus, from among the many educational ideas on the specific transformations in schooling necessary to meet the social, economic and environmental challenges of the 21st century, the members of the Foundational Board of Trustees of Horizons grounded their ideas and hopes in the effects of changing numerous features of Horizons, some of which were underpinned by neo-liberal political thought and others by a general interpretation of progressive educational thought.

To begin, the content of the curriculum was shifted away from a traditional curriculum to one grounded in 'discovery learning', which was captured in the school's mission statement as 'Free to discover, to uncover, create your own path!'

This pedagogical turn meant that learning pathways were constructed upwards from each child's interests and passions, and that self-selected pathways were undertaken in a self-managed context of experimentation, entrepreneurship and risk-taking with minimal instruction and intervention from the teachers. Associated with this pedagogical orientation was the idea that learning was to be focused on the resources of the community and not located in the school building.

The innovative open, brightly coloured and furnished architectural design of the school building located in the city reflected this orientation. Absent from Horizons were the typical resources within a primary school such as a library with a range of books and videos as well as materials for scientific work. Instead, what was prominent was a large bank of computers and mobile phones for children and their teachers, a bright but sparsely equipped art space, a large, beautifully designed kitchen for cooking, eating and socializing, and a lounge area with comfortable chairs and couches.

Horizons' institutional and pedagogical vision relocated teachers as facilitators or 'learning advisers' and parents/caregivers as their partners who worked closely with children in the design and execution of their interest-based learning. This idea of partnership relative to the course of children's learning was instantiated in the 'triangle' in which child, parent and learning adviser were represented as equal partners. Parents/caregivers were conceived as active participants in all phases of their children's learning and were expected to be engaged in the activities of the school community to the maximum extent possible. Children were encouraged to engage in discussions and set appointments with their learning advisers and parents when they required facilitation with respect to one of their self-directed projects through use of their electronic devices, such as mobile phones and computers. Ideas about how children at Horizons could use and extend these electronic resources were borrowed by teachers, parents and children from the everyday values and practices of the business world, rather than being appropriated to traditional school practices, creating the appearance that children at Horizons were apprentices in the global marketplace on their way towards becoming adept with the commerce and communication tools of the 21st century.

Annemarie's Introduction

When Jean asked me to conduct a few demonstration science inquiry lessons at Horizons, I, Annemarie, agreed to do so with a considerable degree of trepidation. Although I had over 10 years of experience studying guided-inquiry teaching in elementary classroom in the USA, I was still 'recovering' from a recent negative experience in which I had attempted to engage a group of upper elementary students in the USA in guided-inquiry science experiences. The activity had not gone well; the children were restless and puzzled; the ambiguity associated with being asked to explore a phenomenon, guided only by a question rather than a series of directions, was more than they could handle at that time. Rather than assume a collaborative stance in which members of the class would persuade others through the power of their ideas and the clarity of the evidence for their claims, children's status in the classroom determined whose ideas would prevail. There was little evidence of learning. In short, I exited the teaching experience humbled and full of self-doubt.

As I considered the prospects at Horizons, the anticipated parallels between the two teaching experiences were disheartening. Similar to my relationship with the students at Horizons, I had been a stranger to the students in the USA; I had no personal relationship on which excellent teaching is built. Furthermore, like the children in the USA, the Horizons children were unacquainted with inquiry-based teaching in science; more than that, they had received little science instruction and had little access to materials that would support their exploration of phenomena. On the other hand, I was aware that the children I would teach at Horizons would be those who had selected science as an interest area; in contrast, the children in the USA had no choice regarding their presence during the science lessons. Furthermore, the children at Horizons were accustomed to teachers assuming the role of facilitator; the approach I bring to inquiry teaching places a heavy emphasis on the teacher as facilitator. Indeed, in our research, we refer to the approach as *guided* inquiry (Magnusson & Palincsar, 1995; Palincsar & Magnusson, 2001).

As I prepared for my experience teaching at Horizons, I wanted to select an investigation that: (a) while not requiring a large amount of time, could involve students in a full inquiry cycle; (b) would not require unusual investigative materials; (c) would pertain to a problem with which students were likely to be familiar; and (d) would be generative, in the sense that students could continue to explore the phenomenon we were investigating beyond the specific inquiry we would do together.

One investigation that met these criteria was the use of a *Cartesian Diver System (CDS)* to explore the question: *Why do objects sink and float?* A CDS is constructed by filling a large test tube with water and inverting a smaller vial, partially filled with water, in the test tube. The larger test tube is then covered with rubber matting (e.g. using a piece of a balloon), which is secured with a rubber band. When constructed well, the vial inside the test tube can be made to sink or float by pressing down on the rubber matting. When pressed, the air in the small vial is compressed and more water flows into the vial, making it sink inside the test tube. When released, the air expands, pushing the water out, decreasing the density of the vial and making it float.

This investigation has the potential to be very productive in the sense that one can explore both floating and sinking with the same materials; furthermore, it is possible to gather accurate data that will support the inquirer to make claims (e.g. noting the change in the number of centimetres of water in the vial when pressing down and then releasing the rubber matting). There is a degree of challenge to the extent that the children need to construct a sufficiently 'sensitive' system such that manipulating the test tube will, in fact, change the floatation of the vial. Further, the CDS can be modified (e.g., by making the same system upside down) so that children can gather further confirmatory or counter evidence.

I had two lessons with a dozen Horizons children, each of which lasted about an hour and a half. On the first day, after a round of introductions, the children were asked to brainstorm answers to the question, *What causes an object to sink and float?* They then were provided with the materials for the CDS and were instructed on how to construct the system, including how to test whether or not they had a sensitive system, and how to observe closely the behaviour of the CDS. They then went off in pairs to build and investigate their CDS. After about 30 minutes of investigation, the class came together again to begin the reporting phase of their inquiry. This is the point in the instruction when the students present – with the aid of posters – diagrams illustrating how they investigated, what they observed and what claims they wish to make from their observations. All of this happened in session 1. In session 2, the children revisited the class claims for the purpose of discussing the claims for which there was consensus, and those on which there was no agreement. This then set the stage for the next round of investigation, which involved using the 'upside down' CDS to explore the same question: *What causes objects to sink and float?* This investigation was followed by another round of reporting out and discussion with the whole class.

In sum, the ultimate goal of the inquiry-based teaching I wished to model was not only to support children's learning of scientific understanding (in this case, understandings about the role of density in explaining floating and sinking) but to support students to experience, understand and appreciate the ways in which these understandings have arisen from the use of the tools, language and ways of reasoning that are characteristic of scientific inquiry (Driver, Osoko, Leach, Mortimer & Scott, 1994; Lemke, 1990; White & Frederiksen, 1998).

OUR TRAVEL JOURNALS

Jean

I was excited by the ease of uptake and the enthusiasm surrounding the creation of a teacher–parent–researcher community (TPRC) at Horizons. Whereas my experiences in forming teacher–researcher communities in the USA were fraught with significant structural impediments, the director, teachers and parents of Horizons appeared to relish the idea of meeting regularly to read about, reflect on and discuss quality interest-based learning. In face of this enthusiasm new structures emerged easily to accommodate the work of the TPRC, such as the addition to the school schedule of a bi-weekly hour-and-a-half meeting time arranged to meet the needs of all members and a shortened school day to accommodate attendance of teachers and parents.

However, the enthusiasm in planning the TPRC did not translate into an accompanying commitment to engage in the range of activities such as reading, reflecting and discussing that were associated with increasing our knowledge and understandings about quality learning and that were co-planned with the director of the school. Instead, our group meetings were characterised by diverse social positions such as polite silences, quizzical expressions, statements of passionate personal beliefs about quality learning, and storytelling about school incidents – in short, social engagement trumped intellectual involvement with the relevant texts to our inquiry. It was unclear whether most of the TPRC members were reading the short classroom-based articles provided, and in the case of those who did, there seemed to be a diffidence about sharing their responses. While some journaling was evident in the beginning of our work together, this activity appeared to fall away over time.

Perplexed by this primary conversational disposition in our meetings and eager to remedy any practices that were not contributing to a more productive learning context, I engaged in discussions with the members of the research group, particularly Ruth and Kane who were native New Zealanders, to try to understand these unexpected dynamics. Their analytic responses centred on the power dynamics at play in this group which raised questions of unresolved authority relative to the social mix of administrative, teaching and parental involvement coupled with the addition of faculty and graduate students from the university (Quinlivan, Boyask & Carswell, 2008).

Although I could understand their analysis intellectually, as an outsider to the embedded school discourses of New Zealand *and* the facilitator of the TPRC, I could not frame a way forward that would both address these power dynamics and refocus our efforts on the stated interests of the group – understanding quality interest-based learning. In reflecting further on this dilemma I wondered whether the power dynamics in the social situation operated to conserve the status quo in the culture of the school as primarily social rather than intellectual, and whether I too was being acculturated towards the social and away from the intellectual without my knowing it. Also, I wondered whether the agrarian, pragmatic culture of New Zealand with a distrust of the intellectual and abstract was also working against the creation of an intellectual learning context in the TPRC.

I was delighted that Annemarie had agreed to meet with members of the TPRC to share her experiences in developing and working in teacher–researcher communities in the USA and, in addition, to demonstrate guided-inquiry science instruction with a group of 12 mixed-age Horizons children who had self-selected science as one of their primary subject area interests. I viewed Annemarie's visit as having the potential to reignite broad and deep interest among the TPRC members in our expressed goal of increasing our knowledge and understandings of quality interest-based learning.

However, once again my assumptions were not met. The initial introduction of Annemarie to the TPRC in which she talked about her teacher–researcher community experiences in the USA did not elicit any more curiosity or enthusiasm from the non-research members than the previous readings and discussions on the same topic. Again, the social dynamic of most of the TPRC members was marked by a civil discourse but without an apparent interest in engaging with the implications of such a community for children's quality learning; only the director of the school could be counted on to contribute a question or comment.

Ruth and Kane encouraged me to think of the problems inherent in the social dynamics posed, by a famous international researcher speaking to Kiwis. Disheartened, I hoped that Annemarie's work with the children in guided-inquiry science would finally fuel open discussions among the TPRC members.

Annemarie

My recollection, supported by viewings of the video recordings of our guided-inquiry science experience at Horizons, is of the ease with which the children engaged in the activity: they eagerly shared their thinking about floating and sinking and, similar to children everywhere (it seems), settled on the explanation that 'heavy things sink and light things float'. The children quickly set about making their diver systems; interestingly, they were more challenged to assemble the CDS than I had expected they would be. Furthermore, their methods of assembly were haphazard: rather than make gradual adjustments to the test tube or vial (e.g. using a pipette to add or remove water), they would begin anew each time that their CDS failed to work as it should, dumping out the water and starting over. They listened very respectfully to one another in the reporting phase of the inquiry. They appeared delighted to have access to materials and were curious about other investigations they might conduct with the materials, in some cases asking if they could bring the materials home with them. And, in the ultimate compliment to a teaching activity, several of the pairs continued the conversation about their claims at recess. One child even reported that he had changed his mind about why the diver would float or sink, having been persuaded by the argument of his classmate; a conversation they had carried on in the evening.

This was, overall, a very positive experience for me personally. With only one exception (one pair became quite frustrated with their challenges in assembling the system and gave up), the children were indeed highly engaged. There were none of the 'management' issues that give teachers pause before inviting children to investigate with such materials as water and rubber bands. There was an exuberance on the part of some of the children. For example, one child excitedly reported that he and his partner had noticed a number of bubbles along the insides of the large test tube; cleverly, they directed the little vial down the sides of the test tube, in essence attempting to 'sweep' the bubbles away. This, they reported, would make it 'easier' for the vial to travel up and down in the test tube. Although these bubbles were not relevant to explaining how the CDS works, it was nothing short of thrilling to see the children entertaining the range of potential 'variables' of which they were aware regarding this phenomenon.

The outcomes were, then, generally positive (from my perspective). Nonetheless there emerged, even in these two relatively brief lessons, tensions that are classic in the conduct of inquiry teaching (Brown & Campione, 1994). These tensions pertain to the role of the teacher in the inquiry process, and the role of social versus intellectual engagement.

In guided inquiry, the teacher is working to shape the problem space so that it is fertile for advancing children's learning; in contrast to discovery learning, there is less emphasis placed on children attempting to figure out for themselves some of the procedural aspects of the investigation. The teacher is constantly making judgements about whether the children's decisions on *how* or *what* to investigate will facilitate their learning. These are not easy judgements. On the one hand, bumbling about with the construction of the CDS does provide the opportunity for the students to notice, for example, how much air there is in the vial, and the relevance of keeping the rubber matting taut so that it makes a difference in the system when you press on it with your thumb. On the other hand, if children are struggling too much to design a sensitive system, they may lose interest; they may never have a system that successfully supports their exploring of the question; and they may not have the intellectual resources left to attend to the 'science' rather than the 'engineering' in the problem.

Another tension in inquiry teaching is managing the social and intellectual demands. Powerful inquiry experiences call upon students to work cooperatively and be respectful of one another but also to challenge one another's thinking; to, for example, be comfortable with calling attention to the fact that the observations made by one member of the group are inconsistent with the observations made by others and to discuss the relevance of this inconsistency. Or, as another example, children might argue that there could be several explanations for an observation, and not just the one that a student has appeared to settle on. This aspect of inquiry teaching is what calls to mind the idea of teaching as 'enculturation'; in inquiry science teaching, children are learning not only about canonical understandings in science, but also about the norms for engaging in argumentation (Engle, 2006; Engle & Conant, 2002). Because this is a process of enculturation, it would be a folly to expect that children who are just being introduced to guided-inquiry experiences would embrace the intellectual roles associated with inquiry teaching; and, indeed, although the Horizons children were remarkably adept at managing the social demands, they made only a few timid forays into argumentation and, interestingly, the best instance of that occurred not in the classroom but off the school grounds.

Jean

The Horizons staff was extremely accommodating in locating the relevant materials for Annemarie's guided-inquiry science work with the children, securing an appropriate work space and relieving teachers from their obligations during Annemarie's instruction so that all of them could observe her. In addition, the research members of the TPRC arranged for videotaping of Annemarie's instruction to accompany their observations. Finally, all of the parents were invited to observe as well.

I observed Annemarie on both instructional days being as much interested in her work with the children as I was in being present for discussion or commentary with the director, teachers and parents who were also observing. On the second instructional day I was struck by the rapt attention of the students both while they were reporting and in their subsequent activity phase. This kind of focused attention to a sustained activity was not something I, nor the other members of the research team, had witnessed and documented in our extended classroom and community learning contexts previous to the creation of the TPRC. In response, I turned to the director of the school to comment on my experience. To my surprise he merely nodded and then turned away. I wondered at his casualness but then noticed that most of the other non-research members who were observing that day were also coming and going from the observation in a less than concentrated manner.

My hopes were still not dented as I prepared for our post-inquiry TPRC meeting with Annemarie. I assumed that the collective experience of observing a small but intensive illustration of guided-inquiry science would fuel and focus discussion on the differences in discovery learning and guided learning, and lead us forward in thinking and reflecting on the nature of quality interest-based learning that would ground the pedagogy of this 21st century school. Also, as several of the children who chose to participate in Annemarie's science work were the children of members of the TPRC, I assumed that pedagogical interest would be heightened. I hoped as well that the short reading we had provided on Annemarie's work might supplement our discussion.

However, on my way to the meeting I encountered a mother of one of the participating children who was also a TPRC member and who had observed Annemarie's teaching. In my enthusiasm for discussion with her I inquired casually about her responses. She quickly and with some degree of irritation stated that she had observed that the children were squirming around on their stools during the reporting phase, and that she thought Annemarie should not have expected the children to sit on uncomfortable stools and be attentive for such a long time. Shocked at this as her first response I waited for her to add additional responses, however, even when I encouraged her to share any other responses, she declined.

The post-inquiry meeting that followed with the entire TPRC did not fare any differently to previous meetings. In spite of all of the members either having observed Annemarie's teaching in situ or having viewed it on the video recording and in spite of our having designed the meeting as an opportunity to share observations and raise questions, there was almost no uptake at this meeting. Finally I began to appreciate that the adult educational context that I had imagined through my *acculturation in the USA as a parent, teacher, learner and researcher* was unlikely to emerge. Left with this realisation I was lost as to how to begin again, where to begin and why to begin.

Annemarie

The tensions described above, pertaining to the role of the teacher in the inquiry process, and the role of social versus intellectual engagement (Palincsar & Herrenkohl, 2002), are an important part of the story of enacting inquiry teaching at Horizons because these are the very issues that I had expected the Horizons teachers, parents and staff would discuss when we convened to debrief the instruction. Several teachers and several parents had viewed the teaching as it unfolded, and all had access to a video of the instruction prior to our meeting for the debriefing. As Jean has indicated above, our hope was that parents' experience of watching their own children engaged in this novel activity would fuel discussion regarding a broad range of issues specific to: learning, development, pedagogy, the design of instructional contexts and the use of critical thinking skills. However, much to my surprise, there was virtually silence when we gathered to debrief.

One parent raised a question about what she had observed to be uneven participation on the part of the students, which, is, of course, an important question for which I was grateful. But, beyond that, there seemed to be nothing about the four hours of inquiry teaching that captured the attention, fed the curiosity or fired the imagination of the group.

Of course, many explanations are possible. Perhaps it was naïve to think it would be otherwise; in addition to the issues that Jean and her research group identified above, the TPRC members had only begun their reading and discussion of inquiry teaching and learning prior to my conducting the demonstration lessons. Perhaps, in the absence of many lenses, the participants were, in fact, unable to see what the children were doing and learning. Given that the school had no specific science curriculum and did not routinely include science learning opportunities in the school day, this activity may have been judged not to be of sufficient value to the school's goals. It is also possible that the pedagogy itself was so unfamiliar to the participants that it was difficult for them to find a point of entrée into the conversation. Perhaps the pedagogy was not only unfamiliar but also contrary to the tenets of 'discovery learning' self-directed by the children themselves that was valued at Horizons? As mentioned above, in guided-inquiry science the teacher is actively shaping what is possible for children to 'discover' in the instruction; hence it may have seemed like poor pedagogy to the TPRC participants but Kiwi civility prevented a direct conversation on this issue.

EMERGING CONCLUSIONS

I am not the same having seen the moon shine on the other side of the world.

Maryanne Radmacher

Upon returning to the USA after nearly eight years of work in New Zealand my sister gave me, Jean, a piece of art work with the quotation above; in response I cried. The teaching and learning experiences I had had in New Zealand, of which the research study at Horizons was a central part, had left me doubting that my acculturated US views of exemplary educational thought and practices would 'travel' well across the globe. They did not fit well into the social fabric of New Zealand, a country that shared Western social and historical roots, so why should I assume that they would fit in non-Western countries? For example, although I had become comfortable with the ideological and pedagogical contestations within the USA in the educational literature and had engaged in these contestations through writing and speaking with my US colleagues, those experiences had not prepared me for the unexpected, subtle, pervasive and distinctly different social discourse surrounding education in New Zealand; a discourse that was more oriented towards achieving a social consensus free of the kinds of open inquiry that I had experienced as generative in intellectual matters. What did this mean for cross-cultural educational work; for example, did Kiwis travelling as educationists to the US experience analogous disquiet in not having their educational assumptions taken up?

We turn now to our questions in the introduction as a way of opening up conversation to issues confronting educators who want to work across borders in the 21st century global world. In thinking about the critical understandings and tools that elementary children need to 'travel' well in and around the world, on the one hand, we are impressed with the civility of the Kiwi adults and children in social situations. This disposition on the part of Kiwis undoubtedly would serve them well in meeting diverse people from around the globe, and is, therefore, a discourse important to cultivate in children in our school settings in the USA and elsewhere – wherever it is absent. However, our emerging understandings from New Zealand also appear to suggest that there may be particular kinds of civil social discourses that work against – rather than in support of – contexts of lively and productive intellectual discourse. In as much as our coming to the richest possible understandings of exemplary teaching and learning rests on knowledge of and engagement with a range of educational ideas, then the cultivation in our children of both a civil social discourse and a disposition to stretch their minds beyond their own acculturated views is critical to their involvement in work and civic engagement in the global world. We would argue that this kind of stretching cannot happen without sustained involvement in diverse but focused learning situations under the guidance of expert others; here the pedagogy of Horizons, in spite of having the accoutrements of the marketplace of the 21st century, was lacking in substance.

But, in addressing our second question, our cross-cultural educational experiences in New Zealand suggest the unsettling recognition that, in fact, educational ideas are more culturally situated and therefore more complicated than economic ones; as a result – unlike economic ideas and practices – they do not travel easily around the globe. Whereas banks, investment agencies and businesses share the same goals of securing and making profit and use the same tools of the trade (stocks and currency) to execute their processes, educational endeavours are grounded in a myriad of assumed cultural values and shaped further in specific instantiations of those values in individual schools and classrooms. Yet international scales of educational achievement such as those of the Organisation for Economic Co-operation and Development (OECD) have assumed an economic model with a global educational currency; objective test scores that reduce educational systems and students to human capital (McPhail & Kaur, 2008). With profit as the clear economic goal in the global marketplace, fast-paced decisions are made without necessary respect for other kinds of cultural values. Yet in educational settings based in democratic values, schools driven by a single profit goal are deeply embedded in moral ideas that are shaped in culturally specific settings. For example, as it is adult members of a cultures who are in charge of shaping particular takes on best educational practices, there will always be a conservative impulse in schools towards maintaining their social system with its moral values, so that their children remain with them and are not lost to new values and ideas outside of their cultural milieu. In Horizons, as an example, we experienced the strength of the convictions of the foundational board members towards their school's vision and practices – a position that moved them to resist other educational visions and practices. Clearly doing cross-cultural educational work involves a confrontation with deeply held cultural values that include national, local and familial hopes and dreams; our own, as well as those we encounter in our global travels.

Having painted a picture of the complexities involved in doing cross-cultural educational work, the question remains of how educationists can address these issues to create fertile alliances and collectively enhance teaching and learning opportunities for students and teachers. First, we think it is critical that we recognise the kinds of sensitive cultural variables that will play a central part in any cross-cultural educational discussion that is likely to be productive. Secondly, we understand that addressing these sensitive issues will require a greater openness and courage than academics usually bring to their work, for as long as our cross-cultural work and discussions remain at procedural or technical levels, no movement towards the moral, social and intellectual problem space involved in the creation of the best possible teaching and learning contexts for children will occur.

REFERENCES

Boyask, R., MacDonald, M., & McPhail, J. (2004). The Discovery 1 Photography Group. *Aotearoa New Zealand Association of Art Educators, 14*(1), 6–7.

Boyask, R., McPhail, J. C., Kaur, B., & O'Connell, K. (2008). Democracy at work in and through experimental schooling. *Discourse: Studies in Cultural Politics of Education, 29*(1), 19–34.

Brown, A. L., & Campione, J. C. (1994). Guided discovery in a community of learners. In K. McGilly (Ed.), *Classroom lessons: Integrating cognitive theory and classroom practice* (pp. 229–272). Cambridge, MA: MIT Press.

Driver, R., Osoko, H., Leach, J., Mortimer, E., & Scott, P. (1994). Constructing scientific knowledge in the classroom. *Educational Researcher, 23*(7), 5–12.

Engle, R. A. (2006). Framing interactions to foster generative learning: A situative explanation of transfer in a community of learners classroom. *Journal of the Learning Sciences, 15*(4), 451–498.

Engle, R. A., & Conant, F. C. (2002). Guiding principles for fostering productive disciplinary engagement: Explaining an emergent argument in a community of learners classroom. *Cognition and Instruction, 20*(4), 399–483.

Freeman, J., McPhail, J. C., & Berndt, J. A. (2002). Significant features of situational interest for sixth grade students. *Elementary School Journal, 102*(4), 335–347.

Lemke, J. L. (1990). *Talking science: Language, learning, and values.* Norwood, NJ: Ablex.

Magnusson, S., & Palincsar, A. S. (1995). Learning environments as a site of science education reform: An illustration using interdisciplinary guided inquiry. *Theory into Practice, 34*(1), 43–50.

McPhail, J. C., & Kaur, B. (2008). In search of a participatory democratic vision in teacher education. In A. Scott & J. F. Moir (Eds.), *Shaping the future: Critical essays in teacher education.* Rotterdam, The Netherlands and Taipei, Taiwan: Sense Publishers.

McPhail, J. C., Pierson, J. M., Freeman, J. G., Goodman, J., & Ayappa, A. (2000). The role of interest in fostering sixth grade students' identities as competent learners. *Curriculum Inquiry, 30*(1), 43–70.

McPhail, J. C., Pierson, J., & Goodman, J. (2004). Creating partnerships for complex learning: The dynamics of an interest-based apprenticeship in the art of sculpture. *Curriculum Inquiry, 34*(4), 463–493.

Palincsar, A. S., & Herrenkohl, L. (2002). Designing collaborative learning contexts. *Theory into Practice, 41*(1), 26–32.

Palincsar, A. S., & Magnusson, S. J. (2001). The interplay of first-hand and text-based investigations to model and support the development of scientific knowledge and reasoning. In S. Carver & D. Klahr

(Eds.), *Cognition and instruction: Twenty five years of progress* (pp. 151–194). Mahwah, NJ: Lawrence Erlbaum.

Quinlivan, K., Boyask, R., & Carswell, S. (2009). Dynamics of power and participation in school university partnerships. *New Zealand Journal of Educational Studies, 44*(1), 65-83.

White, B. Y., & Frederiksen, J. R. (1998). Inquiry, modeling, and metacognition: Making science accessible to all students. *Cognition and Instruction, 16*(1), 3–118.

Jean McPhail
(Formerly at the School of Education
University of Canterbury)

Annemarie S. Palincsar
School of Education
University of Michigan

CONVERSATIONAL INTERLUDE THREE.
ENGAGING WITH DILEMMAS AND POSSIBILITIES

In this last conversational interlude, we wish to highlight the ideas that continue to engage us as educational researchers and educators, raising further questions as ongoing challenges to our thinking and action, as well as suggesting productive possibilities.

One of the themes that continues to dominate our conversations is the allure as well as the danger of emotionality as a site for learning.

Sean Darmody: What is interesting about this idea is that you can do a whole range of things. For example, the object of your fear may well be unreal or irrelevant or a nightmare or whatever but your experience is the same as real fear: and then the role of children's stories and for me our Irish folk stories which are quite horrendous. They get to a stage where you think, 'This story cannot get worse' and it does and it deals with real things ... children will sit on laps of their parents and if you watch them, they're really interesting at about three, four and five. They cover their eyes but they are open and they are engaging in a secure way and the fear is there as the story's told ...

Kathleen Quinlivan: Has anybody written about this in terms of its usefulness as a pedagogical site? Fear as a pedagogical site?

Lia de Vocht van Alphen: There was a presentation today about fear and I went to it and there was a Dewey presentation *(inaudible)* and the person presented it from three perspectives – Rousseau, Dewey and Freire and how they approached it. ... It's a bigger thing than learning. I think in life, there has to be death and sadness and fear and things like that, feelings like that in order for there to be happiness. You can't have one without the other, somehow.

Kathleen Quinlivan: I think it's kind of interesting in relation to thinking about what it means to engage with difference: the notion of fear. That's the whole notion of the other isn't it? It's the unknown ... Actually when you engage with difference that's when there's something that goes down that's not quite so pleasant. Do you know what I mean? I think that there might be a kind of fear [of the unknown/unfamiliar] ... it's very relevant to what happened in that classroom with the kids and also the teacher and with me.

Baljit Kaur: But then how is it that, but why is it that you weren't able to engage with that fear as a pedagogical site? That is the question. I don't mean you have an answer.

Kathleen Quinlivan: No, I do have an answer actually because what I suppose kicks in then is to do with that rationality–emotionality binary and how that's operating. The classroom is a site where rationality is privileged. You can't do emotions.

K. Quinlivan, R. Boyask and B. Kaur (eds.), Educational Enactments in a Globalised World: Intercultural Conversations, 151–156.

Baljit Kaur: ... but as a pedagogical, as a place we are trying to learn something new, actually you do need to take risks into the unknown to learn something new. So there has to be discomfort in that and there is emotionality involved with that except that in our ways of teaching and learning there is no space to do this. So why are we not able to sit with it? Why is it that we make no space for it in our ways of learning? I think it might be to do with privileging the rational much more than emotionality, as you were saying, because emotionality has come to be associated with savagery and irrationality.

Ruth Boyask: But I don't know, just thinking about some of those terms that you were using to talk about things like savagery ... in relation to different cultural contexts, these things mean quite different things and that was some of the discussion today, wasn't it? Okay, emotionality might be important in the US, it might be important in New Zealand and even in Britain in some ways, but not [in] other [places]. But what does it mean within a culture like Singapore where there's even more privilege in having emotion under control? So *(pause)* what am I trying to get at?

Kathleen Quinlivan: I think you're talking about something quite important actually, when you're talking about an educational enactment: it speaks to a context in some ways ... I think it's one thing that we were trying to be able to account for in the way we developed the themes for the book or these ideas; what happens when you talk about material enactments in a globalised world?

Baljit Kaur: So is the globalised world not all that 'globalised' as far as emotionality's concerned? Is that what you're saying?

Ruth Boyask: In some places emotionality is significant and others not.

Baljit Kaur: The meanings that are there are quite globalised and therefore one is talking about a globalised world; however, it's not as if it is a monolithic kind of concept. One needs to think about in what ways are we living in a globalised world and in what ways we're not globalised.

Ruth Boyask: So the globalisation extends across rational discourses and particularly neo-liberal discourses, but globalisation at the level of human emotionality ...?

Kathleen Quinlivan: It's almost like a done deal, isn't it? Like, you know, it's just a taken-for-granted notion now that we live in a globalised world but actually what does that mean in essence? Actually Eve's contribution speaks to some of those issues. She argues that the language of globalisation is just being used to constitute a new kind of colonialism ... Well, not a new form of colonialism, but it is done in the name of globalisation but it's the same kind of 'being done to' in a way that's not respecting the value of indigenous knowledges and practices within those contexts.

Ruth Boyask: Which is similar to the universalising discourses that we were talking about earlier, in relation to things like personalised learning and Every Child Matters. It's that kind of universalisation of difference, and actually Vanessa's comments about consumer identities probably fit in there quite nicely because it's those identities that get transferred across. How do you feel about that, Jean, because it's something that you talk about as well?

Jean McPhail: Well, I was just sitting here thinking, in terms of your question which I think is a good one, is how to make sense of what things actually mean when you live in another culture ... That was a real problem for me in New Zealand that things did not mean *(laughs)* what I thought they meant! ... And of course what was for me extremely challenging was that I never presumed that, in an English-speaking country that had its roots in the same part of the world that Americans had their cultural roots, that there would be that much difference in the meanings of words. But there were [many such differences], so the question of 'How globalised are we really?' – I mean, when you look at education, how it's actually constructed to be part of the neo-liberal discourse now ...

Hazel Lawson: ... the whole notion of, you know, even talking among westernised countries if you like, it's already a problem but when you get to places that aren't represented anywhere at any of these conferences, it's a bit of different game, isn't it? And yet some of those things to do with globalisation – like increasing literacy and all those things that are like part of a global agenda if you like through the UN and things – impact upon places like Mongolia where the notion of disability is entirely different.

Sean Darmody: ... *(Inaudible)* the language, analysis of language. The idea of globalisation I cannot express in Irish ... English is a brilliant language for expressing property and possession but you can't do it in Irish ... Globalised, the consumer owning, I can't express it, therefore I can't think it, therefore it has no impact on me. There is no globalisation in that way unless I think in English or French or something else. When we talked about emotionality and that it's context-based, in Japanese you can't actually say, 'I love you'. [You can only say] 'I have esteem for you' or 'I regard you highly'. You can't express the emotion [of love] because it doesn't exist in the language.

Baljit Kaur: There is quite a bit of work in cross-cultural psychology about meanings of words like, you know, we don't have words in Indian languages like child development, for bringing up children. As Professor Durganand Sinha (a well-known cross-cultural psychologist) once said, 'We live with our children, we don't bring them up'.

Kathleen Quinlivan: So what are the implications of what we're talking about then in terms of the themes of the book? So what is the significance of this, I guess is what I'm thinking ... there's so much debate around whether or not we are in an era of globalisation and people are talking about de-globalisation and all that stuff. It reminded me a bit of Tom Popkewitz actually; he said, 'My interest in globalisation is not that there is such a thing, it's how this moment of globalisation is different', you know, from previous ones. So I think it's obviously something that people are speaking to that we need to engage with in terms of interrogating what it actually means if we're talking about intercultural conversations that move across.

...

Jean McPhail: ... It seems to me that because of the technologies that you talked about and because of the economic globalisation, there's something about consumption that supports economic globalisation that seems to me to have colonised, you know, all of the social systems including medicine, hospitals in the United States.

Baljit Kaur: It's commodification of life that has happened. So things that were not seen as commodities, now are, and people that were not seen as consumers, now are. That's quite a different thing so there is uniformity of objects as well as people that is introduced in this particular turn of globalisation.

Kathleen Quinlivan: This speaks to the 2003 Paul Willis article, doesn't it really? The way that young people are increasingly likely to be defined, and to define themselves, by their ability to consume, and I was interested to know whether that was something that came through in your stuff or not [in Hazel's work in the UK]. Yeah, because his argument is that young people don't define themselves any more by their identities ... you know [by] gender, race, class, sexuality. They define themselves by their ability to consume. And so then that, somehow, has got all sorts of implications for how you engage. So all of those ways that we've always thought of as powerful ways of being in the world, suddenly actually mean something very different in the current context ...

Sean Darmody: But ... globalisation, treating them as consumers, almost negates this possibility, it's like we're different but we're all the same and the possibility for exploring individuality decreases with globalised markets ...

Jean McPhail: ... my sort of off-the-cuff interpretation, well I've thought about this before 'cos I've seen some of this. So here are the Dutch now so there's this sort of global economy that's imposed in the European Union so now we have one currency. Now we're all the same but the Dutch are saying, 'Oh no we're not' *(laughs)* 'I may use that language but –'

Lia de Vocht van Alphen: Yeah, there is a revival and so the currency's put onto people by others, and so people retaliate by getting stronger in their national identity, and it could be sport, it could be the language, you know there could be all sorts of different ways. And there was a real risk, you know people did talk about that too, the risk, because people would lose part of who they were and their culture as a nation.

Baljit Kaur: So what you're saying is that imposed homogenisation is happening in the wake of these discourses about globalisation and in the wake of the economic kind of turn to that, and that people do resist this, so they want to kind of assert or reclaim their particular identities then?

Lia de Vocht van Alphen: Essentially, yes.

Baljit Kaur: And they become more essentialised and I think that does happen at, not just adolescence but also for younger children, even for younger children where we homogenise them so much – they're all four-year-olds, five-year-olds, sixth graders, fourth graders, whatever, everybody's supposed to do the same thing, everybody should be good at everything. Then children, many of them – actually all of them, in certain ways – try and negotiate that very, very actively such imposed defining of their lives and act in reaction to that.

Ruth Boyask: And it's quite interesting the way that those sort of peer subcultures that we were talking about before actually do appear in many different cultural contexts and so you get this sort of, these fundamentalisms around these,

these subcultural groups like the chavs [and] bogans ... A lot of what we're talking about here in regard to these complexities of intercultural conversations really and the difficulties of actually attaining them because of all these complexities around different kinds of identity and different ways of being in the world. But then, the question that we were also asking is, how can we make those happen and under what conditions might we be able to actually engage in some intercultural conversations? To actually use globalisation as some kind of productive force? ...

Hazel Lawson: Can I say something completely different? It occurred to me this morning that I hadn't quite got the hang of what you were meaning by intercultural and that I had only taken it to mean cross-country or inter-country or whatever, and that actually you were also talking about intercultural in the sense of, you were talking about researchers and teachers, and you were talking about children [and adults] and I hadn't got that about the book until this morning.

Sean Darmody: There's another element to intercultural and it's the cultures within the country and it's the class structure perhaps in England. In Ireland it would be the city and the rural that would be different and from *(inaudible)* times they're completely different languages. They perceive the world differently. And its relation to education is crucial.

...

Julie Allan: [Comment after the 2009 American Educational Research Association Symposium] The 'encounter' at AERA provoked some thoughts about the nature of intercultural conversations and the conditions for their occurrence. In the AERA proposal, it is stated that the intercultural dimension of the conversations involves drawing on the insights of others to reveal the limitations and possibilities within our own investigative contexts that we might not otherwise notice. This stands in contrast to what Nicholas Kristof described in the New York Times (18 March 2009, cited by Smith, forthcoming, 2009) as 'The Daily Me' phenomena in which people don't actually want good information, but rather [they want] information that confirms their own existing knowledge and prejudices: 'We may believe intellectually in the clash of opinions, but in practice we like to embed ourselves in the reassuring womb of an echo chamber' (Kristof, cited in Smith).

On the basis of the discussion, there seem to be a number of features which have significance for creating the conditions for fruitful intercultural conversations. I have set out questions in relation to each of these:
- Space: can an open space help to create a flow of conversation?
- Ontology: what are individuals' assumptions about the nature of reality and how do these influence what they hear?
- Epistemology: what are individuals' assumptions about the nature of knowledge? (Otherwise known as the great enlightenment debate.)
- Power: which voices are heard most often?
- Exclusion: what, and who, are missing from the conversations (eg, the developing world)?
- Missing of minds: can 'talking past' one another be heard? Can these breaks/ fractures be seen as productive spaces or as problematic gaps?

- Reflexivity: can individuals articulate moments when they see their own context differently as a consequence of the conversations? Are they minded to do so?

On the one hand, there are the provocative questions that Julie Allan has raised for further conversations. On the other, there is the challenging stance that Jean McPhail and Annemarie Palincsar take, based on their experience about the near impossibility of intercultural research engagements.

Jean McPhail: [At AERA 2009] So in conclusion this, in my mind and Annemarie's mind, raises serious questions about doing cross-cultural research in that one of the issues for me is that with the global economic/business discourse being elevated to the status it is and education riding on the coat tails of that discourse, that when folks try and do real research in other cultures without appreciating, as you were saying, Hazel, the particularities that exist within those discourses and the way those particularities are shaped by the governance and political and social discourse, is actually not easy work. It's not like banking. We don't have a common currency, it seems to me, to trade across even if we do work in western cultures.

We, Kathleen, Ruth and Baljit hope that intercultural conversations will continue in other forms and forums, framed around the emerging and recurring concerns and challenges highlighted above. Because we contend that despite the misgivings on many levels that are evident throughout this book, it is worthwhile, indeed imperative, for us as educators to engage with these challenges. As Maxine Greene (1995) reminds us:

We who are teachers would have to accommodate ourselves to lives as clerks or functionaries if we did not have in mind a quest for better state of things for those we teach and for the world we all share. (p. 1)

REFERENCES

Greene, M. (1995). *Releasing the imagination: Essays on education, the arts, and social change.* San Francisco: Jossey-Bass.
Smith, A. (forthcoming, 2009). The daily me: A response to Tocqueville on democracy and inclusive education: A more ardent and enduring love. Response piece. *European Journal of Special Needs Education.*

NOTES ON CONTRIBUTORS

Julie Allan is Professor of Education and Deputy Head of Department at the Stirling Institute of Education, University of Stirling, Scotland. She is the Director of the Professional Doctorate (EdD) Programme and teaches on a number of undergraduate and postgraduate programmes. She also holds a Visiting Professorship at the University of Borås in Sweden, where she teaches on several courses within the teacher education programme. Her research interests encompass inclusion, disability rights, children's rights, the arts (especially disability arts) and social capital and she has published widely in these areas. She has also been adviser to the Scottish Parliament during its inquiry into special educational needs and has provided evidence and advice on special needs and inclusion to the Welsh Assembly and the Queensland Government, Australia. Her most recent books are *Rethinking inclusive education: The philosophers of difference in practice* (published by Springer, 2008); *Doing inclusive education research* (with Roger Slee and published by Sense, 2008) and an edited volume, *Social capital, professionalism and diversity* (with Jenny Ozga and Gerry Smyth and published by Sense, 2009). Julie is currently engaged in a Council of Europe project, developing teacher competences for socio-cultural diversity.

Ruth Boyask is interested in the interplay between the dynamic and formal properties of education, and as such her research is characterised by diversity and border-crossing. She has led projects and published in areas such as innovations in schooling, participatory research and educational policy. Her curiosity about conceptualisations of difference in educational policy and practice is an ongoing motivation in her work. She explores the enactment of social policy intended to widen participation, and policies that both open and close possibilities for learners and learning. Her academic career started in New Zealand at the University of Canterbury and Massey University. She has previously held a position at Cardiff University, Wales and currently is lecturing in Education Studies at the University of Plymouth, England. Prior to her academic career she was a secondary school teacher in North Canterbury, New Zealand.

Rebecca Carter is a Lecturer in Early Childhood Studies at the University of Plymouth, England. With the aim of equipping future early years carers and educators with the knowledge and skills they need to do the very best for young children, her teaching within a multidisciplinary team focuses on social policy, equal opportunities and diversity, social inequalities, child poverty and multi-agency working. She is the leader for the programme's Research in Early Childhood Studies module, and has a particular interest in participatory research methods, and applied social research that looks at issues around inequalities in the UK and beyond. Prior to taking the position at Plymouth, Rebecca has worked on educational projects in Namibia, Ghana and Kenya and in various community development roles in the UK; these have included managing projects to address health inequalities in East London, support and advice services for refugee families in Manchester, and educational enrichment activities for children in public care. She plans to pursue PhD research into how the UK education system caters for children from transient and disadvantaged communities such as homeless, gypsy and traveller, and families of refugees and asylum seekers.

Eve Coxon is a Senior Research Fellow Lecturer in the Faculty of Education at the University of Auckland, New Zealand. She has also taught, largely at postgraduate level, in the Centres of Pacific Studies and Development Studies at the University of Auckland and supervises a number of masters and doctoral students from all three programmes. Her broad research interest in education policy encompasses comparative and international education, global–local intersections in education policy development in Pacific Islands countries, and educational equity for Pacific communities in New Zealand. She has worked as a teacher, researcher and/or consultant across a range of Pacific countries and for a number of multilateral and bilateral development agencies. In recent years her writing has been published in journals such as *Comparative Education, Educational Philosophy and Theory, World Studies in Education* and *International Journal of the Humanities*, and she has co-edited a number of collections. She is currently conducting research into shifts in modes of educational aid delivery to 'developing' countries.

Andrew Gitlin has focused his research efforts on trying to understand the intimate connections between knowledge and power. In looking at this issue, he has centred his latest work on the exploration of the political dimensions of aesthetics and the implications of this 'deep politic' for schooling. His current scholarship includes *Educational poetics: Inquiry freedom and innovative necessity* (published by Peter Lang, 2005), 'Inquiry, imagination, and the search for a deep politic' (2005, *Educational Researcher*, *34*(3), 15–24), and 'Cultivating the quailtative borderlands: educational poetics and the politics of inclusivity' (2008, *International Journal of Qualitative Studies, 21*(6) 627–645).

Baljit Kaur teaches at the University of Canterbury, Christchurch, New Zealand. Her research is in the areas of historical and cultural studies of childhood, disability and education, currently with a focus on home–school relationships, literacy acquisition and specific reading disabilities, and diversity and social justice issues in education.

Didi Khayatt is a Professor who teaches at York University in Toronto, Canada. Her scholarly work and publications span over a quarter of a century and are mostly concerned with issues of sexuality and equity in education.

Hazel Lawson is Senior Lecturer in special and inclusive education at University of Exeter, England, having previously been a Lecturer at University of Plymouth and Middlesex University. Prior to this she was a teacher for many years in primary and special schools in England. Her research interests are in the general field of special and inclusive education, with specific interest in: the education of children and young people with severe and profound learning difficulties (intellectual disabilities), especially in the areas of curriculum and citizenship education; conceptualisations of diversity and pedagogical implications; and pupil participation and voice. She has a particular enthusiasm for sociological perspectives and qualitative research approaches.

Richard Manning has recently been awarded a PhD in Education by Victoria University of Wellington, New Zealand. He was born in Wellington and grew up in Porirua East; one of New Zealand's most economically vulnerable and culturally diverse communities. Much of his current research interests result from his Pākehā childhood interactions with numerous Māori and Pacific Island classmates, friends, teachers and lecturers. He was awarded a New Zealand Top Achievers Doctoral Scholarship (2003) to commence full-time doctoral studies and was contracted to write community consultation and engagement guidelines for the Capital and Coast District Health Board (2003–2004). Since then, he has been employed by the Treaty of Waitangi Information Unit in the New Zealand State Services Commission (2005–2006) to advise on the development of Treaty of Waitangi education resources. He has also conducted research as a claims inquiry facilitator for the Waitangi Tribunal (2006–2007), before commencing his current position as the Coordinator of the Treaty of Waitangi Education programme at the University of Canterbury, College of Education (2008). Richard lectures in cultural studies and social sciences and is now researching how critical pedagogies of place are applied to remedy colonial conflicts in New Zealand and elsewhere.

Frances McConaughy is a PhD candidate at the University of Utah, USA and she has taught for several years in a health profession programme. Her interests include understanding the structural and cultural influences in identity formation and the educational experiences of both educators and students in secondary and higher education.

Jean Claire McPhail retired from the School of Education at the University of Canterbury, New Zealand in 2007, and is currently engaged in grass-roots prog-ressive political action work in the USA.

Annemarie S. Palincsar is the Jean and Charles Walgreen Chair of Reading and Literacy at the University of Michigan, USA. She is an instructional researcher who wishes to contribute to our understanding of how schools could be more interesting and productive places for youth and teachers.

Hazel Phillips is an indigenous educator of Ngāti Mutunga tribal descent in Āotearoa New Zealand. She is a Senior Lecturer based in He Parekereke, Institute for Research and Development in Māori and Pacific Education at Victoria University of Wellington, New Zealand and has a background in sociology of education. Her passion is working with Māori (indigenous peoples) communities and she is committed to the sustainable cultural, social, political, environmental and economic development of whānau, hapū and iwi (family, subtribe and tribe) that fulfils their aspirations to and expressions of tino rangatiratanga (self determination). As part of this commitment she is dedicated to working for social justice. Her research interests include: the reassertion and reclamation of traditional knowledge and practices; the interface between indigenous knowledge and western science, especially the impact that this has on the construction of Maori identity, knowledge, practices and values; kaupapa Māori (for Māori by Māori) research methodologies and knowledge production; and the politics and practices of inter-disciplinary research practices and ethics. Current research projects include school-to-work transitions for young Māori and Pasifika and the impact of educational and health policies and practices on the cultural identity and well-being of kāpō (blind) Māori.

Lou Preston coordinates and lectures in the Graduate Diploma of Outdoor and Environmental Education in the School of Human Movement and Sport Sciences at the University of Ballarat, Victoria, Australia. Teaching and leading in the outdoors, she is able to share her enthusiasm for activities such as rock climbing, bush walking, and paddling. But she is also interested in exploring less traditional outdoor (and indoor) activities as a means of encouraging ethical connections with the natural world. Her current research, informing the chapter in this text, draws on post-structuralist theorising of pedagogy to explore the value of incorporating a wider array of activities within outdoor and environmental education. She is also interested in the apparent 'greening' of outdoor education and her recent doctoral research investigated the formation of environmental ethics among university students undertaking the outdoor and environmental education course. An overarching focus of her research is on the implications for pedagogical practice in outdoor and environmental education and in education more broadly, especially in relation to the importance of 'place' and the spatial dimensions of pedagogy.

Kathleen Quinlivan is a Senior Lecturer in the College of Education at the University of Canterbury, New Zealand. She works across theory and practice contexts to explore ways of learning that engage with diversity and difference within a range of sites in secondary schools, including classroom and student peer contexts. She has published widely in the area of sexualities and schooling in books such as *Queer in New Zealand* (2004) and *From here to diversity: The social impact of lesbian and gay issues in education in Australia and New Zealand* (Haworth Press, 2004); and in journals such as the *Journal of Lesbian and Gay Studies in Education* and *International Journal of Qualitative Studies in Education*. She is currently directing a New Zealand AIDS Foundation research project exploring the role that gay–straight alliances can play in widening constructions of sexualities and genders within a range of New Zealand secondary schooling contexts.

Mary Lou Rasmussen is a Senior Lecturer in curriculum and pedagogy at Monash University, Victoria, Australia. A principal focus of her research is on issues related to sexualities education; presently she is researching a book on sex, education and secularism. She co-edited *Youth and sexualities: Pleasure, subversion and insubordination in and out of schools* (with Susan Talburt and Eric Rofes, Palgrave McMillan, 2004), and wrote *Becoming subjects*, a monograph on sexualities and secondary schooling (published by Routledge, 2006).

Gill Valentine is Professor of Geography at the University of Leeds, England. Her research interests include: social identities, citizenship and belonging; and urban cultures and consumption. She is a (co)author/editor of 14 books and over 100 articles and reports.

Sue Waite has been Faculty Research Fellow in Education at the University of Plymouth, England since 1998. In the past she has worked both as a teacher and teaching assistant, and as a research council and university administrator. As the daughter of a teacher, her childhood was spent in residential schools for young offenders and 'maladjusted boys'. Her recent research has been centred on learning outside the classroom and she leads the faculty research group in outdoor and experiential learning. She is currently conducting an Economic and Social Research Council-funded project on *Opportunities afforded by the outdoors for alternative pedagogies in children's transition from Foundation Stage to Year 1*. This interest arises from her broader concerns about affective issues in education, which have been the subject of several previous projects for public bodies, including research on continuing professional development materials for the UK Government's Excellence and Enjoyment initiative and out-of-county residential provision for students with social, emotional and behavioural difficulties. She continues to try to develop innovative mixed methods for the exploration of hard-to-measure qualitative data in her research.

INDEX

A
Adult regulation, 15, 18–19
Adult roles, 23
Aid
    aid delivery, 129, 131, 158
    Better Aid Agenda, 131, 132
    New Aid Era, 130–132
    poverty reduction, 129, 132
Anomalous places of learning, 106–111

C
Caring/uncaring
    class identified caring, 28, 29
    race based uncaring, politics of
        containment, 37, 38
    refuge, 28–29, 33, 35, 36, 38$n2$
Child agency, 13, 19, 122
Childhood
    concept, 13
    conception, 13, 23
    constructions, 13–16, 23
    universal ideal, xiii, 14, 15, 23
Children
    active/passive, 13, 15, 17, 22, 23, 98
    competence, 15
    position within school, xiii, 92
Child roles
    Assiduous Protector, 17, 21–22
    Goody Two Shoes, 17, 20
    Little Atlas, 17, 20–21
    Smart Tactician, 17, 22–24
    Vigilant Sentinel, 17–19
Choice, ix, 6, 20, 47–48, 68, 137, 140
Class, xiv, 15, 17, 20, 22, 27–38, 38$n1$, 38$n2$,
    60, 63$n12$, 65–67, 70–73, 81–86, 91, 93,
    96–98, 121, 124$n1$, 139, 141, 154, 155
Colonisation, 109
Communication practices, 98
Conceptualisations of diversity, 116–122, 124,
    159
Contradictory representations
    class, 27–38, 38$n1$, 38$n2$
    race, 27–30, 32–38
Critical pedagogy of place
    critical pedagogy, xiv, 51–61
    decolonization, 53, 54, 58, 59
    Ecoliteracy: reading landscapes as historical
        texts, 56, 59–60
    place-based education, 52, 53, 59, 62$n2$
Crown
    Crown agencies, 55, 58, 61
    Crown representatives, 62$n1$

Cultural diversity
    cultural agency, 130
    local traditions, 130

D
Deficit thinking, 15, 48
Deleuze
    deterritorialisation, 2, 7
    difference, 1–3, 6, 8–10
    the rhizome, 2, 4, 7, 8
Derrida
    aporias, 6, 43
    deconstruction, 2, 6
Destabilisation
    Destabilising gendernormativity, 87
    Destabilising heteronormativity, 87
Development, modernisation, 130–132
Developmentalism, developmentalist
    assumptions, 15, 23, 130
Difference, ix, xiii, xv, xvi, 1–3, 6, 8–10, 31–38,
    41, 42, 45, 48, 70, 72, 79, 92, 97–100, 108,
    109, 115–121, 124, 124$n1$, 129, 144, 145,
    151–153, 157, 160
Dilemmas in cross-cultural educational
    research, 141
Discomfort, xiv, 5, 70, 72, 77, 78, 87, 92, 152
Diversity, ix, x, xii–xvi, 14, 23, 30, 56, 63$n12$,
    65, 66, 77–79, 95–100, 115–125, 129, 130,
    133, 134, 137, 157–160

E
Education, ix, 1, 14, 27, 41, 45, 52, 65, 80, 93,
    103, 115, 129, 137, 153, 157
Education for Development, human capital,
    131
Educational equality, 117
Elizabeth Ellsworth
    pedagogical events, 107
    place and pedagogy, 106–110
Emotionality
    emotionality as a site of learning, 79–80,
        86–87
    theorising emotionality, 79–80
English schools, 97, 115, 124
Equity, ix, xiv, xv, 27, 41, 46, 65–75, 115,
    117–119, 131, 158
Every Child Matters, 43, 116, 120, 122, 124,
    152

F
Femininities, 81–86
Feminism, 74

Foucault
    ethics, 9, 10
    practices of the self, 2
    transgression, 2, 3

G
Gender, xiv, xv, 29, 35, 65–67, 69, 72–74,
    77–83, 85–87, 95, 116, 118, 119, 121,
    131, 154, 160
Generalisation, x, 117–121, 124
Global discourses, x, xi, xiii, xv, 123, 129
Globalisation
    local/global interactions, 129–133, 158
    structural adjustment, 131
Guattari
    deterritorialisation, 2, 7
    the rhizome, 2, 4, 7, 8
Guided science learning, 139, 140, 142–146

H
History
    history education (pedagogy), xiv, xv, 8,
        51–63, 92, 106–110, 112, 145–147,
        160, 161
    identity (teaching about), 72
    In relation to knowledge of te reo Mâori,
        56
Home–school relations
    children navigating, 13–24
    children's perspectives, xiii, 15, 16
    children's voices, 15
    congruence, 15
    and effective learning, 14, 15
    match/mismatch, 14
    partnerships, xiii, 14–16, 23
    policy, 13–16, 23
Homogenising difference, xv, xvi, 36, 120
Human rights, 45, 49, 74, 117–120, 124,
    132

I
Identities, ix, xii, xv, 3–5, 8, 9, 19, 27–38, 41,
    42, 47–49, 58, 59, 66, 68–71, 73, 95–100,
    108, 115–124, 129, 133, 152, 154, 155,
    159–161
Identity formation
    effects of class-based identity, 30–33
    effects of race-based identity, 33–35
    in relation to dominant culture, *different
        from*, 29–30
Identity/identification, xiv, 5, 8, 9, 27–38, 41,
    42, 47, 48, 58, 59, 68–71, 73, 95, 97, 99,
    100, 115, 118, 119, 122, 123, 154, 155,
    159, 160

Inclusion
    form of political engagement, 1
    impossibility of, 1, 2
Indigenous, xiv, xv, 45, 49, 51, 52, 62, 73, 104,
    109, 130, 133, 152, 159, 160
Indigenous knowledge, 49, 133, 152, 160
Intercultural citizenship, 96
Interest-based learning, 138, 139, 141, 142, 145

L
Language contact, 96–99

M
Mâori
    Iwi, 46, 47, 51, 60–62, 63*n14*, 160
    Tangata whenua, 51
    Te Ātiawa, 51, 52, 54–58, 60–62, 62*n2*,
        63*n5*, 63*n6*, 63*n12*–63*n14*
    Te reo Mâori, 56, 60
    Wellington Tenths Trust, 52, 57, 62*n3*
Mâori education, 45–49
Macro-level policy, 117–120
Masculinities, 82–84
Multilingualism, 97, 99, 100

N
National policies, 116, 120, 124
Neoliberal, 45, 49, 131, 132
Nomadic learning to teach, 6–10

O
Outdoor education, 52, 103–112, 112*n4*, 160

P
Pacific
    Pacific education, 133, 159
    Pacific Island countries, 133
    Parent teacher collaboration, 14, 16–18, 20
Performance/performativity, 32, 74, 95–97,
    103, 108–111
Personalising learning, 42, 116, 120, 122, 152
Philosophers of difference, xiii, 1–3, 6, 10,
    157
Place
    cultural landmarks, 59
    ecological literacy, 55, 59
    reconciliation (cross-cultural), 51, 60–62,
        63*n14*, 137–141, 147, 148, 153, 156
Policy, ix, x, xi, xv, 4, 13–16, 23, 41, 43, 46,
    48, 72, 96, 100, 115–124, 129–131, 134,
    157, 158
Pre-service, 60, 62, 63*n5*, 122
Private/Public Worlds, 17, 21, 23, 36, 82, 122
Provocation, 1–10, 79–86

Q
Queer pedagogy, 78, 79
Queer theory, 42, 79

R
Race, xiv, 27–30, 32–38, 42, 63*n6*, 65–67, 72,
73, 118, 154
Refugees, 16, 22, 95, 100, 158

S
Schooling, ix, x, xiii, xv, 14, 15, 23, 24*n1*, 27,
29, 31, 36, 37, 38*n3*, 41, 45, 46, 48, 49, 54,
67, 86, 92, 96, 115–117, 121, 124, 137, 138,
157, 158, 160, 161
Schooling policies, 28, 29, 41, 96, 117, 119,
120, 124
Schools' guidance, 116, 117, 120, 121, 123
Sexual orientation, 70, 119
Social justice, ix, xi, xiv, 41, 45, 49, 65–68,
70–75, 115, 117, 121, 123, 124, 129,
158, 160
Social policy, 46, 157
Social provision, xv, 41, 115, 116, 118, 120,
122–124

Space, xi, xii, 1–4, 8, 10, 14, 16, 21, 24, 42,
43, 45–47, 49, 69, 73, 93, 95–100, 103,
106–111, 118, 122, 132, 139, 143, 144,
148, 152, 155
Specificity, 116, 118–120, 137
Subjectivities, xi–xv, 41, 42, 77, 79, 87, 96,
116, 117, 122–124, 129

T
Teacher–child relationships, trust, 17, 19, 22,
24*n6*
Teacher–parent–child triangle, 16
Teacher–parent researcher community (TPRC),
141, 142, 144–146
Teacher–student relationships, 3
Teaching, xiii, xiv, 6–8, 10, 22, 29, 30, 43, 47,
52, 54–56, 59, 60, 62, 65, 66, 70–73, 79, 80,
83, 87, 93, 96, 100, 106, 107, 110, 116, 121,
133, 137–148, 152, 157, 160, 161
Transitional spaces, 107
Treaty of Waitangi (1840)
treaty claims, 159
Waitangi Tribunal, 3, 51–53, 62*n1*, 63*n6*,
159

U
Universalism, 42, 118, 119, 125*n2*, 134

Lightning Source UK Ltd.
Milton Keynes UK
24 February 2010

150549UK00001B/123/P